Groovers On Manoeuvres

All rights reserved. No part of this publication may be reproduced, stored in a retrieval system or transmitted, in any form or by any means electronic, mechanical, photocopying, recording or otherwise without the prior written permission of the copyright owner.

Copyright © 2021 Tony Wilton
Cover Art © 2021 Tony Wilton
All rights reserved.
ISBN 9798703929049

Groovers On Manoeuvres

Shenanigans from a 7 Month Deployment to the Far East with the Royal Navy On Board the Type-22 Frigate, HMS Sheffield aka 'The Shiny Sheff'

Tony Wilton

For Rick, Howie, Bubbles, Tammy and Jessie who crossed the bar way too soon.

"Fair winds and following seas, Shipmates."

Contents

Acknowledgements	6
Introduction	7
1 Nozzers	10
2 Monster Slippers	25
3 Wanna See a Greyhound	52
4 Thimble Hunt	64
5 Big Dog, Little Dog	114
6 Tigers	131
7 I am a British Sailor...	138
8 Demis Roussos	169
9 We Watched Disney	187
10 Crossing The Line	221
11 I Know the Tampax Song	240
12 Jeans and Strippers	262
13 Hello Glastonbury	297
Epilogue	320
Glossary	322

Acknowledgements

Thank you to all Military Mums and Dads who put up with their Military off-spring dumping tons of laundry on the bathroom floor every weekend. Thank you for putting up with our arrogance and often alcohol-fuelled 'attitude'. Mum, you laughed with me all the way and I admit it, you were right, I should've gone to Art College, but boy do I now have some dits to spin!

Introduction

To the tune of Rolling Stones, 'Satisfaction'.

Chorus
I can't get no satisfaction,
I can't get no split reaction,
'Cos I try, 'cos I try,
And I try, and I try,
And I try, and I try,
And I try, and I try,

I can't get no, I can't get no.
When I'm lying in my rack,
And this bloke comes on the main broadcast,
And he's giving me loads and loads and loads,
Of useless information,
S'pose to drive my 'magination,
I can't get no, No no no, Hey hey hey.

Chorus - I can't get no...

When I'm watching S.R.E.
Not tuned in by Jack Hatty,

And this bloke comes on and tells me,
What a big dog he can be,
But he can't be a dog 'cos he doesn't eat,
The same shit as me, I can't get no,
No no no, Hey hey hey,
That's what I say.

Chorus - I can't get no...

When I'm sailing round the world,
And I'm shagging this,
And I'm shagging that,
And I'm trying to take a day's sea leave,
But the HODs say come back maybe next week,
CINC fleets permission you must seek.
I can't get no, I can't get no,
Satisfaction.

Actually, I can't get any!

Ever fancied working from home? For lots of people, it's a dream. But what if you have to share that home with 270 other people, all dressed the same as you? What if 30 of them actually share *your* room, and all the windows have been bricked up? What if there's no lock on the bathroom door, and you spend half your waking life scrubbing and cleaning and re-scrubbing and re-cleaning the same bits of your house, night after night regardless of whether they are dirty or not? What if there's no reception on your TV, so you instead choose to watch the same videos over and over again, and you're only allowed three small cans of beer a night? And you can't even go for your dinner until some chap inspects your living room cleanliness while you stand to attention in acknowledgement of his authority.

What if, every three weeks or so, you were graciously allowed to leave home and venture into town? A town, nay, a country which, strangely and as if by magic, is entirely different every time you stepped outside of the front door. Now, if you lived like that for seven months of the year and were a young bloke in the prime of his life, I am willing to bet that you would get screaming shit-faced every single opportunity you got.

> Welcome to the Royal Navy, shippers! Pull up a bollard, I'll spin you a dit!

Chapter One

NOZZERS

Every child has a dream of what they want to be when they grow up and my dream was seeing the world on a warship, sailing the 'Seven Seas'. As far as I was concerned I came from a forces family, on my Mother's side at least. Her Dad and his 2 brothers were in the Army, Navy and Air Force during World War 2. Their Dad was a Petty Officer during World War 1 and his brothers, of which there were many, were in the other forces also. There were loads! Great Grand Parents, Great Uncles, Great greats and Super greats! The family tree on my mother's side read like a military roll-call. As a result, I had wanted to join the Royal Navy as soon as possible and on the day I hit my 16th birthday I insisted on being taken to my nearest Armed Forces recruitment centre in Truro, Cornwall. Over the next couple of months, I undertook tests designed to evaluate my grey matter to see where I could fit into the naval family. I had already a bit of knowledge about how the Navy worked and decided that I wanted to join the Weapons Engineering branch for two main reasons.

Number 1 – My brother was already in the Navy as a Weapons Engineer and number 2 – The badge looked cool. It had a Sea Wolf missile pointing from south to north and a torpedo from east to west. Four lightning strikes fired in from either corner. I had assessed the coolness of the badges worn by other trades, the Stokers looked ok with a massive propellor while the WAFU's had little aeroplanes while anything to do with supplies, logistics and admin had a tidy little star, but the WE branch - That was the one for me! What a way to choose your career path, who had the coolest 'badge'.

I was required to sit a 'multiple guess' quiz to establish if I had the grey matter to become an Artificer Apprentice. Because of my impatience, the test result would replace my, recently taken GCSE results along with serving to see which of the three engineering areas I had the best aptitude for. Despite wanting to be 'Weapons', the test would determine if I should go for a career in Marine Engineering, Weapon Engineering or Air Engineering. It was engine rooms, weapons systems or fixing helicopters. Results were quick and not surprisingly I failed to get the required score for Artificer but did score enough to become a mechanic. If I had waited and been a little less impetuous I could have walked straight into an Artificer role on the back of my GCSE results rather than taking the Navy's in-house aptitude test but sadly that was my nature all over.

About a month before my starting date I received a letter from the Navy detailing a list of kit I needed to bring myself along with a travel/rail-warrant. 'D' day soon arrived and my folks drove their 16-year-old, wet behind the ears, still just a school-boy, son the short half-hour trip to Bodmin Parkway railway station where I swapped my rail-warrant for a one-way ticket to Plymouth. It was then only a forty-minute hop up the line to Plymouth station. On my arrival at Plymouth, I was herded with all the other scared lambs onto coaches for a short trip over the River Tamar back into Cornwall and to HMS Raleigh, home of Royal Navy basic training. Stuck on the side of a hill which descended from the town of Torpoint down to the River Tamar, HMS Raleigh was fondly referred to as Legoland for its boring brown square accommodation blocks.

It was July the 3rd 1989. I didn't even want to wait and enjoy the summer holidays. I just wanted to get on with the adventure of joining the RN. Basic training was my first taste of the big world. I knew it was unlikely that I would be running 50 miles each day with a ½ ton rucksack on my back. I was joining the Navy not the SAS, but nevertheless, it still hurt like hell to be 16 yrs old and getting screamed at by every person you looked at. Fortunately the Navy, I suspect like the other services had a method of breaking you in relatively gently with the first week being known as 'New Entry'. Each 'division' consisted of about 25 lads who were handed over to some salty old 'Father Figure' Chief Petty Officer whose job was to bring you up to speed with the very basic rules around Naval life, routine, lingo and what was to come. Brand new recruits were known by the nickname of 'Nozzers', my first introduction to an entirely new language unique to the Royal Navy, Jack-Speak. The first day saw us getting lots of new kit thrown at us, getting the mandatory head shave and doing some basic admin which included the writing of an 'HMS Raleigh' postcard which I had to send to my parents to let them know I was alive and had arrived safely. I had to write what I was told and it was something along the lines of, 'Dear Mum and Dad. I have arrived safely at HMS Raleigh. It is very nice here and I am looking forward to my training. The Chief Petty Officer is a nice bloke. Love Tony.'

The picture on the front of the Postcard was of HMS Raleigh's official crest along with a few sailors marching and someone sailing a small boat, presumably after substantial instruction. After writing and handing back the postcard to be 'vetted' and no doubt censored to remove our real thoughts and emotion, we were taken on mass to a large room which was a laundry. The place was full with row upon row of stainless steel sinks apart from along one side which was a line of wooden worktops. On these counters were tubs containing both black and white paint. We were instructed to grab a tub of each colour then proceed to 'mark' our clothing and uniform using little wooden blocks which had metal letters pressed into them. Mine was appropriately 'A WILTON'. We marked everything from trousers to towels. Everything!

During that first week, we were taught a variety of things, some obvious and some not so obvious. How to shave properly for example (regardless of whether you need to yet or not), how to clean boots, how to hand-wash, iron and most importantly fold your new uniform in a very methodical, precise and specific way. This was to get us into the habit of being super smart and hygienic. After all, after this training, we were going to be living for months on end in a grey metal box, either above or below the sea. We were given instructions on how our kit was to be laid out for inspection, how it was to be placed in a tiny locker besides our bed and how to keep our accommodation spotless, well beyond spotless, almost surgically clean. We also got some hints and tips on how to 'bullshit' the staff by stacking our super-duper white sailor hats in a pyramid much to the amusement of our instructor.

Our uniform was a little odd, to say the least. Our flat white sailor hats had the name the ship on which we served written on it in the form of a black silk ribbon with gold embroidered lettering. All of us new recruits had HMS RALEIGH on ours. The 'A' of the word 'Raleigh' was to be placed directly above the nose as this was the centre letter of the text 'HMS RALEIGH'. The ribbon was then tied to the side of the cap with a neat bow over the left ear, the 'tails' of which cut and shaped into neat points. We soon learnt the trick of holding the hat in the steam above a boiling kettle. This caused the ribbon to shrink and tighten around the band of the cap. Our best uniform was the stereotypical dark blue navy jacket and flared trousers, big square blue collar and a brilliant white lanyard around the neck along with a band of silk. We were issued two sets, one with gold badges and one with red badges. The gold badged set was our Number 1's, for dress best and Number 2's for, well, second best I guess.

Our working rig was known as our Number 8's or just 8's for short and was standard blue long sleeve shirt and dark blue trousers, worn with a blue beret and our beret badge consisting of a silver anchor inside a gold-coloured circle. To this day I have no idea why each of our uniforms was allocated a number. I am sure some historian somewhere can tell me. Finally, our evening rig (that's what we were told to call our uniform from now on) was known as Number 5's. This consistent of straight-legged black trousers and a 'white front' top which was a white cotton shirt with a square neck. They were intended to be *very* tight-fitting and it took several attempts for new sailors to figure out how to put them on, and even longer to work out how to take them off. The rest of the week was filled with marching, admin and some mild 'beasting' designed to get our bodies ready for the remaining seven weeks.

After completing our first week we left the safety and security of 'New Entry' and were allocated to a Petty Officer, thrown into another accommodation block and given the name of 'Benbow 27 Division' named after Admiral John Benbow 1653-1702. Our Petty Officer would ensure we were always where we were meant to be, our kit and the general standard of presentation was up to speed and any welfare issues were taken care of. Okay it wasn't the Army but we still had to be fit and had our fair share of assault courses, weapon handling and squad runs to endure. On top of all this was training unique to the Royal Navy. Replenishment At Sea, or RAS, was taught and practised which was a very confusing procedure of getting objects from one pretend ship to another pretend ship by using a rifle to fire various rope lines between both of the pretend ships, attaching thicker and larger ropes then steel cables which would eventually enable us to traverse objects across the gap between the two ships. This was the Navy's way of stocking up on supplies at sea which included fuel. Learning to tie knots and hitches was on the agenda as well as practising how to tie the moorings on a steel cable for holding a ship alongside. HMS Raleigh had a large room full of ropes and bollards kept for that sole purpose. Overall my 8 weeks of basic training at HMS Raleigh thankfully went by without any major events. Been shouted at was ok once you got used to it. The only thing that did get to me was the timekeeping, something I counted as a strong point. Recruits were always given 2 minutes to complete a task that should take 10 but that is all part of the 'induced stress'. One thing our division was not too good at however was marching and drill in general. Out of the 3 divisions, Benbow, Cunningham and Drake we were by far the worst. Every couple of days throughout our training we would be drill bashed on the parade square by a Royal Marine Sergeant with a hair allergy. He was a decent bloke really and maintained a sense of humour which was lost with the Navy instructors. I suspect it was because he knew he was as tough as old steaming bats whereas the Navy instructors just wished they were.

Towards the end of our training, about a week before our 'Passing Out' ceremony one of the 3 divisions would be selected to perform the role of Guard, a role which appealed to us all for a couple of reasons. Firstly because you wore a flashy white belt and gaiters and carried a gun and therefore looked a bit cooler and secondly because you were the last division to march on and first to march off afterwards meaning less time stood still on the parade ground. We would also get to stand right at the front of the parade ground in front of the families and do some cool drill stuff flinging our SLR rifles about. To select the 'Guard' each division was drilled to see who was the snappiest, the slickest, the best, the smartest. To our surprise just prior to us going out on the drill square as we waited in the drill shed for our turn to shine, our Petty Officer instructor who had nurtured us and fathered us throughout the whole of basic training took us all to one side.

"If you little fuckers get Guard I will be fucking pissed off!" said our instructor Petty Officer Rosie Rosevear, a portly bloke with red face and a well-loved, groomed and slightly too perfect beard.

"Don't think I'm pissing around, I fucking mean it," he continued. "If you get Guard I'm going to be in here doing a shitload of extra drill myself and I don't need that!"

Rosie made his feelings quite clear. He knew that us being awarded the honour of passing out as the 'Guard' would require him doing a ton of additional drill training probably during the times of the day he would have been taking a round of Golf somewhere. He would have to march on with us and perform the same stunts, tricks and bullshit 'fling arounds' with his rifle as we did. So it came as no surprise to find out he was seething when the Drill Staff broke the news to him that Benbow division had been the best of the three divisions and as a consequence been selected to as Guard. This also came as a small shock to us as up to this point we felt we had been pretty shite at drill bashing. Another Petty Officer instructor from one of the other divisions collared us as we were being marched back to our barrack block.

"You lot are in the shit," he snarled, "one fucking request, just one fucking request from Petty Officer Rosevear and you couldn't even let it go. Well, you're fucked now!"

We were completely clueless as to what he was going on about. During basic training, you had to everything to the best of your ability or you got hammered later. Naturally, we wanted to do our best but for once our instructor did not.

"He's looked out for you lot," he spat, "he has stopped me from filling your little fucking heads in and giving you shit and *this* is how you reward him you little fucks!"

It was times like this I was grateful that Petty Officer 'Dickwad' was not our instructor. He had the most frustrating of personal issues know too many as 'small man syndrome' and was one of the few people who got real pleasure from inflicting pain on others. I had no time for the guy. The phrase 'I wouldn't piss on him if he was on fire' being so apt.

The day before our 'Passing Out' parade they made their pathetic feelings known and we returned from a day of training in high spirits only to find that the entire barrack room had been bonfired. Not literally of course, but the contents of all our lockers including best uniform, boots and personal items had all been piled into the centre of the room in a heap and every available box of washing powder or 'dhoby dust' as I was to call it from this point on had been emptied on to the top of the pile. We even found some stuff had been launched outside the windows and was in a snotty heap outside at the bottom of the block. Rosie and Dickwad had been in and trashed the lot.

The day of my 'Passing Out' arrived and was attended by my Grandparents, parents, brothers and sisters. After the other divisions, Cunningham, Anson and Drake had marched on to the parade square and were formed up and stood to attention the Lieutenant in charge of us bellowed out the order for us to march on to the parade ground, *"GUARD! Guard by the right QUICK MARCH!"*

We marched from the drill shed and formed up on the square directly in front of the podium where some high flying Admiral stood watching us but most importantly, close enough for my folks to see. We did some snappy drills showing off our newly found skills of standing perfectly still in a straight line and looking awesome before we gave a 'General Salute' with our SLR rifles with the shout of *"GUARD - PRESENT ARMS!"* from our 'two ringer.'

The icing on the cake was marching off to the anthem of the Royal Navy, 'Heart of Oak'. I'd only been a 'sailor' for 8 weeks but I could already feel my chest rise with pride! I'd gone from 5th-year schoolboy to Royal Navy personnel in a few short weeks and I was chuffed to fucking bits!

When the parade was done and dusted we were all allowed to leave the drill shed and run back to meet our families where I was predictably plastered in kisses from my Mum before being whisked off to a local Torpoint pub, the Carbeile Inn for a slap-up steak meal. I'd made my family proud!

A week of annual leave at home in Padstow passed uneventfully during and before I knew it I was back on a train, this time to Fareham, Hampshire. The next few months of my Naval service would be taken up by 'trade' training and, as per the badge I was keen to have on my arm dictated, I was shipped off to HMS Collingwood to begin training as a Weapons Engineering Mechanic.

All new 'junior rate' recruits joining the Royal Navy regardless of trade do their basic training at HMS Raleigh and I had done my 8 weeks with lads who were going to be posted all over the UK to various Navy bases in order learn a variety of trades. Artificers who also did basic training at HMS Raleigh were there for a for an additional few weeks and the officers did a far longer but arguable more in-depth course at Britannia Naval

College where they learnt to say *barth* instead of *bath* and also how to hold a spoon correctly without offending the Queen. As for the trades, well the Marine Engineers went to HMS Sultan in Gosport also in Hampshire. The Seamen and Chefs stayed put at Raleigh to continue their trade training.

My arrival at Collingwood meant going back to the bottom of the pecking order. It was good to be the senior class at HMS Raleigh if only for the last couple of weeks. Although things were a lot more relaxed at HMS Collingwood or as we soon learn to call it, Colling-grad, but we still marched everywhere but now we were given green canvas 'man bags' to store our course books in. Parades were still performed weekly and there were still inspections each evening but we could definitely relax more. I was thrown into an accommodation block with a heating system on life support and ceilings so near collapse you had to consider wearing a hard hat. The long corridors which ran from one end to the other had large open plan rooms sprouting off them. The only privacy was a massive full length infested curtain which could be drawn across the corridor to hide the four beds and stop people waking you as they ran down the corridor or worse, staggering back to their pits rat-arsed at the end of a night out.

The camp as a whole was well run. Sport was mandatory and team sports were encouraged. Every Wednesday there was a disco or 'Bop' above the NAAFI and local ladies came by the busload attracted by cash naive young sailors pay packets and vast amounts of cheap alcohol. Every Friday, provided you were not part of the 'Duty Watch' you could either travel home or enjoy the delights of the local taverns. It didn't take me too long to figure out that getting involved in some more specialist jobs within the establishment meant you were taken off the duty-watch completely and I soon managed to land myself helping out with the running of the Bop. It meant I had to operate the lights and smoke machine during the discos plus help with selling tickets and clearing all the shit up at the end of the night. The downside of this was that I couldn't get pissed during the Bop but it also meant I saved some cash, but I was at least excused more agonising duties and got to look swanky for the chicks, well at least in my mind anyway. Very important for a 16-year-old fast approaching his 17th birthday!

During the next few months, I learnt about making fuse testers, soldering, cutting the isolating wire to a precise length and bending wires at an exact right angle. I made some amazing little bits of kit, even constructing the aluminium case for the outside. Then some hairy arsed Chief Petty Officer would inspect it, mark it out of ten and write your name on the bottom with a fat black marker pen. It was all boring stuff, even more so if you didn't have a clue about electronics. I learnt some technical stuff about amplifiers and diodes but from all the work the only thing I can remember to this day was the equation for resonant frequency due to it being presented in the form of a song. I began to wish I'd picked another trade.

With trade training completed and out the way the final stage before being allowed to go to sea was the safety stuff. This was more like it! I loved it! I underwent Naval fire-fighting at HMS Phoenix then sea-survival at Horsea Island in Portsmouth. The firefighting was a real head rush. When a ship catches fire there is no dialling 999 and waiting for Trumpton to turn up. We fought the fires ourselves but in contrast to that of the civilian fire service, our priority was saving the ship not saving life.

Dressed in a Fearnought suit made of compressed wool we were thrown into an enormous metal box built to represent some ship's compartment. The entrance to the rig was a couple of stories vertically straight up on the roof and in via ships hatch. Once inside we would scale ladders, navigate feel your way around, open watertight hatches all in the pitch black while a large oil fire roared away under your feet - and I do mean *pitch* black - all done whilst wearing the Fearnought suit, full breathing apparatus, large compressed woollen mittens, anti-flash hoods and the baddest bad-ass steel top capped boots you have ever encountered. On tapping your way around the edge of the compartment using the back of your free hand to locate the bulk-head in zero visibility, dragging 'charged' hoses, you and your fire-fighting team would fumble for a hatch opening, lift the hatch and placing a nozzle set to 'spray jet' tight into one corner of the hatch opening, ensuring a 'water-wall' was placed at the top to prevent flames and fireballs coming up into your compartment and toasting you all, then the team would descend the ladder and fight whatever fire we found in the compartment below. It was brilliant!

After completing the fire-fighting course it was then sea-survival. This consisted of two different elements. One was keeping a ship afloat when it was damaged and the hull had been breached by either collision or hostile attack. This meant mending holes as fast as you could as seawater fired in under high pressure, propping up and 'shoring' falling and twisted deck-heads and in amongst all of this as you waded in varying depths of sloshing seawater flooded compartments, running very high voltage power cables from emergency junction boxes through the compartments. This training, in common with the fire fighting, was something the Navy made as realistic as possible and for much of it we used a pretend section of ship called 'Havoc' which we descending into via a watertight 'ships' door and made our way through Havoc fixing holes through which was gushing tons of water at immense pressure while the lights flickered around you before failing completely. The compartments would slowly and painfully fill up with water to the top with your working room and breathing space reducing second by second as you bobbed on the surface of the floodwater, your head moving ever nearer the deck-head and if you failed to get the holes plugged your only choice was to abandon the compartment to the sea, get you and your mates out before sealing the hatch behind you. While all this went on, the Havoc rig was thrown about on giant hydraulic rams to simulate a rough sea. No pressure then?

The vessel sinking always going to happen and your fate was deliberately thrust upon you by the training staff as they needed to see what you were capable of and if you had the sense of mind to judge under pressure when a compartment was lost and that you had the balls to seal the hatch even if that meant leaving sailors trapped within. Another immense buzz and I loved every minute of it.

The second element to the sea survival course was about what to do if the first had failed. When all hope was lost, how to abandon ship and survive in the sea for as long as possible with or without a life raft. It meant jumping into the freezing sea from a decent height in a rubber suit and life jacket, swimming to the nearest life raft which always deliberately floating upside down, getting it turned the right side up and then climbing in. Once inside you would activate the emergency radio set and erect the telescopic aerial and transmit a distress signal. Easy really.

Finally, I was trained up and ready to join my first ship.

Chapter Two

Monster Slippers

The Navy News - A fantastic publication for Matelots (pronounced *mat-lows,* slang for ratings of the Royal Navy), ex-Matelots and the families of Matelots, who suffer long periods of both domestic bliss and sheer hell whilst their fathers and sons, and more recently daughters and wives, float off around the globe. Plus, of course, anyone else with a healthy interest in all things associated with the senior service. As I said, a fantastic publication.

Eagerly awaited by all, one of the most popular sections of The Navy News for serving members at least, was the 'swap drafts' section. Swap drafts are situated towards the rear of the paper, possibly due to the reluctance of the management to recognise that the humble sailor may be unhappy about the posting to their next ship or draft; after all, this would determine the course, quite literally of that sailor's life, and to some extent the life of his family over the next 24 months or more. The concept was simple really. Able Seaman Jack Tarr gets a 2-year draft or 'posting' to HMS Rustbucket but isn't overly impressed as HMS Rustbucket is off on a deployment counting waves in the South Atlantic for the next 9 months and Jack Tarr has just become a daddy. Jack Tarr puts an ad in the 'swap drafts' section at the back of Navy News. Able Seaman Jezz Staines who is the same rank and trade spots Jack's advert and fancies swapping drafts as Seaman Staines has been posted to Plymouth dockyard's 'Untangling Old Rope' Department for the next 2 years and can't think of anything more boring. Seaman Staines and Seaman Tarr both agree to swap so both lads write to their respective management and their posting are swapped. Everyone's a winner, well they are if you can find someone to swap with.

The swap draft gave somewhat limited hope to those wanting a chance to try another one of Her Majesty's big grey war canoes but alas my experience of swap drafts was that is was a waste of time. I was quite enjoying time in the UK with my new fiancée and I was hoping not to be sent to a ship that would take me away from her for any great length of time. I had been in mob a little while now and already had a couple of lengthy deployments under my belt which, whilst fun, was no conducive with romantic relationships. I had recently passed the exams for promotion and was sent back to HMS Collingwood for my Leading Rates trade training. To my frustration, shortly before completing my course, I received notice that I would be drafted to HMS Sheffield, or the 'Shiny Sheff' as she was fondly referred to by her crew. The Sheffield was all set to deploy on a seven-month trip, taking in the Far East, the Middle

East and an awful lot of places in between. I did not want to go.

"Are you the twat who's trying get off the Sheffield?" I looked around the table in the canteen; eight pairs of eyes were staring right back at me. It was October 1994 and this was my first day back at the Fleet Maintenance Group, Devonport – the stopover for engineers just leaving or awaiting their next surface ship or submarine.

"Yeah!" I chuckled, hoping that Mr Friendly would chirp up again but I was met with silence and straight faces so decided it would be better to just shut up and sit down.

The Fleet Maintenance Group worked out of HMS Defiance, a shore establishment set within the dockyard at Devonport, Plymouth. The dockyard itself was probably one of the most historically wealthy places in the UK. The South Yard dated from the end of the 17th Century and contains an array of slipways, buildings and docks from that period and those build subsequently over the next couple of centuries. The older South Yard is also full of some magnificent buildings which would have been fit for grandeur if they had been constructed almost anywhere else. In their shadow stood one of the few remaining working sets of hangman's gallows in Britain – a reminder that the penalty for committing arson in a Royal Dockyard was death right up until 1971.

Wide streets with the lightest of traffic weaved between the 18th-century buildings, along the waterfront and over an uneven road lined with train rails reserved for the nuclear train which bore the responsibility for moving large submarine reactors to the newer end of the dockyard. The train certainly kept the vast number of commuting cyclists and motorcycle riders on their toes! The North dockyard was far busier than the South and was considered the real business end. It was full of large modern cranes, industrial style units and large wharfs to berth our warships and foreign vessels, both military and civil. Fast food huts painted imaginatively in Navy blue selling pasties, sandwiches and drinks were found every five hundred yards or so. Hell, I believe these days there may even be a MacDonalds in there somewhere. Busy Sailors and blue Bedford rascal vans scurried about purposefully like worker ants diving in and out of doorways and workshop entrances.

As a member of FMG, I was tasked with minor repairs and maintenance on-board ships returning from sea. I spent the next couple of months walking around the dockyard avoiding work as much as possible. I hated that place and am full of admiration for those who live out nearly their whole 22 year careers there, and then some. I would question their mental health. They are either headstrong or plain mad. It was, however, a far better place if you were partway up the hierarchy ladder and enjoying some of the benefits of rank but for me, nope. I was on the bottom 'rung' of scramble net.

My first experience of the dockyard was a stressful one. Through no fault of the Navy, the blame lay entirely with the Army. On completion of my initial engineering course at HMS Collingwood in 1990, I was sent to Devonport dockyard to join HMS Defiance as a baby engineer with nothing in the way of practical experience of Naval life or engineering. Defiance was my first 'working' concrete ship. Being quite tired, comfortable and somewhat sleepy during the train journey trip from Fareham to Plymouth, I dozed off, waking moments before arriving at Exeter St. David's train station where I was due to change trains for Guzz, the slang name us seafaring Naval folk gave to the city of Plymouth.

The majority of the sailors based in England were either 'Guzz' Ratings for Plymouth or 'Pompey' Ratings for Portsmouth depending on the type of ship you were drafted too. Primarily Destroyers and Aircraft carriers were stationed at Portsmouth whereas Plymouth was home to the Royal Navy's fleets of Frigates.

Whilst on the train I had left my military kit bag in the safety of the guard compartment in a separate carriage; it contained my uniform, my shiny parade boots, my gas mask, my beret, my cap and a Christmas present from my mum to keep my feet warm during the cold nights at Collin-grad, I mean Collingwood.

So, a few minutes before I was due to arrive at Exeter-St-Davids train station I stretched, yawned and got up to go and recover it from the guard compartment but found it had disappeared. Then mild panic set in as I recalled a group of Pongos (That's our fond term for Army folk) who'd been sitting near me as I'd drifted off to sleep. They'd been nudging each other and giggling among themselves like sniggering schoolgirls when I woke up. Putting two and two together didn't take me too long. Glumly, I reported the missing kit bag to the British Transport Police and then headed off to join Devonport dockyard in a pair of blue denim jeans, a T-shirt and a pair of trainers, wishing that I'd had the foresight to ensure my uniform when I first had the chance during basic training at Legoland aka HMS Raleigh. My Divisional Officer seemed sympathetic enough, at least on the surface and tasked a Petty Officer to find a van to drive me across the River Tamar back into my homeland, Cornwall, so I could buy some second-hand uniform from HMS Raleigh's stores. Here, a wealth of DC, 'declared clothing' could be haggled for from Jack Dusty. 'Declared clothing' was the leftovers from those who had not completed their basic training and had returned all their kit before being ceremonially booted from the establishment, unworthy of wearing a Square Rig.

Later that week and much to my surprise I received a phone call from the British Transport Police with some good news! My kit bag had been found. There was some bad news, however. It had been hit by a train, or ten, after somehow falling onto the line. I headed off to Plymouth's main train station to collect my ruined belongings, from the British Transport Police. I still remember my embarrassment, and the patronising grin on the copper's face as he itemised the property that had been received from the line finishing the list with a monotoned adenoid voice.
"And finally, one pair of monster slippers," smirked the Transport Rozzer.
Holding up a pair of large brown furry feet complete with claws and denim patched soles. An addition that my Mum had sewn on to them as I had worn through the original ones such was my love of my nasty warm 'Monster Slippers'.

This return to Devonport dockyard in 1994 was far less stressful. Although I was still the *twat* trying to get a 'swap draft' from the Sheffield I was, at least, still amongst my own kind and had some experience and credit to my salty swagger. More relief came in the form of 'Mac' McKay, a familiar face from my time on board the dry-docked Aircraft Carrier, HMS Illustrious. A short, stocky, spotty and scruffy-looking bloke with a puffy face and greasy brown hair, Mac was famous for being able to thread his gold necklace through a freak hole which had appeared at some time in his foreskin and then to swing it in circles in front of him, like some demented, desperate for attention, cheerleader who had just discovered that the college football team liked her party-trick with her newly acquired nipple tassels. Mac was the first person to mention to me that the 'Andrew', that'll be another slang term for the Navy, was planning some voluntary redundancies and that members of the Weapons Engineering branch were in the line of fire to get some.

We spent the next few weeks pestering anyone ranked *Charge Chief* or above in an attempt to gain more information about dates and numbers of redundancies, along with long drawn out 'stand-easies' with a pasty and a copy of *The Sun* newspaper trying to calculate the vast wealth that would come our way should we find the chocolate bar which contained the golden ticket. Gradually, more of my shipmates arrived from the Illustrious. She was in Plymouth, reaching the end of her two-year re-fit, and was soon to be re-floated and sent back to her homeport of Portsmouth, leaving behind a thick residue of engineers and mechanics all running around without a place to call home. As luck would have it they were all rounded up and sent off to work in the dockyard with us. This made it far easier to loaf off work. You weren't missed as easily as some other poor bugger would get collared to do the work meant for you.

My recent 18-month sentence on the Illustrious, or Lusty had been fairly uneventful aside from a brief liaison with a stunning lady sailor. She was petite, with a perfect Babs Windsor chest, short black hair, gorgeous blue eyes and a soft Newcastle accent. The last

I heard, she was discharged from the Navy after getting the hots for another lady sailor on her next ship. I told myself this may have been a ploy to get herself instantly kicked out and avoid the eighteen-months notice required to leave the service. My ego certainly prefers that to the theory that snogging me put her off men for life. At the time Gayness was still banned from HM Forces.

HMS Illustrious was big by our standards and she took up nearly the entire length and width of one of the dry docks in the dockyard. With walls of light brown stone resembling giant steps from the top of the dockyard wall to the bottom, the dry dock was home for the Lusty for several months. On one occasion when the opportunity arose, I descended the steps and into the bottom of the dock and strolled along directly beneath the Illustrious to a point where when I was certain that I was standing centrally, I reached up and placed the palm of my hand against her belly. A very surreal feeling, knowing that 22,000 tons of aircraft carrier was only three feet above your head supported only by beams of wooden shoring, yes wooden!

Because she was stripped of all habitation, initially the crew of the *Lusty* were accommodated in HMS Drake, another concrete ship hugging the perimeter of the dockyard, but as work on the ship progressed personnel were moved on-board and into their respective mess decks. As there was not a great deal of equipment up and running for me to keep an eye on most of my time was spent trying to accidentally destroy the bomb-proof Watchkeeper's clock that had to be taken everywhere with the 'Weapons Engineering' watch-keeper.

As the on-duty Watchkeeper, I had to check various compartments and offices within the ship. To ensure I completed these round properly keys were hung in each compartment of the ship on the Watchkeeper's list. These compartments had to be visited hourly and the key inserted into the heavy, round, lunch box sized, victorian looking, leather-cased clock, and turned a full 360 degrees, Doing this would mark a thin paper roll which was loaded inside it to record the time of visit and number of the key. Sounds easy enough and if I'm honest it also comes downright tedious but on an Aircraft Carrier, that means an awful lot of walking and climbing ladders. What made this task even more difficult was that the regular semi-civilised aluminium ladders normally found within Naval ships had all been removed for the duration of the refit. The reason for this was unknown to me but I imagine the ladders were being tested to ensure it retained the strength to take the weight of a 20 stone duty Matelot carrying a crate of 'Angry Apples'. Then I suspect it would be refurbished or even replaced before being refitted to the Lusty towards the end of her time in refit. Every aluminium stairway was replaced with a wooden ladder which had all been placed at a 45-degree angle. They had no handrails, were about 18 inches wide and were knocked together in the dockyard by a hungover YTS Jan-dockie and a bent hammer and each creaked uncomfortably like the Mary Celeste under a Matelots weight. These wooden ladders were a nightmare for anyone with vertigo as glancing down you could see straight down several decks through the widely spaced wooden rungs. The view made better by the neat and orderly line of hatches, one directly beneath the other.

The watchkeeper's clock itself was a real pain in the ass to carry around, a clockwork 'big brother' to keep tabs on us plus it was a sturdy old thing, but after numerous 'accidental' drops through four or five decks the paper roll within did sometimes become jammed. Mission accomplished. I still count HMS Illustrious as a ship I served on I was officially one of her *ship's company* however I just didn't get the chance to go to sea on her. A big disappointment as I imagine a ship as big as the Lusty would have been an experience. She would no doubt get the good ports and visits especially after her re-fit as the Navy would be keen to show her off. I suspect many of those ports would've been US side of the Atlantic.

So it was, I joined HMS Sheffield in January 1995. No-one had answered my request to swap, so I was stuck with her, or rather, she was stuck with me. She was the third British Warship to bear the name Sheffield. The first, being a 'Southampton' class cruiser and had seen action during the Second World War. The second, commissioned in 1975, was the first of the Type 42 destroyers but was struck by an Exocet missile during the Falklands conflict in 1982 killing 20 of her crew. She was the first Royal Navy warship destroyed in action since the end of World War Two and her sinking sent shockwaves around the world. The Sheffield I joined in 1995 was a 'Type 22 - Batch II' Frigate, coming it at a mere 4,900 tonnes and boasting a crew of 270. She was armed with a variety of weapons – Seawolf anti-aircraft missiles fore and aft, STWS torpedo tubes on the port and starboard waists, either one or two Lynx helicopters, and port and starboard 20mm and 30mm cannons. Ironically, she also carried four Exocet anti-ship missiles, the very missile responsible for her predecessor's demise. Sheffield was due to leave on a 7-month deployment in the spring so I spent the next two months getting familiar with my role on-board, learning my duties and responsibilities along with the layout on the ship. Although I had spent 2 years on board HMS Brazen, another Type 22 frigate, there were many differences between both ships. Brazen was a batch I and Sheffield a batch II. The longer sleeker version, new and improved one of Her Majesty's big grey ass-kicking war canoes.

Stepping on to the flight deck at the rear (aft) of the ship, day-to-day access was gained by entering '1' deck just forward of the aircraft hangar on the starboard side, that's the right-hand side to all you landlubbers. 1 deck was the exit/entry deck. Decks below were then numbered 2-deck, 3-deck etc. A large number '1' or '2' was painted at various points along the corridors and within compartments to remind the lost, confused and bewildered which deck they were lost, confused and bewildered on. In addition and to add to the confusion everything *above* 1 deck was numbered 01, 02, 03 and so on.

On a Type-22 this entry point on 1 deck would bring you into a well-lit passageway about five feet wide and nine feet high lined with pipes and cables running almost the full length of the ship. Most compartments and offices found on this deck were administration or belonged to the Weapon Engineering department and were buzzing with computers and power supplies, with the exception being the officers' mess, known on-board a ship as the 'wardroom', and the officers' cabins.

As with all Royal Naval vessels, the walls or 'bulkheads' within the ship were painted an identical ash grey, with the monotony broken only by frequent silver fire extinguishers and bright red metal boxes fixed to the bulkheads containing breathing apparatus or 'BASCCA'. From here, various hatches could take you to the decks above or below. Located within the deck above was the Operations room, highly regarded as the nerve centre of the ship, together with more weapons compartments, radar compartments, the captain's working and living spaces and the ship's bridge. Descending to '2' deck brought you level with the senior ratings' accommodation and mess decks – the home of the Chief Petty Officers and Petty Officers.

A Royal Navy Petty Officer is the equivalent rank to a Sergeant in the Army or Air Force with a Chief Petty Officer being a Senior Sergeant. The Chiefs were usually in charge of a particular item of equipment, office space or had responsibility for a large area within the ship such as the Upper Deck Weapons or the Engine Room. The Navy then had two further tiers above CPO, that of Fleet Chief Petty Officer and Warrant Officer. This was as far as a lower deck rating could go before joining the - *cough* - elite by gaining an Officer's Commission. Also located on 2 Deck was the galley, dining hall, toilets or 'Heads' as the Navy say, and showers, along with the NAAFI shop.

Approximately halfway along 2-deck was the 'Ship's Control Centre'. If the Operations room was the brain of the vessel then the Ship's Control Centre was surely her heart. From here, the ship's engines, propulsion and electrical generators were regulated, along with fresh water and sewage all essential for the smooth running of the frigate. The junior rates' mess decks were found on 3-deck. The Junior Rates were the soldiers of the ship known as Able Seamen and their corporals, referred to in the Navy as Leading Rates or Killicks. The 'Killick' a reference to the Anchor they wore denoting their rank. To some these lower deck Messes were a place of scandal and excitement, partying and excessive drinking; to others, they were a prison cell.

The engine rooms took up several decks and were found in the centre of the vessel. These huge Olympus turbines engines were nursed and tended by a host of Marine Engineers. The throaty and industrial noise they created was unique and strangely comforting after you got used to it. Understandably, a lot of preparations have to be done with a ship and her crew before any deployment. There's an intense training programme by all on-board, along with a methodical examination of every nut and bolt, circuit board and micro-chip. It's a long and tortuous process, but the time seemed to fly by and before I knew it the time to leave was upon us. The last evening I spent with my girlfriend Abby was pretty crap. Over the previous couple of years, I had made regular trips up to London at the weekends, where she was studying at university and needless to say there were a few tears before I left but that was to be expected, seven months is a bloody long time to be away from those who gave a shit. I was thrown into '3 Golf' mess, the '3' denoting the deck on which the mess was situated, and the 'G' indicating how far along the length of the ship it was. The compartments ran from forward to aft, A, B, C D and so on. The compartment forward of us would be 'F' and aft, 'H'.

3G mess deck consisted of approximately thirty-six bunks and was divided into port and starboard sections. In other words, there were two 'mess-squares' where the lads would live day-to-day. Each contained a television; the starboard mess had the additional benefit of a stereo but the port mess controlled the all-important beer fridge. We were directly below the galley and the dining hall, so we had a minimal distance to walk to feed our faces. 3 Golf mess deck, in common with every mess deck in the Navy, was crammed full of a broad range of characters. We had blokes who were dedicated to the progression of their career with blokes who would have been right at home outside football grounds kicking the shit out of rival fans. We had Nozzers who were just fresh out of the box and blokes who weren't that far from collecting their pension. Nevertheless, we all had one thing in common. We were about to embark on a seven-month piss-up.

Entering or leaving harbours of notable importance usually meant a routine known as 'Procedure Alpha' and leaving Plymouth was going to be one such occasion. Early on March the 14th 1995, we slipped our mooring at Frigate Alley, all available personnel from the ship's company gathered smartly on the port side of the upper deck in their best uniform. This gave us a fantastic view as we crept slowly past the other ships resting in the safety of the dockyard, passing the loved ones waving at us from Devil's Point, the closest vantage point offered for those left behind. As we passed Devil's Point, it felt as though you could lean across and touch them and I wondered whether anyone had jumped from the deck of a ship in a last-ditch attempt to avoid a deployment or win a sweetheart's kiss. I had said my farewells to my parents when I'd left home in Cornwall the day before.

"Goodbye Guzz! Goodbye Express-Pizza! Goodbye Union Street! Goodbye Mum!"

Adrian 'Bruce' Willis had joined the ship around the same time as myself, and it was an early sign of things to come when we were pursued from Plymouth by a small fishing boat overflowing with totally shit-faced friends of Bruce, who had all emerged from his local pub to see him off. As they bobbed toward us waving cans of beer, their little vessel came worryingly close to colliding with us. This was the last straw for the Ministry of Defence Police who, in *their* little boat, intercepted the fishing boat for a quick word.

We soon sailed passed Drake's Island and the breakwater allowing the Captain to put his foot down and within no time we were steaming at twenty-five knots with the UK behind us when the ship's main broadcast clicked on, followed by a second or two of silence before:

"FOR EXERCISE! FOR EXERCISE! FOR EXERCISE! FIRE! FIRE! FIRE!"

It was only to be expected. You are always guaranteed a wake-up call in the form of a fire exercise or something similar within moments of leaving, usually a well thought through distraction to stop a Matelots mind dwelling on the fact we were sailing away from their loved ones for seven months. These fire exercises are usually pretty mundane affairs, and more of a disruption to our loafing than anything else, though I'm sure all sailors would reluctantly admit that they were essential – Practice makes perfect, and it stops the crew drifting around in a miserable, moping, zombie-like state. Some exercises were small and some big and on this occasion, they were doing things properly. The Marine Engineering Officer had been spotted strolling around in his 'fresh out of the bag' crisp white overalls which meant we'd be charging the size two fire hoses with water and wearing and using breathing apparatus equipment, instead of pretending to. The battleship jungle drums had beaten their usual warning five minutes before the exercise kicking off, giving us the chance to safely store equipment that would otherwise get damaged in the mad panic of the ensuing moments. Knowing that this was going to be a bigger than average exercise, I'd been tempted to go to my emergency station straight away, but I had to pretend that this was an everyday small fire, and so I remained at my office with my coffee.

The 'first wave' attack party, who would initially fight the fire with the aid of simple fire extinguishers and breathing equipment, waited for the instructions as to its location. The speakers of the main broadcast crackled again.

"FIRE IN THE GALLEY, ATTACK PARTY MUSTER AT THE SCENE OF THE FIRE, SUPPORT AND CONTAINMENT PARTY MUSTER AT THE AFTER SECTION BASE!"

The Attack-Party now knew where to run. Meanwhile, a support party consisting of five sailors ran to one of the large damage control lockers, usually favouring the one furthest from the location of the fire allowing them more time to kit-up and make ready. On the Sheffield, there were two of these lockers, one forward and one aft, and both located on '2 Deck'. Once there, they would crack open the metal doors and with some additional help dress in large, woolly 'Fearnought' suits. These one-piece compressed woollen overalls were excellent at keeping out the intense incinerating heat of a major fire, and along with anti-flash white head coverings, gloves, outer mittens, helmet, boots and breathing apparatus was the best the modern Royal Navy had for the task.

While the Support-Party dressed, a containment party would be mustering at the section base. Along with fire-fighting equipment inside the Section-Base lockers was a variety of damage control equipment so Jack could stop the ship sinking. From here the Containment-Party were directed to compartments directly next to the scene of the fire. Their job was to spray jets of water onto the bulkheads, cooling the sides of the compartment affected by the fire. This procedure, known as boundary cooling, was vital. Without it, the metal bulkheads would simply melt under the intense heat of the fire.

Our priority when fighting a fire was to save the ship rather than saving life. Without the ship, everyone would perish so it was a no brainer. The fire exercise was expected to last a couple of hours sending us to the next level up on the scale.

"HANDS TO EMERGENCY STATIONS! HANDS TO EMERGENCY STATIONS!"

All of the ship's personnel were now involved and I went to my Emergency Station post. In the past, I'd been a member of the Support-Party for an Engine Room fire I can confirm this is a highly stressful role to have, especially for a 17-year-old as I was at the time. I'd also tried my hand at various roles within the fire party, but now my role was to use my knowledge of the radar and computer systems to keep the ship running, rather than be directly involved in fighting the fire. I had to sit in the Operations Room and act like a coiled spring should the systems crash. To add some realism, various lighting and electrical circuits were disrupted, smoke canisters were deployed and selected personnel were required to act as casualties to test the medical staff's ability to treat burns and smoke inhalation. The next hour was dominated by organised chaos – This stuff is great for morale especially at the start of a seven-month deployment away from home, honest!

When the exercise eventually finished, then necessary the tidy up began. Mopping up free-standing water from the passageways and recharging the breathing apparatus was a bigger pain in the ass than the exercise itself. Later as the early evening drew in and the crew was a bit more back into a ships routine, the duty-watch personnel from each mess would clean the ship for the nightly ritual known as 'evening rounds'. The living quarters, bathrooms and main passageways were scrubbed and then inspected by the duty Officer of the Day. Once that was over, those of us who were now 'off-duty' could settle into our evening meal and our beer ration. We couldn't go out anywhere and with this being a warship of the Royal Navy out on active duty, there was sadly no possibility of getting pissed, well *officially*.

Each sailor was permitted three tins of beer or per night, but a smart beer-bosun, whose job it was to manage the supplies for the mess deck, could hoard mountains of the stuff for emergencies, stuffing it away under seats, behind clothing lockers and under bunks. This was a far more simple task than it appeared. Not everyone drank their allotted three tins every night, but the beer bosun's paperwork showed that they did. If the records showed that a mess deck of thirty ratings drank their entire allowance of 90 cans every evening, when in reality only twenty tins had been drunk, this left seventy additional beers for the next night, and so on. This could work forwards, too, in the sense that you could drink tomorrow's rations – Or even the next week's today! As this was only the start of the trip, nobody had got on anyone else's nerves or pissed anyone else off enough to warrant starting a punch up, so the music got turned up to full volume and we settled into a drinking session, the gentle soothing tones of The Prodigy masking the sound of the sea striking the sides of our vessel.

3-Golf mess consisted of a right bunch of reprobates. We had a load of 'Weapons Engineers' along with a couple of apprentice Artificers who were expected to rise rapidly through the chain of command and beyond on some accelerated promotion scheme, but in a change to what I was used to, 3-Golf also had Matelots from the Navy's other branches. I was a member of the Weapon Engineering branch, a killick greenie. Killick referred to my rank and 'greenie' being a slang term for my trade, and up until now, I had lived on-board ships in mess decks only containing other Weapons Engineers. 3-Golf had a mix. Diversity for tradesmen! Radio Operators, Seamen aka 'dabbers', dabbing paint here and there, and even a Surveyor whose job was to make maps and chart the geographies of the ocean, YAWN! Sorry for a moment I began to nod off! Our surveyor bore more than a passing resemblance to pop singer Jimmy Somerville. Well, that's what we told him, anyway.

Some of the Matelots had the trademark tattoos and shaved heads, with one lad, in particular, standing out in this respect. Known as 'Bubbles' he was plastered head to toe in tasteful ink work. Bubbles was a Cornish boy like myself and along with Charlie Worker, who was known as 'The St. Austell Slayer' due to his passion for getting pissed and having a flashpoint lower than nitro-glycerine, we made up the Cornish contingent of 3G Mess. Two Northampton lads, Mick Bridger and Chris 'Lordy' Lucan would always end up fighting each other – If Lordy Lucan could be found. Like his namesake, Lucan would frequently disappear, usually being flown home from lengthy deployments for one reason or another. Richie Richards, another killick greenie, was a slender bloke sprouting an impressive mop of blonde hair. He also had a foghorn surgically attached to the front of his face where his mouth should have been. This earned him the alias of 'The Mouth on a Stick'.

Along with numerous other lads of varying ages between 17 and 40-something, we were to travel the globe, ruling the waves, defending the realm and searching for cheap beer and cheaper laughs.

So back to the deployment and the first part of our plan, or rather, the ship's plan as we weren't involved, was first to sail down to the Middle-East where we would float around engaging in random checks on shipping and generally flying the flag for Great Britain Limited and Her Majesty Queen Elizabeth the Second. The Royal Navy had a large presence in this part of the world, even before the 1991 Gulf War, mostly working with local governments to stamp on those found breaching trade embargoes, especially during the Iran-Iraq war of the '80s and trying to keep things ticking along smoothly. Although the '91 Gulf War was supposedly resolved with a gentlemen's agreement between Saddam Hussein and George Bush Senior some 4 years previous, a lot of tension remained and several countries had their forces showing a substantial presence in the area. This was both reassuring and good for morale. Foreign Navies were genuinely good for a laugh and a scrap when on a 'run ashore'.

During the evening and early hours of the following day we had sailed south across the Bay of Biscay and started down the coast of Portugal, settling into the old routine of work, system checks, exercising both ourselves and the ship and then back evening rounds with an inspection, evening meal, beer ration and a videotape thrown in the VCR machine to stop everyone getting too bored. Within a couple of days of steaming we had passed the south-west corner of Spain and turned left, or 'port' into the Mediterranean Sea via the narrow Strait of Gibraltar.

We sailed east through the Med where some amazing European Ports sat teasingly off our port side. Warm Mediterranean evenings, beach side bars, scantily clad women and exotic cocktails, We missed them all. Instead, we steamed East – Fire exercises, damage control exercises, man overboard exercises and in the evening more beer – Until we reached the northern coast of Egypt. This opening leg of the deployment left us all feeling a little short-changed. Don't get me wrong, we all loved being on-board ship. We are the Royal Navy, sailors of her Majesty's fleet, men of steel with hearts of oak, but alongside steaming the oceans in 5,000 tonnes of long grey sea-Ferrari we still appreciated the chance to hop off and hit a bar to two. How else are we going to tell stories of our brave heroics to the local ladies? The tall tales of battling sea monsters and pirates were not going to tell themselves! Until Egypt, we'd not even seen any notable landmass. The only indication that we had left British waters was the change of weather, which was warming up nicely.

Leisure time on board ship saw many lads and lasses sun-bathing on the upper-deck, taking care to lie on a towel as the metal deck did tend to get a little 'Tefal' hot.

After ten days which seemed like an eternity, we stopped at Port Said in Egypt situated at the Northern end of the Suez Canal. Here a handful of the lads went ashore so that they could be bussed off for an overnighter and on to visit the Great Pyramids. They would meet up with the ship again at the bottom end of the canal. I had put my name on the Pyramid list but I didn't get my name picked out of the raffle. Understandable as there were quite a few of us wanting to visit the pyramids. I would just have to wait six months until our return passage through the Suez to try again.

Any ship transiting the Suez Canal is contractually obliged to embark some of the local traders, among them a genuine Egyptian barber along with an odd little chap known as the 'Gully-Gully' man. There were ample money-making opportunities presented to the locals by the numerous foreign ships and sailors transiting the canal. For a short time, the ship transformed into some type of exotic bazaar. When you walked out onto the flight deck it turned into a scene from Lawrence of Arabia. At least twenty traders stood behind an array of wares laid neatly out on dusty mats to a backdrop of stunning sandstone buildings and an enchanting waterfront, all of it neatly laid out on our flight deck (that's the large flat helipad area at the back of the ship) and sailors were soon crowding around and bartering furiously for trinkets, t-shirts, towels, jewellery boxes and so on. Lads were snapping up the vast array of fake Fred Perry shirts on offer, others tempted by a bronze ornamental dish or two. As a Suez regular, I tried to avoid such bargains. I'd had my fingers burnt before on-board HMS Brazen when, as a very naive baby sailor I'd paid five quid for an 18-inch diameter metal plate decorated with a couple of pictures. To promote trust and goodwill, I had handed the git a £20 note, stupidly expecting change. He was off over the side and onto his termite-infested pooh stick before I could shout Anne Robinson.

I blame my naivety on a huge number of stupid comments and fuck ups in my late teens. Just wish I'd had someone about to give me a clip round the ear but I guess that's part of the learning process.

The 'Gully-Gully' man was a little old Egyptian magician so named for his constant muttered of 'Gully! Gully! Gully!' and was always worth watching for a laugh. He would mesmerise his audience in the dining hall. Standing at the front of a dining hall full of sailors the Gully-Gully man, dressed in a traditional white one-piece robe, he would start his act by pulling fluffy yellow baby chicks out of tin cups and from behind peoples' ears. The chicken trick grew more complicated as his inventory of chicks increased. They came out of his pockets, from behind his back and even from their groin area of Leading Seaman Smith who sat quietly in the front row. His act would end with him yanking a long line of four-inch-square flags from his mouth, standing to attention and saluting when the Union flag appeared. This always ended in a round of applause and a few quid chucked his way. The Captain dropped in for the Gully-Gully man's first performance as a gesture of goodwill but was soon off to his normal duties of running the ship and left the rest of the crew to get a share of Egypt's answer to Paul Daniels.

The only local on-board who wasn't directly after your cash was the pilot, who was needed for his knowledge of the local shipping lanes. He came on-board to guide our sleek grey messenger of death through the canal and safely out the other end without bumping into any nasty rocks or running onto a sandbank. It took one full day to transit the Suez Canal and is only wide enough for one-way traffic, therefore ships would stack and wait their turn patiently. Many on board viewed the transit as the day-one of the infinitely impossible task of working off the beer belly. There was a running route around the circumference of the upper deck, starting from the boat deck just behind the funnel. 21 laps was an approximately one mile. In the cooler parts of the day, it was awash with dozens of sailors sprinting, stomping or shuffling up one side of the ship, crossing from starboard side to port by the forward Seawolf missile launcher and coming back down the other side, or 'waist' and back to the boat deck. A half-fit Matelot could run a lap in about 40 seconds, though a few of our complement were not even half-fit, more like a tenth fit or even 'barely living'.

Everyone had to run in the same direction – either clockwise or anti-clockwise – As there was no room to pass each other on the three-foot-wide Olympic track, which inevitably led to the quicker lads and lasses bunching up behind the slow ones. It often resembled a scene from *Convoy*, with Kris Kristofferson's *Rubber Ducky* being played by a twenty-stone Matelot sucking oxygen in through his arse. Jogging around the ship, I marvelled at how narrow the Suez Canal was often only 20 or 30 feet of clearance on either side of the ship. Despite the scenery, it wasn't a good idea to take your eye off the way ahead for too long, however. There was a very real potential of tripping up and flopping over the three-foot guard rail and into the 'oggin 40 feet below or braining yourself by running full tilt into one of the huge watertight doors or hatches which could easily be swung open into your path. But probably the greatest hazard came from the poor buggers working inside the ship on the deck below, who had to put up with the sound of 20 pairs of fat-arsed 'soles' banging on the deck above their head. An hour of this would drive anyone crazy and would be enough to turn the next 'run ashore' into a chance for the long-suffering watch-keeper to find the culprit adjust the balance. Karma can be a bitch!

After our transit, we emerged from the South end of the Suez and the ship cranked things up a yet another gear. I firmly believe that through all of the skylarking and pissing about, the Royal Navy trains and maintains the best and most professional Navy ever to have sailed the world. We may not have the physical resources or vast numbers enjoyed by other nations, but all of the exercises and constant drilling of procedures, undertaken to the tune of constant grief from the ratings, have produced the very highest quality of sailor. The same can confidently be said about the British Armed Forces as a whole. We've never been the best-equipped or best-paid, but we have always been and will always continue to be the very best. This is reflected in the genuine respect in which British soldiers, sailors and airmen are held by foreign forces. I digress.

We continued steaming south through the Red Sea and towards the Gulf of Aden, where we entered the realms of Nuclear Biological and Chemical Defence (NBCD) drills and performed another exercise accordingly. NBC is a serious threat to a ship and her crew, and even more so in the Middle East. Although in more recent history no weapons of mass destruction had been found in Iraq, this didn't mean there had never been any – In fact, we knew there had because Saddam Hussein had gassed thousands of his own people. If his mustard gas, Sarin and Tabun reserves had been spirited away and were now in the hands of people who didn't like us, it was by no means inconceivable that a British warship could be attacked with them. With this in mind, the 'Citadel' was drilled.

The Citadel was a system of closing down the entire ship and making it completely gas-tight. Doors, hatches, ventilation, the lot were shut and sealed tight. This is a procedure known as 'NBCD State One Condition Zulu Alpha' and the aim is to prevent the penetration of any gases or chemicals. It's foot-to-the-floor stuff: as soon as the alarm is sounded and the ship will begin to snake through the sea at full power, making sharp and severe, high-speed turns as she twists through the sea. The idea being that this will throw up as much spray as possible which, combined with pre-wetting spray systems (external water sprinklers on steroids) help to keep the outside washed free of chemicals. Meanwhile, all watertight doors and hatches are closed, and there is greater control on ventilation for the obvious reasons. Access to the upper deck is forbidden to all but specific personnel through dedicated and complicated airlocks systems. To re-enter the ship the sailor has to enter via a 'cleansing station' leading to the junior rating's showers. Here, highly trained decontamination personnel, aka the chefs who were cooking your breakfast 2 hours previously, strip, scrub and wash you. As a final precautionary measure, the air pressure within the Citadel is kept significantly higher than the pressure outside, this ensures that if any breaches do occur then the nasties will be blown out from the ship, rather than sucked in.

I have to say that, I was terrified at the idea of an NBC attack. Convulsing and drowning in the mucus from your lungs while your eyes and mouth burn intensely is not the Rambo-style demise that might appeal to most of the medal collectors. The threat might have lessened since the gulf skirmishes of the past that Saddam was renowned for, but it was still there, and we had no wish to get caught with our pants around our ankles. With the day's Citadel exercise over and the routine mundane chores completed, the ship's company were left to their own devices. Drinking beer, smoking tabs and playing cards.

We had steamed out of Plymouth, down the East coast of France and Spain, passed by Gibraltar, across the Med and dropping down through the Suez Canal and we were only in week two. They never mentioned this kind of crap at HMS Raleigh when I joined.

Chapter Three

Wanna see a Greyhound?

Entering the Gulf of Aden we steamed east along the southern coasts of Yemen and Oman. The journeys around this area are usually pretty uneventful other than our constant drilling or NBCD and fire exercises but then we turn North West, enter the Gulf of Oman and head towards the Strait of Hormuz. Here we start to play seriously. This narrow channel has been a sensitive area for years and is as close as Iran gets to having any significant impact on sea power. Realistically, it is the best opportunity that Iran has to strike at us. Transiting here requires us to take precautions and we heighten the readiness of the warship to respond instantly to hostile action or engagement from aircraft, other vessels and missile battery pot-shots. Personnel close up to 'Action Stations' and we sit and wait.

To keep a ship at a state of Action Stations for a prolonged period is not ideal. It is comparable for holding your breath and getting ready for a fight. A dump of adrenaline that needs to stay constant rather than 'fight or flight' as nature intended. The journey through the Strait of Hormuz is thankfully over quickly and HMS Sheffield can relax a little. I love the stillness of the water in the Persian Gulf. They are almost mirror-like, perfectly still and smooth like a vast expanse of polished glass. It almost feels like vandalism to cause a wake behind us. Our engines set at a cruise we gentle sail south-west to stop at a port I know well.

Dubai – Many people who have flown out to the Far-East have been offered the chance to stopover or change flights at Dubai in the United Arab Emirates and I would encourage anyone whoever gets the opportunity to spend a night in this beautiful city to grasp it with both hands. Take a couple of nights there if possible. Dubai is a jewel in the crown of the United Arab Emirates and at the time felt like a second home for me and some of the other sailors who were going through their career on Gulf trips. The attractions are not immediately obvious but those looking for culture with a drop of Lawrence of Arabia shouldn't be disappointed. There is an abundance of gold shops lining the streets and electrical shops stocking state of the art high tech products at bloody good prices. I bought some cracking cameras and car stereos from the high street shops in Dubai City and never once met a dodgy salesman or was sold a duff product. You even get to do a bit of 'Life Of Brain' haggling and doing so will ensure you get a few extras thrown in. Geographically Dubai is surrounded by some serious desert, the Arabian Desert. Big gas-guzzling American trucks and cars are everywhere and with petrol prices as cheap as you'd expect from a country swimming in oil one can easily see the tax free attraction for the expats who set up home there.

The majority of these ex-pats are genuine people and often willing to play host to the invading British sailors, usually stockpiling lager in a similar way to our beer bosun. We found rugby matches against the ex-pats one means of getting out and about. No one cared who won the match as the piss-ups afterwards were legendary.

Another attraction to this area was the large number of British air-hostesses stopping over in Dubai's many hotels and British nurses earning wages more worthy of their skills and far in excess of what they would earn in the UK. These girls were simply bloody good fun to get pissed with and were usually just as glad to experience a bit of the home atmosphere by hanging out with similar-minded British sailors. The stop into Dubai made the ship's company comfortable and was our first decent chance to get hammered, properly hammered. Dubai's nearest major seaport was Port Jebel Ali, primarily a container port with brand new 4x4 Chelsea Tractors scattered liberally about the dockyard looking abandoned and forgotten encased in a healthy film of desert sand. It made you thirsty for a beer just looking. This was a berthing spot for most Navies visiting the area but the British and US seemed to have the monopoly.

We arrived in Jebel Ali at beginning of April. After one of our first nights out on the beer, some of the lads returned to 3-Golf to recover. It'd been a long day in the desert heat, hanging out at hotel bars and pools along with a little bargain hunting for new gadgets but now we were back on-board after a short taxi ride back from

Dubai and we could relax with a couple of last-minute beers from the fridge in the mess square.

The mess square was exactly that, a square with hard moulded plastic seats permanently fixed to the bulkheads, their cushions velcroed on. Suddenly a stark bollock naked 'Taff' Selfridge strolled in as pissed as a handcart. Taff was a Leading Radio Operator, a Welsh lad who liked his beer, he was quite a decent bloke, not easily flustered and mild-mannered but certainly not someone to cross. He knew his trade and had a fair amount of respect from the other lads as he had been in the Navy a few years and had already done his fair share of deployments.

"Ere lads," said Taff, "wanna see a greyhound?"

Without giving anyone time to object Taff turned his back on us, dropped his head and proceeded to fumble around with his 'twig and berries'. He then bent forward and whilst keeping his feet firmly on the ground placed both his hands on the deck in front of him. The lads stared in nervous disbelief with a collective 'What the fuck?' etched across everyone's faces. The site of the hairy arse would've set us off in fits of laughter on its own but Taff had tucked his nuts between his legs so they squeezed through the insides of his thighs popping out the back. Like two veiny pink boiled eggs both knackers, trapped in their new position, were strained to bursting point. It was like the rear view of a greyhound dog but with rather fatter legs, a hairier arse and two dirty great big pink bollocks. If that wasn't enough, Taff started to bounce up and down on his feet before hopping off into the darkness towards the bunks behind the mess square.

A drunken Mick Bridger was momentarily distracted from his phone-call home to the UK but soon regained his train of thought, or what was left of it as most was shot away by that evening's alcohol consumption. The internal telephone within the mess decks that Mick was using could be patched through to an out-going line from the ships Headquarters (HQ1). We were allowed to book ten-minute spaces in which we could phone home to loved ones in the UK. The connection, made with the help of the HQ1 watch-keeper sat next to his little telephone panel some fifty yards along the length of one deck was hit or miss. The phone lines weren't 100% reliable and your ten-minute slot had to be booked in advance by popping into HQ1 and looking at what slots were available on the phone timetable. If you had a good watch-keeper connecting the lines (and no one waiting in the next slot) you could drift significantly over your ten minutes.

Sat on Mick's right side was Lordy Lucan looking quite content and almost comatose in his alcoholic state and lying next to Mick on his left, slouched over onto a supporting elbow was Bubbles wearing only a pair of standard-issue Jack Blair Bermuda shorts and a *very* sunburnt bald head. The mouth on a stick was sat next to him followed by Jim Bowen, a killick dabber with a cracking fifties 'Teddy boy' hairstyle. Bubbles, who was also several sheets to the wind, was being generally anti-social and developed a hatred for the small mess table booting it across the mess square with his size 9 flip-flop.

After a good twenty minutes of drifting in and out of varying states of drunkenness, some basic conversational skills involving grunts about Mick's crap attempt at divorce, swearing and comedy farting, Taff Selfridge strolled back in *still* completely naked. Where he had spent the last twenty minutes was anyone's guess but he had decided not to be a greyhound anymore. Tonight Matthew I am going to be 'The Fly!'

I'm not sure which must have been more painful to perform out of the fly or the greyhound but each was equally disturbing. 'The Fly' involved placing both hands under the scrotum and lifting everything skywards, pressing the whole lot against the stomach. Looking down onto the arrangement one would see a site which could, vaguely and with a fair dose of imagination resemble a fly's snout and it's two bulbous eyes glaring back at you, the abundance of pubic hairs made interesting attention to detail in finishing the fly's head.

"I think I will land on Taff Selfridge," said the fly which for some reason had a comedy French accent.

"bzzzzzzzzt bzzzzzzzt bzzzt!" it continued.

With that Taff got sloppy and one of the fly's eyes dropped away to hang where Mother Nature intended.

"Oh no, my eye 'as dropped off!"

Taff gathered the rogue eye back up with his hand but with a little too much enthusiasm and he gave a pathetic cough as he strained his knacker. Everyone winced and Taff bent forward and limped out of the Mess Square nursing his pet genital insect and disappeared from view once again into the dark abyss of the bunk areas.

Mick had by now been on the phone to his ex-wife for a good half an hour and decided that he wanted Lordy Lucan to speak to her instead and thrust the phone receiver at him. As Lordy chatted away to Mrs Bridger a debate started between Mick and the rest of the lads over Mick's marriage. He had only been married for about six weeks before deciding enough was enough and getting divorced. It now looked as though they now wanted to get back together again.

Lordy had been doing a fine job yapping to Mick's wife when "Bzzzzzzt bzzzzzzzzzzzzzzt bzzzzzzzt!"

The fly returned and hovered a couple of inches from Lordy's head. Not exactly impressed by the visitor Lordy decided to pass the phone to the fly so it could speak to the former Mrs Bridger.

"Ello, bzzzzzt I am the fly!" said the fly as Taff waved his scrunched up bollocks at the receiver of the phone.

The fly was by now starting to get on everyone's nerves so Lordy decided to squat it and he clouted Taff square in the nuts with the heavy old telephone handset causing Taff to collapse in testicular pain for the second time in ten minutes. More 'Balls Eye' than 'Bulls Eye!'

The phone was returned to Mick who quickly wrapped up the phone call home.

"Off you scoot then," he chirped before replacing the receiver.

Mick then looked around the room. His eyes appearing to operate independently, each taking a turn to roll upwards into the eyelid.

"Woooooooooaaaaaaaooooooooo where's my wallet man?"

Mick looked around the room and deciding that as he couldn't see it the next best thing was to pick up and throw the small table that Bubbles had already kicked over.

"Leave the table, Mick," suggested Big Jim Bowen, "enjoy the table where it is, enjoy the table karma man!"

This appeared to do the trick and Mick decided to sit back in the corner where he dropped immediately into booze-induced coma.

Enough was enough and everyone decided to bugger off to their scratchers to get their heads down for the night leaving only Mick, Lordy and me in the Mess. Mick had fallen from the seats and now lay face down asleep on the deck. The mess carpet had absorbed all sorts of nasties in its short life, so much so that ours had actually shrunk about an inch around the edges, and I half expected Mick to leap back to life as the 'Odour la piss e beer' would be enough to raise the dead.

There was an unwritten rule regarding blokes that fell asleep in the mess square so Lordy made efforts to haul Mick up and get him into his pit. Blokes would routinely wake with eyebrows missing, legs shaved or their clothes stitched via homeward-bound tacks to the mess cushions rendering them paralysed until help came. This was quite tame in comparison to going to sleep in other mess squares elsewhere on-board, especially if you were their guest in the first place.

Ships often contained five or six different mess-decks, larger ships had more messes and smaller vessels less. This also included those occupied by senior ratings such as Chief Petty Officers and Petty Officers. If a Matelot was invited into another Mess for a beer you could be assured that one beer would turn in to several beers quite quickly. The chances of an early sober and unscathed escape were not good. Most regular pub-goers are familiar with the notion of 'breaking the seal' where every other drink demands a corresponding visit to the Gents. Well, the 'Heads', or toilets were usually located some way along a passageway on the deck above and therefore to ensure the 'guest' returned from visiting the loo an item, usually, a watch was required to be handed over before them leaving and held as security. The chances of escape being slim it was a sure bet that if someone was invited to another mess for a beer he wouldn't be returning to his mess until the early hours of the next morning.

This courtesy was also afforded to civilians who found their way on-board. Often under the guise of the ex-pats mentioned earlier, these 'lambs' would not have a clue what they were letting themselves in for. When a twenty-stone nicotine sweating walrus sporting tattoo's of 'spot the beaver?' says to you, "If yer going for a piss, leave yer fuckin' watch"'

Suddenly Omega's become worthless wind-up's and slip from the wrist very quickly. But don't panic, it's a security deposit and it'll be returned when you do.

QUICK DIT WARNING! This method was preferred to the one used by the Stokers mess on board HMS Brave.

During a deployment as West Indies Guard Ship (WIGS) they had obtained a full-blown genuine antique cannonball as a 'Gizit' on a visit to the Caribbean and had decided to weld a short length of chain to the cannonball with an equally iron age bracelet on the other end, medieval ball and chain style. This was then padlocked to the victim's ankle ensuring they returned from their visit to the loo and continued drinking. As the chain was only a couple of feet in length the wearer would have to walk with a distinct stoop. This idea didn't last too long though as one day whilst entertaining a young lady sailor in their mess-deck, the Stoker's used the ball and chain to prevent the young 'Jack with bumps' from running back to her own mess-deck. The lads placed the key to the padlock, which was now securing the ankle of the lady sailor to the cannonball, inside an empty beer can and then placed the can into a bin along with the further empty beer cans that had built up during that day's beer session.

As it was her birthday the Captain also intended to give her a small present in the form of a balloon and a can of beer in his cabin. I guess some Commanding

Officers have some strange habits. Unaware of the impending treat at the Captain has in store, Wren Smith sat half-drunk in the Stokers mess-deck.

"Wren Smith, Captain's cabin..."

The main broadcast piped for the lady sailor to attend the Captains cabin. A small panic ensued as everyone scrambled to find the padlock key ripping open the gash bag and searching feverishly for a can that rattled but in the chaos empty tins were strewn all over the mess, making the task even more difficult.

"WREN SMITH, CAPTAIN'S CABIN!"

The key was lost.

The birthday girl struggled up to the Captains cabin via the whole length of one deck and three sets of ladders carrying the cannonball ankle chain. Needless to say, the skipper was less than impressed with Wren Smith's new buoyancy aid and seized the remainder of the Stoker's beer banning the entire mess from any more beer for fourteen days.

Back in 3G mess HMS Sheffield Lordy was attempting to wake Mick and was being as delicate as an ape in the process which was kind of appropriate as he was as hairy as one.

"Mick, Mick, MICK!" he shouted, poking him sharply, "come on Mick, you can't sleep there!"

"Fuck off."

"Mick!"

"Fuck off!"

"Mick!"

SMACK!

The first punch caught Lordy mid stomach as did the second. Mick, who was a keen rugby player, then rose to his feet and butted his head into Lordy's stomach and running forward slammed him into the bulkhead. Another couple of punches to the torso and Mick appeared to drift off to sleep again whilst remaining in situ stood pinning Lordy against the bulkhead. Lordy was a little confused by this and paused to consider a plan of action. Before he had thought of one, Mick stood up and staggered over to the doorway leaving Lordy recovering from the assault in the corner. Then lowering his head Mick charged again this time managing to build up a little more momentum. A perfect flying head-butt straight to the stomach and Lordy was again left considering his options whilst wondering where had all the air gone that had been in his lungs moments before.

"You twat!" he laughed nervously.

The sense of humour tactic worked on Mick who believing Lordy was taking it as a joke released his weighty presence and sat next to him.

Thud!

A change of mind and another punch, Mick hadn't finished and now decided he wanted to fold Lordy in half so started again preparing for another charge. This time however he was a little faster and head locked Mick who possessed the alcohol-induced reactions of a startled sloth.

"Le'go," Mick grunted.

Chris choked him harder.

"Le'go!" Mick's head and face were now turning bright red and he started to tap Lordy's arm in submission.

"You can fuck right off," said Lordy nervously.

"Com'on le'go, I can't fuckin' breathe."

"You can fucking talk!"

Unwilling to commit murder, and also largely because Mick could fix things in the Communications Room that Lordy couldn't, he decided to release him from the vice-like headlock he had placed him in. On release, Lordy took some very large steps towards the doorway and once there turned to check that Mick wasn't lining up for 'Round Two'. Mick just sat there listing a little to the starboard side, raised a two-finger salute fell over and passed out.

Chapter Four

Thimble Hunt

There is a very common saying that the quiet ones are the ones to watch out for and Bruce Willis was, on the surface, a quiet one. Adrian Willis or 'Bruce' to us lot, joined the ship about one month before this deployment and in that time he hadn't done anything out of the ordinary. He had hardly done anything at all, we barely knew him. He worked his day on board and went home each evening unless of course, he was on-duty. While the ship was in Plymouth he could just pop across the water to his home town, Saltash and I guess for this reason no one got to see the real side of him.

He was in his late thirties and therefore had a few years of service under his belt but like most Matelots looked a fair bit older than he was. Bruce was a 'three badger' though how he kept hold of his three 'good conduct' badges was beyond me. One chevron stripe, resembling a lance-corporals stripe was awarded for every 4 years of good conduct. A maximum of 3 stripes was awarded and no more. They were worn on the upper left arm of the dress uniform or No's 1's as they were known. This would often confuse when having Army lads on board. The 3-badge lads would get called 'Sarge' by the visiting squaddies. Bruce's 'good conduct' secret was not to get caught. He wasn't the biggest of blokes either. Smaller build than average, skinny in fact. It soon became apparent that Bruce's only real vice was *'Drrrink!'*.

Dubai, Jebel Ali and the Middle East, in general, were early stops in this trip and most major dramatic, or rather traumatic events were yet to come. They traditionally saved themselves until mid-deployment, or sometimes later when everyone began relaxing believing that they were on the home straight. Perhaps someone would break a leg in Gibraltar on the way down or a quick inter-ship fight would occur when two rival ships berthed in the same port but most things tended to happen after some time had elapsed and the crews started to get bored of the same old faces smiling at them over a pint. Time passes *incredibly* slowly on a deployment.

Port Jebel Ali was our middle-east substitute for Devonport and the one thing it boasted, way back then, was its very own 'fast-food' outlet. It took the form of a small wooden shack with a bloke inside flogging egg-roll type things, I would best describe it as a tortilla style omelette wrap with some hot sauce and a slice of tomato thrown in. They were bloody lovely and cost about one 'Icky', about pence at the time. A small band of hard-core disciples gathered there each morning for their stand-easy snack.

Having already spent several days berthed alongside in Jebel Ali we were now under 'sailing orders' and were off out to sea for a few days. All seemed fairly normal, I got on with a few mundane checks which were required on the navigation equipment before sailing and then set about finding a place to hide from the boss. Different ship, same shit!

In an effort to get a decent coffee without being caught loafing in the mess during working hours I decided to catch up with Bruce Willis, despite it being early days I had been out with Bruce on the beer a couple of times now and was beginning to view him as a dependable oppo. I had seen him earlier that day before 'turn-to' so I took a slow amble around the upper deck to find him and catch up on the previous night's events. Bruce worked on 'upper deck weapons' where he and the Upper Deck Weapons Chief Petty Officer shared a small workshop on one of HMS Sheffield's bridge wings. Bruce's boss, in stark contrast to mine, was fairly laid back and had a sense of humour.

"Bruce about, Chief?" I asked.

"Nope," came the reply, "I ain't seen much of him at all this morning."

I'd already been in the mess-deck looking for him so I wandered off to try a few more haunts around the ship, the Chief Stoker's office was a favourite spot or anywhere else where he could get a brew but I was out of luck. I couldn't find the scrawny bugger anywhere.

An hour or two passed and I slowly grew more concerned for my shipmate. We were due to be sailing shortly and it was a matter of minutes before we would be closing the ship and getting 'specials' underway. These 'specials' or Special-Sea-Dutymen (SSD) were required to close-up (that's Navy speak for 'go-to') certain positions and duties when the ship was about to undertake a task or manoeuvre which presented a threat or risk to the vessel. In this case, the threat was that of colliding with the jetty or other ship alongside. My Special-Sea-Duty position was to sit in the Operations room ready to spring into action should a radar set fail or something similar go pear-shaped. Nine times out of ten I couldn't fix it. I was a shit engineer, but I always knew a man who could. It's not what you know, but who you know' as the saying goes.

Bruce Willis was also required to close-up as a Special-Sea-Dutyman although it escapes me what exactly he did. He was still nowhere to be found so I did the uncharacteristically responsible thing and decided to tell a grown-up. I first chose to share my concerns with a few lads from the mess, seeking reassurance I suppose. We all agreed after a little chat about consequences that somebody more important, and resembling a bigger grown-up should know we told the Joss, aka the Ships 'Master-at-Arms.'

BOOM! All hell broke loose and I was now praying that Bruce really was missing, for *his* sake.

"D'ya hear there?" The pipe started, "This is the X.O."

Pause (likely hiding a sigh of disbelief about what he was about to say)

"It has been bought to my attention that a member of the ship's company is unaccounted for." The Tannoy clicked on and off as the Jimmy caught his breath.

"It is imperative that anyone knowing the whereabouts of LWEM(O) Willis should report those whereabouts to the Quartermaster immediately. I will remind you that the ships is under sailing orders and we are due to sail in under twenty minutes."

Less than five minutes elapsed before the Jimmy made his next pipe.

"D'ya hear there? This is the XO..."

He *loved* the sound of his voice.

"...commence Operation Thimble-hunt, commence Operation Thimble-hunt."

Operation '*Needle-haystack*' would've been more appropriate but the term 'Thimble Hunt' gave everyone a little more hope. We all reported to our departmental head offices where the duty senior rate proceeded to take a name check of who was there. We already knew that Bruce was missing so checked off our names to the 'charge-chief' accordingly. The ship was then searched methodically from top to bottom by a selected few but with much more haste than normal. It confirmed what we already knew, that LWEM(O) 'Bruce' Willis was not anywhere on-board. The next area of activity came from the flight deck where the gangway was positioned along with the Quartermaster and a very frantic Executive Officer.

The next line of enquiry for the Jimmy was to see if LWEM 'Bruce' Willis had returned from his night out. A couple of the lads came forward stating that they had seen Willis floating around the ship at the start of the day wearing his dark blue work overalls and looking a little worse for wear from all the beer from the previous night's run ashore. This information was backed up by finding his trademark T-shirt and jeans on his bunk, in fact, it was his *only* pair of jeans. Bruce, the only man in the world who can go on a seven-month deployment with just two T-shirts, a toothbrush and one pair of old blue denim jeans for the entire trip.

Back on the flight deck, you could see the stress on the Jimmy's face as he tried to figure out his next move. His body language was a dead giveaway; he was sweating, fussing and fidgeting. His preferred tactic appeared to be constant attempts at getting both clenched fists into his gob at the same time and chew on his knuckles. At long last, his thought process came through and a very dim light came on above his head.

"Right!" he declared with puzzled furrows on his brow, his eyes scanning the dockyard cranes for inspiration, "I'll take two men and the Master-at-Arms and search the dockyard."

Was this guy for real? But then again I suppose he didn't have any other options left to him at this stage.

Port Jebel Ali was bloody enormous. I mean huge, small city huge! It was well over 100 square kilometres of buildings, locked warehouses, parking lots, container stacks, office complexes and even accommodation and sure enough, he wanted to search it. An eerie and somewhat surreal calm fell over the ship. The dockyard was normally a place where we could come and go quite freely, walking on and off the ship pretty much as we pleased but now we were being ordered told to stay put, it almost felt like we were on the naughty step. Everyone was feeling guilty despite knowing we hadn't done a dam thing wrong but at the same time it was a little bit of excitement to give us a little buzz and a laugh. A little anarchy and chaos are good for morale.

The vast expanse of the dockyard was going to be a nightmare to search. How on the earth the Jimmy intended to do it was a mystery that even Scooby-Doo and Shaggy would struggle to get their heads around. Sailing from Jebel had now been delayed for about three hours and the meter was running. Each hour was costing the ship thousands. This was 'Pay & Display' for ships and the X.O. had lost his token.

Tick tock tick tock...

Another hour passed, during which time the ship's company took full advantage of the circumstances to do as little work as possible, then the news came that a rather angry looking Jimmy was storming back along the sand dusted jetty towards the gangway. He was striding with purpose, like the Gestapo Officer he aspired to be, little puffs of desert sand exploding from the ground each time his heel struck the floor. About fifteen feet behind him followed a very bedraggled and tired looking Bruce Willis covered a thin layer of fine sand dust. He was wearing his overalls and appeared to be completely unaware of why everyone was stood on the side of the flight deck laughing at him. The gangway was hoisted up as he stepped off it onto the flight deck and a matter of seconds after Bruce was back on-board the ship Special-Sea-Dutymen closed up to their positions and we prepared to get underway slightly later than planned. I wanted the 'Lois Lane' exclusive so grabbed Bruce before anyone else got a chance.

"What the fucking hell happened to you?" I asked.

"I went to get a bloody egg roll di'n' I,'" said Bruce in a soft Lancashire drawl.

"Eh?" I puzzled.

"I went to the egg man to get an egg roll for stand easy."

Stand Easy is the Royal Navy equivalent of a tea break and lasts a strict twenty minutes from 10:00 to 10:20 hours.

"It's three o'clock in the afternoon mate, did he have to go and find the chicken to lay the egg?"

"Nah, I thought I'd have a little lie down while he made the roll. There was a lorry trailer behind the old boy's shack so I got underneath it for a nap. Next thing, the fucking Jimmy is shouting in me lug'ole. Ain't the bloke got a fuckin' sense of humour?"

"Not any more he ain't Bruce, no."

We both giggled, Bruce's laugh being somewhat more nervous than my own. It turned out the Jimmy and his little team *had* searched the area around the egg shack. A couple of times in fact but no one had thought to look underneath the numerous abandoned lorry trailers dotted about everywhere.

'Hands to harbour stations, hands to harbour stations. Assume N.B.C.D. state three condition yankee. Close all screen doors and hatches. Hands out of 'rig of the day' clear off the upper deck.'

In layman's terms that meant we were, at long last sailing. Up the revs, handbrake off and out onto the big blue mirror-like waters of the Persian Gulf.

Bruce was fairly quiet over the next couple of days. A visit to the Captain's table, where discipline offences were dealt with, was not the major bollocking we all expected him to receive. They didn't have anything to throw at him from the Naval discipline book. He wasn't adrift, Naval terminology for being late back to the ship from the previous evenings shore-leave. He just happened to wander off to grab a bite to eat at 'stand-easy' but got distracted by a large imaginary duvet and pillow his imagination had placed underneath a dockyard lorry trailer. The end result was a small fine from Bruce's next pay packet for not correctly filling out the 'Ashore-On-Duty' book.

"I wasn't ashore-on-duty," complained Bruce afterwards, "I wanted an egg roll! What's on-duty about getting a fucking egg roll?"

Over the following couple of days, we had to put up with Bruce complaining that he was the aggrieved victim of a miscarriage of Naval justice but realistically he didn't have much to whinge or drip about. A small beer ban, that was it. He got very little sympathy for his little incident but did get lots of pats on the back for giving us all a good laugh and something to write home about.

It wasn't long before we reverted to the hum-drum sea routine of popping to work all day, loafing about cleaning, doing some routine maintenance, keeping watches, fire exercises and each evening drinking as much beer as was possible, watching videos and generally doing 'sweet Fanny Adams'.

A few days later and a few laps of the Persian Gulf and we were given a new toy to play with to help cure the boredom. There is only so much sailing round in a circle one person can cope with so to help lighten the mood we were presented with a nearly new, low mileage, genuine and authentic United States Navy sailor. To promote relations with our US colleagues and the chance for a few of the lads to have a laugh, the opportunity to conduct a 'sailor' exchange arose. We sent a few of the lads over to a Yank ship and they sent a few over to us, one sailor per mess-deck was the rule.

A change is as good as a rest. We *reluctantly* offered up Andy Mathews, a decent but somewhat annoying lad who could only be tolerated in small doses. In exchange for Andy, we were given Ralph Stephens, U.S. Navy Seaman first class, A.A., R.A.C. and bar. A home-grown, southern boy and fine upstanding member of the ship's company of FFG-41 the USS McClusky aka 'The Mighty Mac'.

The Yank, or 'septic tank' as he became known, seemed to be somewhat of a disappointment for us at first. For starters, he was completely tea total, not at all what we expected. This attribute is something that nowadays I view as quite an endearing feature. A trait which I feel expresses a person's contentment and inner strength and wellbeing, but it is also fuck-boring, especially when you are in the bloody Navy! I mean, honestly, tea total! Who the hell did this guy think he was?

We didn't care how Andy Mathews was doing on the USS McClusky and hadn't given him a second thought since he left. Indeed we half expected the Americans to signal us any moment, begging us to take him back.

In the meantime, Ralph entertained us with his naive devotion to the American ideal. A skinny guy with match sticks for arms and legs, but a gaunt drawn face which was home to a big smile however and combined with his parrot style crest of hair he was more Stan Laurel than US military action hero. He was also proving to be a typically true US patriot and a July 4th junkie however the poor lad fell flat on his arse when he commented on our unquestionable allegiance to Her Majesty Queen Elizabeth by shouting, "You see no bitch on this bill." Whilst waving a US dollar note. Not the things to yell on British Warship. A minor beating followed, but only a small one as he was, after all, a guest.

Ralph did not hesitate in making himself at home and later in the day, he started voicing his opinions again.

"You guys had everything," he blurted, "the biggest fucking empire the world has ever seen. You had the whole world in a vice!"

Ralph began digging himself a hole by first attacking our monarchy and how the British people were in the dark ages to have a Queen rather than a President. He continued to dig himself deeper by making constant references to the father of the United States, George Washington. At this point, one of our baby engineer artificers chipped in. Noddy Holder told the Yank that Washington was born and bred in Lancashire, England. The Yank went quiet.

Washington was, as you'd expect U.S. born but judging by his silence the Yank didn't know that. Well done Noddy, if you can't be right, be wrong at the top of your voice.

Ralph enjoyed minor celebrity status as our guest although 'novelty' rather than a guest would've described him more accurately and after one fairly mundane day of work we received a visit by HMS Sheffield's Flight Commander, Lieutenant 'Shiner' Wright GM. Shiner was one of the few officers who was openly welcome into our mess-deck. *All* mess-deck visitors had to knock on the hatch above and request entry. Those are 'dem rules! Shiner could knock and stroll done the ladder without a reason. He was an officer who the lads had overwhelming respect for.

He popped down from time to time down to play Uckers. A game that Shiner instigated by declaring confidently, "There's not a white person in this whole world who can beat me at Uckers!"

Ralph got nosy.

"What's your race?" he asked in admirably blunt straight forward monotone that only someone raised in an unconscious oblivious and multi-cultural country like America could.

"My father is white and my mother is Malaysian," Shiner answered in equal monotone.

The GM after Shiner's name stood for 'George Medal' and was a sign of a very colourful career so far. The George Medal is one of the highest decorations a person can receive in peacetime. Awarded to military and civilians alike, it was given for acts of great bravery. Shiner had joined the Royal Navy as a chef before transferring to be a Royal Navy Search And Rescue diver or 'dope on a rope' as they were fondly referred to. Then on to the officer's mess by becoming a Navigator and Flight Commander on Lynx helicopters. While working as a Search and Rescue (SAR) diver Shiner would be dangled out of Sea King helicopters in the most horrendous of weather and hoist folk from the decks of sinking ships, boats and yacht's wrenching them from the jaws of certain death in gale-force winds and big seas. It was while in this role that Shiner, along with his mate Dave Wallace saved the lives of forty people trapped on a sinking Pakistani container ship, the MV Murree, off the South Devon coast in October 1989.

They initially believed that the ship had fourteen people on-board but on arriving on the scene found that there were, in fact, forty all desperate to get off a ship which was sinking and at some rate. In between the huge lunging swell Shiner and Dave were dropped down to the sinking vessel and successfully winched the entire crew and their families to the relative safety of the Sea King helicopter even placing some of the children into zip-up bags, however during final moments of the rescue the high-line transfer wire from the Sea King became trapped around a handrail on-board the Murree. Remaining cool, Shiner and Dave remained on-board the sinking ship, untangled the mess and realising they had cut it too fine, signalled the Sea King to get clear of the vessel leaving them with no time to save themselves. Suddenly and almost without warning, the container ship's fw'd end disappeared under the water and the MV Murree went nose down and vertical launching the stern approximately one hundred and fifty feet out of the water. She was going to the bottom imminently with Shiner and Dave the only two persons left on board

"I'll see you on the other side mate!" Dave shouted to Shiner.

Then they jumped the 100 or so feet into the sea below.

The British television programme, '999' reconstructed the whole affair and Dave spoke of how he could see the rust on the hull of the vessel as it glided past him to the depths just feet away as he fought furiously against the drag to get back to the surface. Both men had leapt from the stern of a vertical container ship into rough seas and having survived the initial jump, both men re-surfaced and were hoisted back to the safety of the Sea King like drowned rats. Braver men simply do not exist. The eyes of the MV Murree crew were fixed on both their rescuers, wide like saucers. During the flight back to 'terra firma' the second officer of the MV Murree, Irfan Jafri wrote a short verse of thanks on one of their life jackets and handed it to Shiner.

'To the Angels who come in the guise of men, the Lord has chosen thee to perform the most profound of his miracles, saving life. You are what the world was made for.'

For their actions both Shiner and his oppo, Dave Wallace received the George Medals.

The mess was in a fairly sociable mood for the remainder of the night with stockpiled beer flowing freely as Uckers, a Matelot's version of Ludo was played. Shiner had made himself at home supping tins of McEwans Red Death while defending his unbeaten Uckers title against the American. The rest of us kicked back and chilled out. One month down, six to do.

Travelling the globe has it's hazards especially when you are being constantly reminded that you are 'an ambassador for your country'. There are rules everyone must be aware of prior to attending any foreign country. It's all very well knowing which port you are sailing in to but it is a different matter if you are not clued up on local customs and etiquette especially if the culture divide is more like a chasm. European countries are a doodle, as is the US with our main concerns being their rather serious and humourless law enforcement officers but things get a little more tricky when entering Middle Eastern states for instance. Some are far stricter than others with a requirement for all of us to behave for fear of offending someone. Going out and getting shit-faced in Denmark would be a far cry from doing likewise in Qatar for example. If you stuck gold with a lady sailor and decided on some public displays of affection in Dubai for example, you could easily be looking at jail time. On that basis, a crafty hand job from Jenny Wren in a hotel bar was definitely out!

It was for this reason that the ships appointed a liaison officer for each port of call. The liaison officer, usually a Lieutenant or Sub-Lieutenant was assisted by a senior rate, usually a Chief Petty Officer, to help him out with the logistics of telling two hundred and seventy

Matelots not to belch, fart, pick their nose, snog girls, snog boys, hold hands or get there knob/tits out in public.

Shiner was nominated as the liaison officer for our visit to Kuwait City and the Chief Petty Officer on my section, Brum Edwards, was the appointed liaison 'Chief Petty Officer'. Aware of my talent for drawing fancy doodles Shiner approached me to draw some cartoons for his video presentation to the crew. I was happy to help him out and composed a short animated film which involved a young sailor stood in his best glad rags drinking 'tape head cleaner' aka ethanol, as a substitute for alcohol. We were aware that alcohol in Kuwait was almost impossible to get hold of and therefore the ex-pats resorted to a mix of ethanol and tonic water. The problem was that long term abuse of this cocktail left the drinkers with badly degraded eyesight and with enough of the stuff, eventual blindness. Given the long term consequences, it was common sense that short term exposure would also be unhealthy so Shiner set out to make the crew aware of the risk.

In my simple movie, made with a cartoon pad and the 'freeze-frame' facility on the ships handy-cam, Able Seaman 'Shit-Fer-Brains' took a long swig from a can of tape cleaner, immediately both of his eyes popped out their sockets and he fell over dead. I filmed it by recording a series of cartoons like a flick book, with each frame captured for a fraction of a second. When the tape was run back I'd created a full-on animated feature about 10 seconds in length. It wasn't exactly Steam Boat Willy, but it made me chuckle. Wilt Disney!

Further issues Shiner wanted to tackle was the standard of acceptable dress whilst ashore and the use of sexual protection. For this task, Shiner employed the acting talents of the ships Meteorological Officer persuading him to place a condom over his head and inflate it. Breathe in through the mouth, out through the nose. An everyday pub or rugby club occurrence. We filmed our scenes in the comfort, security and relative privacy of the ships computer room where we knew we would be undisturbed apart from the constant humming and whirring of the giant weapons computer. After filming the 'condom on the head scene', the poor METO was then asked to humiliate himself further and dress in certain female attire.

This section of the video was aimed at getting our female crew members to dress a little more conservatively in Kuwait and was scripted as follows.

"The humble lady sailor should not dress too provocatively."

Cue METO wearing white cotton knickers, a bra, suspender belt, a fetching blonde afro wig and hairy gut bursting out over the top of his suspender belt.

"However there is no need for her to go over the top."

Cue METO wearing a Fearnought fire fighting woolly bear suit with breathing apparatus and head over.

Our make-do government information film continued.

"A nice compromise is to dress conservatively."

Cue the METO finally modelling an ankle-length black dress, knitted cardigan and same blonde afro.

In the run-up to the filming I had volunteered to be the official prop-man and I jumped at the chance to obtain stunt knickers from the girl's mess. Rather strangely not once were my motives questioned by the young lady sailors who only asked me to return them once I had finished with them.

April 28th and we eventually arrived at Kuwait City. Predictably as soon as shore leave was granted the majority of the ship's company headed towards the MacDonald's Restaurant situated in the centre of the city. Who says Matelots have no sense of adventure? The lack of booze sadly took its toll and the Kuwait City visit was fairly uneventful especially in respect of high spirited shenanigans. We certainly found ourselves pining for the bright lights of Dubai.

But it wasn't all dull, dull, dull and a small bit of light relief was still to be had one afternoon when the ship arranged 'Damage Control Olympics' on the jetty and invited some of the Kuwaiti Navy to challenge us in a variety of sporting events such as the famous, 'Knock over a wooden pallet over with a jet of water from a fire hose' race and 'Get changed into a sweaty NBCD suit' relay race. Apparently, it is the taking part and not the winning that counts. It was desperation and couldn't even be counted as a good effort. Clearly, some young officer had been tasked with setting up some competitive shenanigans with the locals.

This visit was especially frustrating for me as we would be in Kuwait City for the first of May - May Day! A day that was dear to me as May Day in my home town in Cornwall is celebrated by meeting up with old friends, coupled with drinking copious amounts of real ale and us locals dancing around the town with a large black 'Obby 'Oss. I could bore you with more details but it is one of those things where folk say 'you have to be there!'

Anyway, knowing I stood no chance whatsoever of finding any beer ashore I did the only thing I could and grabbing my accordion, yes you did read that correctly, my accordion, which I had the foresight of bringing with me for the seven-month deployment, and stuffing four cans of McEwan's Red Death about my person just before midday on Monday, May the first, 1995 I walked on to the upper deck of HMS Sheffield and strolled right up to the pointy end of the ship, turned and sat down. Then whilst supping from the first can of Red Death I played Padstow's May Song. The locals looking up from the dockyard must've thought I was barking but for a few minutes at least, Kuwait City became a little more - Cornish.

Gulf patrols are pretty straight forward and after leaving Kuwait we drifted about the perfectly still and pristine mirrored waters for a while before a brief stop in Bahrain helped us relieve a little of the 'Persian Gulf' monotony. Don't get me wrong, the Persian Gulf and the countries which surround it generally conjure up many emotions including thoughts of romance and adventure but there is only so much a Celt with a fondness for ale and shenanigans can take.

Bahrain is one of the more liberal countries in the Gulf. Made up of several islands, both natural and man-made, Bahrain offers the opportunity to relax a little more, let your hair down, enjoy a relatively normal night club complete with a proper bar.

I took full advantage of this and along with many other lads found myself in a very modern club which could have easily been at home in Soho or downtown Miami. At some point I found myself dancing, well trying to dance, on a metal walkway suspended above the main dance floor with loads of other people. A mix of locals, working visitors, tourists and lads from the ship, we were jammed in and loving it. For a small moment, I felt I was still in the UK. Only the heat and the languages ringing in my ears me reminded me that

I was still abroad. That was until I heard a familiar 'Black Country' accent from a very sweet and scantily clad blonde.

"Are you British?" she asked.

"Yep," I confirmed, "I don't need to ask if you are!"

She laughed.

"Can you do me a favour?" she moved her mouth closer to my ear as the club music was deafening.

"That very much depends but go on?" I leant in with slight anticipation.

"My mate has coped off with yours," she informed me, "and that means I'm on my own."

"Tony!" I offered my hand.

"Nice to meet you Tony!" she took my hand and pulled me in, kissing me on the mouth.

An hour later I was in her hotel room. Jack, the lad her mate had fancied and her mate, Gillian were already in another room just down the corridor and it was obviously by the amount of DNA that had been swapping in the club that the night was going well for both of them. Gillian was an olive-skinned stunner also from West Midlands, he *very* shapely form complimented by long silky brunette hair. A Brummie Catherine Zeta-Jones!

My night required a bit more negotiation. Black Country 'Mandy' told me she was an air hostess and this was her first over-nighter since leaving 'Air Hostess Training Academy'. I didn't know whether to believe her or not but she then showed some evidence that she was not used to such a hot country. She had made the cardinal error of sunbathing during the day by the pool of their hotel without sunblock and as a result, her back was 'well done'.

This supporter her story of naivety and newness to her job, a seasoned Cabin Crew would surely not make such a mistake. Mandy went on to tell me how she got engaged the previous month and was having doubts as her new career had suddenly become more fun than she'd thought it would be.

During the chat about her life at home, her new job and deciding if she was doing the right thing in 'getting hitched' she asked if I would be kind enough to rub aftersun on to her bare back. Naturally, I obliged.

About 10 minutes later and Mandy was lying face down, naked on her bed and as I applied the cream to her sunburnt shoulders her back arched and bum began grinding down on to the duvet. Watching her stunning naked size-8 frame and long wavy blonde hair as she pleasured herself by having dry sex with her bedsheets would normally have been enough, but thankfully the alcohol I had managed to drink in vast quantities from the club had deadened some of the obvious physical downsides I would normally be cursing myself for. After another few moments, her legs parted and her perk backside lifted into the air as she pushed herself onto her knees.

Her talk about engagements and weddings stopped. Negotiation over I took off what was left of my clothes and climbed on the bed.

The sound of the pre-booked wake up call the next morning hit me like 'Action Stations' on board. I leapt from the bed and grabbed my clothes.

"Fuck!" I greeted my companion.

Suddenly I started to recall parts of the conversation from the previous night where Mandy had been telling me that her hotel was only 10 minutes down the road from where we think the ship was berthed.

"Where's your mates room?" I asked as I hurriedly pulled on my jeans.

It was 07:05 and I had no idea where we were.

"284," she said confidently, "I'll ring her."

After a couple of unsuccessful attempts at calling her room, I gave my friendly 'Fly-Me Air Hostess' a goodbye kiss and ran up the hotel corridor. After a minute of frantic knocking, Gillian opened the door of room 284 wearing only a black satin slip.

"Jack!" I shouted, "we have 30 minutes to find the ship!"

"Fuck!" came the reply, "Alright Tone, two secs."

Running from the hotel into the empty street it became apparent we were in trouble. The hotel appeared to be surrounded by something resembling a desert wasteland, not deserted, but desert itself. I hailed the only car I saw which as sheer luck would have it, was a taxi. Unluckily though it was driven by Bahrain's version of Captain Slow. He's not James May, He's James May's much slower Arabic Uncle!

Through a combination of panicked raised voices and maritime charade shapes, Captain Slow nodded that he knew where our ship was berthed and turned her car in the slowest three-point turn in history.

After a stressful 10 minutes in the Top Gear Fuel Economy Challenge, we saw the Port and Great Uncle May pulled up and let us out. We showed our appreciation with about £50 in Bahrain Dinars and ran.

Running, hangovers and Matelots don't mix and my watch showed that we have 5 minutes to make the gangway. My lungs soon gave out and with lactic acid screaming through my legs the world's biggest Caterpillar Dump Truck rolled up and stopped beside us. The Bahraini driver waving at us to jump on board.

With Jack and I stood on a ladder clinging to the side of an Earth Mover the size of an apartment block, we pulled up at the gangway of HMS Sheffield with less than a minute to spare. We ran on to the flight deck as the Joss watched us holding up the timepiece on his wrist. As our feet hit the flight deck the Quartermaster ran across to us laughing.

"SAFE! SAFE!" he shouted throwing his arms out to the side like a baseball umpire.

The Joss walked away in a huff.

After the fun of Bahrain we were heading once again to Jebel Ali. No problems had been encountered on this Gulf tour and in contrast to the last time I had been here, five years before it was completely stress-free. The only real threat that bothered us was the vague chance of a left-over mine popping up.

The Royal Navy currently possesses some of the newest and hottest technology available to mankind however when protecting a ship from mines the old Royal Navy still resorts to the good old Mine 'Look-Out'. To the untrained eye, it looked like a sailor sat in a small tent perched right out on the pointy end of the ship with a pair of binoculars scanning the horizon for floaters. That's because it was a sailor sat in a small tent perched right out on the pointy end of the ship with a pair of binoculars scanning the horizon for floaters. During the 1991 Gulf War Mines were dished out quite liberally by the Iraqi Navy to add to those already floating around the waters long before that.

One of the more mundane tasks on a warship is 'store ship'. Much like doing a fortnightly shop at the supermarket but on a larger scale and equally as boring. The day prior to leaving Jebel Ali for the last time, and with it the Persian Gulf we had our expected 'store ship' but this one had some notable extras. A regular everyday 'store ship' involves re-supplying and re-stocking all provisions before sailing. All junior ratings, and some of the senior rates too, would be instructed to line the corridors and passageways throughout the Sheffield. A couple of decent-sized delivery trucks would have arrived on the jetty before this and the entire contents from the trucks would be unloaded by hand with each box being passed from man to man along the chain until it reached the storerooms, way down deep inside the belly of the ship. It would involve stocking up everything from meats, tinned food, dried food, nutty bars and rice to the more boring stuff like deck polish, clothes, rags and bars of soap. A long line of sailors would stretch from the back end of the lorry to the storeroom. With a surprising amount of co-ordination the line of blue-shirted, shaven-headed ants, passing along their bounty from one to the other. The occasion crate of fizzy pop may get damaged during this operation and the odd can find its way into Able Seaman Smith's pocket but all and all it was a boring and laborious task which some lads tried everything to avoid helping with. On this occasion, however, we took on crates and crates of bottled water.

One crate per man. Storage space on a warship is already extremely limited and in complete disregard to the normally religiously strict controls on storing 'loose' items within a ship, we were told just to stack all crates of water in the mess square. This made it a little more difficult to move than normal.

So, the reason behind this mass hoarding of bottled water? Our next stop!

Our six-week visit to the Gulf states wasn't everyone's cup of tea but I loved it. If only to re-visit some ports that I had first been to in 1990/91 during my visit as a spritely 17-year-old. A little part of me felt that I belonged in the Persian Gulf, there was a familiarity with it that I find difficult to explain but it is a little bit like when you return to a favourite childhood holiday destination. On leaving the Gulf we sailed south-east passing Pakistan on our port side and headed down through the Arabian Sea towards India. Falling back to our long haul routine of cleaning, fire exercises, man overboard drills, routine equipment maintenance, chipping and painting the ships structure and sunbathing. Everyone had their role. Small or large, everything needed doing to keep the ship running smoothly and keep us busy. No dramatics or theatre, just time to kill writing letters home, and getting familiar with the mess-decks video collection.

Rounding the bottom end of India we slipped between Sri Lanka and India and headed up to Chennai or as it was known at that time, Madras. We had been reliably informed that the evaporators which were used to transform the saltwater which surrounded the ship, into freshwater for us 'skin and essence' young specimens of perfection to use for cooking, cleaning, washing and drinking wasn't efficient enough to cope with the disgusting state of the water we were expecting to encounter in the harbour at Madras. Nowadays the thought of drinking harbour water from anywhere in the world turns my stomach but back then opening a tap on-board ship felt like opening a tap at home which was sufficient distraction for where the water actually came from.

After pulling alongside and seeing 'home' for the next four days I was grateful for the foresight of the management in purchasing the bottles of mineral water, I would have even volunteered to bring the lot on-board myself if I had known in advance what awaited us. There was no way of flowering this up. It was quite simply a shit hole. That general description is not intended to offend anyone but it is, I feel, an honest one. The benefit of travelling to these cracking holiday destinations and foreign exotic lands in a warship is that we get a 'warts 'n' all' experience of these places probably not too dissimilar from the view afforded to back-packers, a breed of traveller I have a huge amount of respect for. The jetty and surrounding area appeared to be one massive open-air shitter. Thick brown 'substance' everywhere, including up the harbour walls. Rats were openly running about like schoolchildren on a cross-country run. Large power cables designed to provide visiting ships with power were liberally scattered about the roads and walkways with the insulation on most looking decisively dodgy and not too dissimilar to the hem of a hippie's best pair of denim flares.

I have only once before experienced such a shit-hole and that was Djibouti on the East coast of Africa with HMS Brazen. I can remember watching little kids trawling through our rubbish bags after it had been chucked into the dockyard skips. They were pulling the paper gash bags to pieces and removing anything vaguely useful including the paper gash bag. They took old boxer shorts, empty shampoo bottles, toothbrushes, broken chairs and food scraps! It wasn't long before the lads stopped throwing out rubbish and slowly and deliberately replaced the rubbish with more useful items. The rubbish got less and less - rubbish. Strangely lads no longer needed half of the T-shirts and shoes they had amassed and, placing them into brown bags, bypassed the skips choosing instead handing them directly to the kids.

Even Matelots have hearts, made of oak.

Madras made us realise that our problems seemed relatively minor. OK, so we had to bring our own water to the party. At least the ship could still draw in water to keep machinery cool. The machinery wouldn't care what state it was in. A mate of mine on-board HMS Brave didn't have the same luck when visiting the Caribbean. When they berthed alongside one particular island paradise they were immediately joined by millions, and I do mean millions, of squidgy jellyfish. These little transparent tennis ball sized sucker-fuckers were sucked into the system and the Marine Engineers (Stokers) spent their entire visit pulling them from the filters non-stop, Twenty-four hours a day, rotating shifts. All this while the rest of the ship went out on the beer and made the most of the islands hospitality. My oppo, Richie, must have really enjoyed his visit to the Caribbean as another memorable moment for him was setting a new world record time for being mugged after 'on entry to a foreign country'. It took about 20 seconds after stepping from the end of the jetty and strolling out of sight of the ship and the Quarter Master with his SA-80 rifle, for Richie to be done over. Although I had the 'from the horse's mouth' version from the man himself my imagination tends to think it went something like this.

"Oh my, isn't Jamaica lovely, look at the beautiful view, what I wouldn't give to live in a place like this..."

"HEY MAN - GIMME YA FUCKIN WALLET!"

"Well, I say, that *is* a large knife! I'd imagine it's very sharp too. Well, kind sir, please take all of this money I am carrying which, incidentally, is all the money I have for the duration of my visit to this beautiful Caribbean Island of yours."

Poor Richie, literally.

Meanwhile back in Madras with a days work completed on-board the time was upon us to piss off ashore and see the sights. I teamed up with Mick Bridger and Charlie Worker and together we went for a wander into the city. Nothing planned just a quick recce to see what's what. After negotiating a safe footpath through the landfill site which was the jetty we strolled out of the dockyard towards the main gate I was suddenly aware of one feature which was not that dissimilar from one in our own dockyard back in sunny Plymouth. There was an abundance of train tracks embedded into the road surface and I assumed, like the ones in Plymouth, they were disused. Oh, how wrong could I be? I was ashore less than ten minutes when I was nearly hit by a passenger train. No warning toots, whistles, signs or green cross code men, no automatic barriers or human beings waving a flag, just 'look left, look right, think train!' Mick, Charlie and I walked through a large, open imperial era wrought iron gate following some of the locals as they left the dockyard. I momentarily looked at the guy in front and wondered why his walk turned into a brisk skip and then glanced left to see the front of a huge blue and white train, complete with bright headlight and passengers dangling from the footplates and hanging from the doors, heading right towards me.

"fu'kin hell, RUN!" I blurted, shoving both the lads forwards on their shoulders.

We bounded forward 5 or 6 steps to get us clear of the train tracks and then turned to look at the beast as it rolled past us. After some short bursts of nervous laughter nervously we turned around and continued to walk towards the city.

Not only did this place look horrible, but it smelt like shit too and it wasn't long before we found out why. Hygiene and sanitation didn't appear high on the cities list of priorities. The first seriously stinky thing we encountered was a dead horse, the carcass still attached to the cart that had no doubt contributed to the poor animal's early demise. It was laying half eaten half with the onset of decomposition. Bones painfully pushing up through its skin like tent poles failing to hold up a half-erected tent. Birds and dogs had been feasting on the horse but even they knew when meat had passed its sell-by date. It had been there for some considerable time but none of the locals batted an eyelid and they strolled past merrily going about their business. It didn't take long for us to grow tired of walking in the immense Indian heat so the three of us decided to hail a 'putt-putt'. If only to get away from the stares we were getting from everyone. I don't recall where other members of the ship's company had gone for their first day ashore but we did feel very much alone. In the blink of an eye a three-wheeled cabriolet version of Del Boy's Reliant van pulled up and Mick, Charlie and I shoe-horned our 'wider than the average Indian' frames onto the rear bench seat. This one had a pilot and co-pilot and I think both of them had seen us coming a long way off.

"Tour of Madras?"

"A what?" Mick puzzled abruptly.

"Guided tour of Madras, we will show you the city Sir?"

A few raised eyebrow glances between myself, Mick and Charlie and we agreed.

Mick shrugged, "Yeah, alright then."

We roared off. Two strokes and what sounded like no more than twenty horsepower pulling three heavyweight British sailors a skinny Indian cabby and his co-pilot. I wondered if one of these machines would ever find itself into MaxPower magazine. I bet someone could spend a few quid doing it up, multi-disc CD, in-car DVD, turbocharged, supercharged, stripes and leather bucket seats etc. then spend weekends pissing off boy racers. Whoever has seen 'Octopussy' with Roger Moore would know the desired effect when James Bond is escaping the villains on a putt-putt being driven by Indian tennis ace, Vijay Amritraj. Vijay blips the throttle, pops a power wheelie and fucks off up the road leaving them in a cloud of dust and two-stroke.

Although there were no villains in sight, the way we were charging through the hectic multi-lane mad-ass road network made me think otherwise. I was shitting myself. With no regard for anybody's safety, our driver played chicken with every single vehicle on the road. We were even aiming at some head-on for Christ's sake! The rules of the road went totally out of the window along with my dinner. It seemed totally irrelevant which side of the road we were supposed to be on, we simply used both and for added terror opposing traffic was flying down both sides of us, like everybody in India was driving at us from all directions. It was utter mayhem. Pedestrians were doing suicidal mad dashes across the heaving roads in the tiniest of gaps between cars, lorries and buses allowed. The nauseous stench of the place combined with the heat and mixed with the extremely nasal full strength diesel and four-star exhaust fumes from the 1940's Madras vehicle fleet made it near impossible to breathe and left me feeling trapped and claustrophobic. What exasperated matters further was that in a putt-putt we were the lowest on the automotive food chain. Eventually, we stopped at a massive interchange with nothing in the way of traffic lights, just a gathering of revving vehicles all waiting for their turn to play 'British bulldog' with the traffic crossing from the other roads. The very instant we were stationery we were surrounded by an army of beggars.

At first, we all missed the obvious. All we initially wanted to do was to ignore them but the 'beggars' made that impossible for us. They stood right by the side of our death trap cab and stared right into our souls, wanting. One, two then three, four... They started flocking like paparazzi mobbing an unfaithful footballer at the airport. As this one exceptionally skeletal bearded chap stood talking at us he lifted his arms to reveal two stumps emerging just below his elbows joints. I was speechless and just sat there staring at him from within the putt-putt. Then before I could blink my head was thrust back into the seat we were off again charging through the traffic. After less than a hundred yards we stopped again just long enough to survey the surrounding traffic junctions and attract the attention of yet more beggars and notably almost all were deformed, but all through physical trauma rather than birth defects and almost always the injuries were missing arms or hands. This process of stop, start, stop, start went on for another thirty minutes or more before it dawned on us that we were travelling in one *very* big circle. After conferring with Charlie and Mick we concluded that we were being literally taken for a ride and tempers flared. After a large vocal protest from the backseat accompanied by threats of physical violence the pilot and his navigator pulled over, for their own safety. Mick, Charlie and I made our escapes from the rear of the putt-putt as quickly as possible. No grace or poetry, we just forced our way out of our yellow coffin.

We were now loose on foot in downtown Madras and without any real plan decided to follow the signs to a nearby zoo, at least the signs were partly written in English (How rude of foreign countries not to write *all* their signs in the Queen's English, eh?) Strolling along the edge of the busy Madras highway which was a heated mix of dirt and badly constructed roads and partial pavements, dodging more dead animals, mostly dogs, left to rot where they fell. We had been asked for money by quite a few people by this point and we were becoming more acclimatised to the varying physical deformities of the beggars which had been sent out to work but even that didn't prepare us for the next chap. He didn't say a word to me, I don't believe he could have if he wanted too. He just stared at the three of us, or rather he stared through the three of us.

Lying on the roadway between two parked 1950's style Austin cars was a light blue canvas mat about four feet long by two feet across. Lying face down on this worn-out old mat was a skinny seriously malnourished torso. His scraggy bearded head with tangled dirt and lice-ridden matted hair was resting on the edge of the mat with the right side pressing down hard on to the floor. His lifeless zombie eyeballs were bone dry and tormented. The twisted male figure was naked apart from a piece of blue cloth covering his buttocks. His lower back appeared to be completely snapped backwards just above the buttocks and he was, quite literally, folded in half. Both legs ran up and over his back and were nothing more than skin-covered bones, his feet touching the floor next to his face.

A human being snapped in half and folded flat!

His 'Twiglet' shaped arms were lying lifeless and equally broken and every place where his body came into contact with the ground had developed a layer of toughened skin. This thick padded skin ran the length of his chest and even on the side of his face, well the bits we could see anyway. Toughened skin similar to that found on the sole of a foot. I guessed his age to be in the mid-twenties. Disturbingly I was told that he was the main source of income for his family, a career cripple deliberately deformed hideously at birth in order to bring in some money and sadly he wasn't a unique case. Children broken and used for this purpose, family income.

If there was ever such a place as a living hell then this young man was in it. He wouldn't even have been capable of a dignified suicide.

We depressingly continued our trudge following the signs towards the zoo and it wasn't that long before we found it. A long dusty white wall with a 'budget' archway plonked without ceremony halfway along. A picture of some happy animals and a hand-painted 'ZOO' being the only indication that it wasn't somebodies garden wall. After strolling in without being challenged about payment we found our first attraction. A large pile of earth with some rocks pressed into it on top of which stood a man with a stick. Great fun was had watching this nervous-looking zoo keeper teasing a Cobra snake into striking at him. We moved around and watched some fat crocodiles lounge about in the Indian heat. The animals looked to be as fed-up as we were but at least they appeared to be catered for, far better than the people *outside* of the zoo. After 30 minutes and now severely bored, having lost any enthusiasm for life we hailed another putt-putt and instructed the single pilot to take us back to the ship. Not a word was spoken by the driver during the whole trip. No eventful near misses with passenger trains as we walked back in, I don't think I would've noticed one coming anyway. The image of the guy laid on the mat was ingrained in my head.

Leaving Madras behind was certainly not a sad occasion. I imagine India is a beautiful and enchanting country, I just didn't get to see that side of it.

We still had tons of bottled water left and we were informed that it would be advisable to continue using it for a couple of days as it would take a good while for the systems to flush through completely with new water from a big clean ocean. Naturally, we did so without question.

Quite a few of the ship's company got struck with the classic 'Delhi-belly' myself included. I had tasted some of the local delicacies whilst in Madras and was now passing chocolate lager as a result. I pride myself on going native where possible eating local and I certainly couldn't visit India without having a curry so a Madras in Madras seemed most appropriate.

My Granddad was a *huge* curry fan, I'm told a result of his time in India during World War 2 and it had rubbed off on me. I have consumed mountains of the stuff over the years. Whenever I drove home for 'weekenders' I would dive into Mathew's 'Wai-Kui' Chinese Takeaway in Wadebridge and pick up my favourite. Chicken curry with boiled rice, number forty-three! It got to the stage where I could phone and just say, 'Forty-three please!' my call being recognised straight away.

"Ok Wilton! Twenty minute!" Came the reply.

I, therefore, felt duty-bound, whilst in the Navy to try chicken curry in every port I stopped at. All in the name of vital 'Nobel prize-winning' research of course. Denmark, Norway, West Indies, Sardinia, nothing compared to 'Wai-Kui' at Wadebridge.

Even when I returned home from the 1991 Gulf war having served with my brother, unusually on the same ship, HMS Brazen, the first place we both stopped was Mathew's.

"Hey, where you been?" quizzed Mathew in his oriental tones, "haven't seen you for bloody ages."

"Been down the Gulf Mathew."

"Good job you no die, lose *bes'* cus'omers!"

I couldn't help but agree with him, I was also pretty glad we weren't killed. Two brothers serving on-board the same ship during a conflict was a tad unwise, a bit of a public relations disaster should something have happened but there were so such problems. Saddam's Navy never emerged as any credible threat as we sank it all!

Returning to the subject of curry, connoisseurs the world over however will no doubt declare that the curry crown sits firmly on the head of the Indian.

The 'Indus' Indian takeaway in Plymouth supplied many meals to the Weapon Engineers mess on board HMS Illustrious as she sat stranded in dry dock. A favourite for me being the 'Fal'. Hot didn't even begin to describe it. A fuel rod from a nuclear power plant on meltdown would have been easier to consume, and I would watch in awe as one lad, 'Brains', who bore a striking resemblance to a stick-thin version of the 'Yorkshire Ripper' slowly savoured every 'Fal' soaked chip that he shoved in his gob. It was proper rocket fuel and fuck did your arse sting when it fired out your bottom end the next morning.

It was fair to say, like massage parlours and dodgy dingy ale taverns, fast-food joints and historic Naval dockyards went hand in hand. My love of take-away pizza is probably a result of this traditional union and with tempting offers aimed directly at the Naval messdecks including, 'ORDERS OVER £100 RECEIVE A FREE BLOW UP DOLL' who can refuse?

So there we were, floating off across the 'oggin leaving a trail of dirty water behind us.

This 'dirty water' often took many forms. I am unsure why, despite the majority of lads being fairly normal, the Armed Forces seem to attract some of the biggest sexual deviants the world has ever known. I have met a few in my time and heard some stories that would make Madam Whiplash blush but none more so than 'Rolf' Harris, a killick stoker on HMS Brazen in 1991. Before joining the Royal Navy, Rolf used to work in a land down-under and whilst living there he would take every opportunity to visit Thailand during his summer holidays. He came back with a strong Aussie accent and a very personal photo album which he proudly showed on request with every lady he had encountered whilst there. The photos, clearly unacceptable for any passport use, simply showed a spread-eagled 'lady-garden' with some DNA evidence of Rolf's visit. No faces, no catalogue pose, just an open mott-shot! Say "Cheeeeeese!"

Rolf had no morals what-so-ever and this was evident when he stopped for a natter whilst he dipped the freshwater tanks in 3R mess deck on-board the Brazen. The tops of two metal tubes were located in the sleeping area of the mess deck, each with a screw-top lid, and the on-duty stoker would visit several times a day to unwind a weighted flexible steel rule down into the tube and measure the level of water in the tank, much like checking the oil on a car engine with the dipstick.

Rolf, whose turn it was to dip the tank that night, spoke about his final holiday to Thailand before coming to Britain.

"Well, I 'ad this bird right, a fit little thing. I'd been pissin' up all night and thought she would do me fine before I went back to me hotel."

Rolf casually nattered away like he was talking about a shopping trip as he spun the handle, unwinding the large steel rule down into the tube which disappeared into the deck.

"Anyway's I took her out the bar, faced her against the wall outside and pulled up her skirt and pulls aside her knickers."

His enthusiasm for the story begins to build.

"So I slips it in her from behind, I threw it up, she was bloody loving it," Rolf chuckled, enjoying this trip down memory lane.

"I'm bangin' away, getting in me rhythm and I guess I must've been there a fair while so I thought I'd reach around and give her a little bit of stimulation to help her along too."

Rolf winds in the steel rule.

"Anyways, I reach around and, bugger me, she's got bollocks!"

The faces on the lads listening changed instantly from that of excitement to abject horror.

"What did you do?" chirped a voice from the mess square.

"Well, fuck it I thought, I kept going," Rolf confessed casually without a blink.

Stokers eh?

Due possibly to naivety but definitely stupidity the only other time I can recall a tale of such misguided gender recognition was when a young stoker who I shall call 'Spike' due to his hairstyle, again from the Brazen, hired the services of a Spanish prostitute outside a club in Barcelona. Shortly after dropping to her knees to play the pink flute, the young Marine Engineer decided to run his fingers through her long blonde hair but when running his hands down the sides of her face found a good couple hours worth of coarse stubble. In contrast to Rolf, however, a horrified Spike didn't hang around for his 'home run' and he withdrew the transaction and ran back to find his 'run-ashore' mates who were bimbling off down the street completely unaware of the incident.

Now you'd expect most people who'd made such a fuck up would have kept their gobs shut but young Spike wasn't the sharpest tool and he decided to tell all his mates once he got back on-board which meant by nine o'clock the next morning the entire ship's company of HMS Brazen knew as well.

Although, as previously mentioned all the Armed Forces have their deviants, for some unknown reason the Navy seemed to attract more deviants than any of the others. Those long periods at sea have fuck all to do with it. They were already deviants *long* before joining, although in defence of the vast majority of decent high moral Matelots, not all of them are like it.

Whilst serving on HMS Illustrious I had the pleasure to work with Daz White who looked like a cross between 'Steve Wright' BBC Radio Two DJ and 'Walter the Softy' from the Beano comics.

Daz was certainly one to look out for when on a run-ashore, the Navy term for a night out of the town. We spent many a night out on Union Street in Plymouth along with most of the Royal Navy. Union Street was one long row of pubs, clubs, fast food, thick-cut doorman and girls in short skirts. Police riot vans and fights every 50 feet was the norm. One particular evening out whilst in one of Union Streets classier night clubs, Daz, who was not on his 'A' game, was overcome with a sudden feeling of sickness. He grabbed the nearest pint glass and promptly vomited right into it. It was that or the on the carpet. The cries instantly went up from the lads stood aimlessly around aimed at Daz's inability to handle his booze so to silence to critics he decided to neck the contents of the glass that he had just bought up. Low mileage second-hand lager! He got about halfway down the glass when a surprisingly fit young lady approached him.

"I suppose you think you're clever?" she asked.

"Yeah I do," said Daz who stopped drinking straight away, wiping his spare hand across his mouth to regain him some limited respectability.

She took the warm glass and its remaining contents from Daz's hand.

"If I take a swig," she smirked, "then you gotta drink what I give to you?"

Daz wasn't expecting for a second that she was serious so he agreed, hoping to call her bluff. We then watched in utter amazement as she placed the glass to her bright red lips and drank. She only took the one mouthful but it was enough.

"Right, now it's my turn," she declared and disappeared.

I took it upon myself to follow the girl who went straight into the Gents toilet, grabbing the nearest empty pint glass en-route. Once inside she walked up to the long urinal tray and lowered the glass into it running it the entire length of the trough. She scooped up all sorts, urine, vomit, pubic hair, the lot and some of those little yellow cubes for good measure. She left the toilets looking very pleased with herself and returned to Daz.

"There," she said smiling smugly, "drink it!"

If Daz was a bit nervous he didn't show it. He snatched the glass, took one long deep breath and drank. He downed the contents as though the bell had just rang for last orders. I urged just watching. He drank all but the yellow cubes and slammed the glass down empty onto a nearby table.

"Cheers!" he said proudly.

"I'm impressed," said the girl and promptly walked away smiling to herself.

30 seconds later Daz hurled the whole lot back up again onto the floor. Little surprise considering. I could not work out what either the girl or Daz got from the little exhibition of stupidity other than health problems.

Daz was full of tales of sexual conquests and after witnessing his performance with the vomit drinking I didn't have any reason to doubt them.

One of his most memorable stories was as follows:

Once upon a time in a Plymouth far, far away there were two little sailors. Daz and his 'run-ashore-oppo' had been out on the piss and whilst his mate, who had not succeeded in trapping a local maiden, sulked in the corner of the Royal Navy Arms on the Barbican contemplating another night alone with Palmela

Handerson and her five sisters, Daz was busy scoring with a fit young minx who had caught his eye earlier in the evening.

Daz possessed boyish good looks and I suspect a lot of his success was due to older women wanting to mother him. That and a little cockney charm which he used with devastating effect.

The end of the night came around and while Daz had pulled the Minx, he did insist that his mate accompanied them both back to her house.

"If my mate can't come, I ain't gonna come," he slurred.

The male 'bond' can be unusual and unexplainable at times but the Minx didn't see a problem with it and all three walked home to the Minx's place which, as luck would have it, was quite near the dockyard. It was four floors high but a very narrow building squashed tightly between several houses of similar construction.

All three farted about in the living room for a while necking more beer and rooting through the Minx's album collection before Daz was invited upstairs for some bedroom gymnastics. His mate took up the offer of the spare room on the first floor and promptly got his head down. Daz, meanwhile, was fumbling around in the bedroom on the top floor with his conquest for the night and after throwing each other about in several different positions the Minx found herself on all fours with Daz behind.

They continued playing for some time, longevity is always helped by vast quantities of booze, before Daz announced his intention was to take her from behind in a non-biblical manner.

"I don't fucking think so," she protested, "if you wanna put it there, you can piss off downstairs with your mate!"

Daz, being a twat of the first order, tried a second time to ring the back doorbell.

"Right, that's it. OUT!" she yelled and with a swift boot, Daz found himself outside the firmly shut bedroom door holding his jeans and shirt.

"Fuck off downstairs!" she scorned, "you can let yourself out in the morning!"

She sounded the generous sort letting him stay at all after that performance. As Daz made his way downstairs he tripped over several times, being ninety-nine per cent pissed he was some difficulty finding light switches. The overall layout of the house wasn't helping things and after eventually finding the spare room he crashed out on the floor with his mate still sound asleep on a single mattress in the corner. Barely a moment had passed when he found himself desperate for a dump of massive proportions. Getting up off the floor Daz searched furiously for the light switch but couldn't find it. He fumbled his way out onto the landing and gingerly made a search of the other floors in the house but alas was still failing to find anything that resembled the heads. The sweat was now starting to bead and run down his forehead. Panic was setting in.

Daz was touching cloth!

He decided that there was only one thing left that he could do. In a display of ingenuity that only a seriously pissed idiot could come up with he would suspend a sock underneath his squatting rear-end and curl off a chocolate Mr Whippy into the sock. The plan was strangely admirable in theory and brilliant in execution. The only worry that had crossed Daz's rather inebriated mind was whether it would be all fit in the one sock and be solid enough to go in without dramatics. Luckily Daz managed to release an amount sufficient to ease any bowel discomfort, at least until later in the morning when he could find a proper loo. Without requiring the use of a second sock he used it to wipe his backside and then tucked it inside the first.

This had all taken place within the confines of the spare room while his mate slept on oblivious.

One problem remained though, where to put the sock?

Suddenly Daz had a second 'Eureka' moment! He would open the window and throw the sock as far as possible into the street outside. No one would be any the wiser and he wouldn't piss off the Minx by leaving a sock full of chocolate log in the spare bedroom. The last thing he wanted was to see her out on the tiles on some future night and have her tell the story to her friends while pointing Daz out in disgust.

Opening the window he took a couple of steps backwards placing himself about six feet from the window sill. He had long given up trying to find a light switch but throwing the curtains apart along with opening the window had given a welcome shaft of street lighting into his cell. He twirled the heavily laden sock around his head like a highly trained Ninja warrior.

The ancient 'shit-socki' weapon flew with unprecedented accuracy straight through the opening in the wall but it was far from the hurtling meteor Daz had expected. Its velocity was somewhat slow and disappointing and the trajectory fell well short of what he had planned. Nevertheless, it had left the room and was now somebody else's problem. Mission accomplished, Daz could now grab a couple of hours sleep.

Morning arrived bringing with it glorious rays of sunshine, the birds were singing and a few early risers were out and about in their cars gliding along the street outside. Daz stretched out and feeling a lot less pissed than he was just a couple of hours previously scanned the room to gather some reminders about what had happened during the early hours. The first thing he noticed was the temperature, he had forgotten to close the window and it was still a bit on the cold side, even more so as it was about 0700 hours, he still had a good forty-five minutes before his shore leave expired and he would be due back on-board. He chuckled to himself about the sock and looking across the room saw his mate who was still in the land of nod having spent the entire night lying in a state of alcoholic coma unaware of the 'fun' that Daz had been having.

Daz was pretty feeling good with himself. The Minx probably wouldn't be up for a while and if he saw her again he could blame the booze for his poor aim and inability to get the right hole. He stood up and rubbing his eyes approached the window curious about where the sock had landed. Glancing out Daz spotted his sock hanging lifelessly on a steel railing below like a used condom. It looked somewhat dishevelled and suspiciously empty. Suddenly he stopped breathing and froze. The room was pretty much unknown to him and for this reason he hadn't paid much attention to the decoration however a feeling of dread suddenly overwhelmed him. He turned slowly and took a long stare at the pale blue walls around him. They were speckled, *brown* speckled and it had dried solid.

The flight path of the sock had been abysmal because all of the poo had left it via the minute holes in the fabric of the sock ably assisted by some serious centrifugal force generated by Dazs twirling. In short, as Daz swung the sock, shit sprayed through it and pebble-dashed everything including his mate who was still fast asleep on the mattress. To make matters worse the sock he had wiped his arse hadn't stayed put inside the first and was sat on the floor, poo-side down and probably stuck to the carpet by now. Suddenly the floorboards above creaked and movement was detected elsewhere in the house then Daz distinctly heard the sound of a toilet being flushed upstairs.

"FUCK!"

Shaking his mate from his deep slumber he dug around the room for his shoes.

"What's going on? Where's the fire?" Matey asked.

There was no time to explain. The two of them ran like the wind towards the dockyard like two 'Keystone Cops' rejects, Daz's mate didn't bother to ask why they were in such a hurry.

Things ended happily ever after. I gather Daz saw the Minx out and about but she never said anything to him, taking the easy option of just staring daggers each time she saw him. Matey must have forgiven Daz for covering him with crap because sometime after the whole affair he acted as Daz's 'best-man' at his first attempt at matrimonial wedlock.

But I'm not finished with poo stories just yet. A second young sailor, also from the Lusty-Illustrious who decided poo-play was in vogue was a chap going by the name of 'Rat.' He was, as the names suggests, a very small and slightly built chap with pointy features, a gaunt face, a 'Plymuff' boy through and through.

During our draft on board the dry-docked HMS Illustrious, the lads from the Weapons Engineering Department had the pleasure of working with a rather fit but very prim and proper young Wren writer. She was the admin girl for the department and was extremely reluctant to get her hands dirty in any way. The general annoyance was a result of her delusion of self-grandeur which frustrated some of the lads and her noticeable donning of a pair of black leather gloves when picking up a fire hose drove them mad. We were a couple of years into having female Matelots serving on board Naval ships and it was still a source of tension as many men did not think that a female could push her own weight. Life on board a ship was not a picnic and should some serious incident like a fire occur, everyone, and I do mean everyone, will fight it. To lose a ship to fire could result in a massive loss of life, not to mention the cost to the taxpayer. To watch this young lady pick up a brass nozzle while turning her nose up at the thought of actually having to point it towards a fire was a red rag to a bull and wound up many of the lads. Lady sailors who joined the Navy before Wrens being sent to sea were permitted to 'opt-out' of any sea drafts. She was one of the 'none sea-going' Wrens and had no intention of getting her feet wet ever, so a dry-docked HMS Illustrious was a massive inconvenience to her despite a reassurance that she would be drafted off long before it was ever re-floated. She kept her special 'fire exercise' gloves in a draw in her desk in the Combined Technical Office (CTO). Slowly the rumours spread that some sexual deviant from the department had removed the gloves from the sanctuary of their drawer and used them for a posh wank whilst thumbing through the 'reader's wives' section of an adult rag. This made everyone chuckle each time we saw her pulling them on to her soft and blemished hands.

Young Rat, however, was never one to miss the chance to go one better, and realising that the young Wren was likely to be unaware of the crusty DNA sample which lurked within the depths of her leather gloves decided to leave her something else. Keen to impress his peers he removed a glove from her drawer one evening and crept off to the heads with it. He hung it below his backside and began to pull faces, replacing the glove as soon as he was done. Unsurprisingly it didn't take long for the Lady Wren to notice the stinky chocolate eclair which had taken residence within her glove and the shit quite literally hit the fan. Rat came forward and took responsibility for the whole thing and after writing a very long, and vetted, letter of apology to the young lady in question plus receiving a fairly hefty fine, Rat was promoted to morale officer and given a crate of beer by the mess, although he had to wait a few days to drink his reward as he was given some additional duties to perform throughout each day in punishment or his act to accompany his fine. The Navy calls these 'additional' punishment duties, 'Number 9's'.

Boredom during long periods at sea could be a bit of a problem and back on board the Sheffield a few of the lads got together and decided to run a fun, friendly and relatively harmless satirical television news program which was broadcast every other day. It had real mischief potential and was ripe for abuse!

Each mess-deck had its own television set and hopefully, it's own VCR, usually accompanied by a healthy pile of 'Only Fools And Horses' videos. At a specified time, providing the producers had gathered sufficient material, the TV would be switched to the 'internal' channel and the lads took a seat to see which members of the crew had made a big enough twat of themselves to appear on, *'The News!'*.

*"*This is the *NOOOOOOOZE!"* announced the intro, followed by a spaced-out looking newsreader appropriately known as 'Space' to his mates whose day job was a Petty Officer Weapons Engineer, closely resembled 'Beaker' from The Muppet Show. This 'news' programme was broadcast to all of the mess-decks on

board, including the Officers Wardroom and the Senior Rates Mess via the Ships Recreation Equipment or SRE, which was the posh name the Navy gave its internal TV systems on board. Space was the news anchorman.

One of the shows regular contributors was the Supply Officer who had aspirations towards a comedy career. He was a 'two and a half ringer', a respectable Lieutenant-Commander by day and his party-piece was animal impressions.

We gathered around the TV and were on the edge of our seats.

"Here comes a big dog! WOOF WOOF WOOF GRRRRRR WOOF WOOF!"

Honestly, you could have heard a flea fart.

"Here comes a little dog! Woof woof woof grrrrrrr yap woof woof."

"Big dog, WOOF! Little dog, woof woof."

What the fuck was this bloke on? This guy was responsible for ships logistics on a massive scale. Supplies, weapons, spares, fuel and managing and overseeing ships admin stuff and he sat happily in front of 270 blokes on a 'closed circuit' TV system almost every other night and gave us 'Big dog, little dog'.

Jesus-H!

That said and done, what Space's '*NOOOOOOOZE*' broadcast did do was allow lads to take the piss out of each other, stitch up their oppo's, settle scores and generally screw people over good and proper and I felt it was too good an opportunity to miss.

I had become fairly handy with the camcorder. In conjunction with this and my growing dislike for my section Chief, Brum, I decided to broadcast a little documentary on the life of a WE Chief. Well, one particular WE Chief anyway.

Brum was desperate to get promotion to the next rung of the ladder, Charge Chief. He could've been a half-decent chap if this ambition hadn't caused him to combust up his own arsehole. The guy would've sold his own off-spring to the Gestapo if it won him a favour. A little pissed off with his attitude to both me and Fez, the pair of us sneaked into the computer room one evening following a tip-off that he was sound asleep whilst at his 'defence station'. Basically, he was sleeping on watch.

We crept around the corner of the office and slowly zoomed in on the unsuspecting and completely 'dead to the world' Brum who was snoring his face off and nodding more than Churchill the dog. We filmed as he slept for a few minutes which included some close-ups and commentary. That night, just an hour before the broadcast Brum phoned our mess-deck.

"3 Golf Mess, Bubbles Speaking."

Then a pause.

"Tony! Its Brum Edwards for you!" shouted Bubbles.

I walked over and took the phone.

"That bloke is a fucking nobber!" observed Bubbles, who was not known for his diplomacy.

"Yep?" I gave my customary greeting into the phone.

"Tony, I've heard that you and Fez may have videoed me earlier when I was in the office?" he enquired.

"Nah, dunno what you're on about Brum." I lied.

Brum flew straight into one.

"Tony I'm fucking warning you, if that video finds its way onto the news I am going to fucking kill you."

Well, if ever there was a way to win over my generous side, that wasn't it.

"Brum I have no idea what you're on about," I replied, digging my heels in.

I was now trying so hard to sound sincere.

Brum slammed the phone down so and I pressed the receiver to cut the line and tapped out the internal number for Petty Officers mess.

"Fez, Brum is on the warpath mate. He is going fucking ape about the video!"

Fez burst out laughing.

"The fucking wanker shouldn't have been caught napping then," Fez laughed.

That evening the tape was broadcast on the 'Noooooooooze' to the soundtrack of 'Little Green Bag' from the movie, Reservoir Dogs. The video started with the door to the computer room, then slowly creeping around the row of large cabinets and panning across to the top of the compartment. First, there was a pair of black steaming bats, standard Naval footwear on board, then as the camera panned to the left a pair of hairy stick legs poking out of some standard tropical issue blue shorts. Sat on the deck with his back leant up against one of the cabinets with his hands wedged in his pockets was Brum, catching flies and snoring away oblivious. We zoomed in and took a moment to get his dribbling gob in full glorious Technicolor before slowly retreating out of the office, filming as we went.

He hit the bloody roof.

The next morning he met us in the computer office.

"I want that fucking video Wilton or I'll take you to the Captain's fucking table!"

He stamped his feet and was close to tears like a spoilt child until the Deputy Weapons Officer, Lieutenant Phil 'Gazza' Gascoigne, wandered over to see why one of his Chiefs was suffering some form of cardiac episode. Brum told Gazza about the video to which Gazza summed up my feelings perfectly, "Just leave him alone

Chief, Wilton's got redundancy and probably doesn't care anymore."

Now *that's* a boss!

"We've all seen the video," he continued, "no one cares. You're a big boy, deal with it."

Gazza then strolled off leaving a gobsmacked Brum alongside Fez and I grinning widely. I could feel how much Brum wanted to swing for me. Gazza was one very chilled out and laid back Naval officers. I'd heard rumours that his career was more of a hobby than a profession and he was a man of other means and income but I never found out for certain. He was definitely a top boss.

Gazza was right, I had indeed found the chocolate bar with the golden ticket and had learnt that my request for voluntary redundancy had been accepted. I was winding down and wasn't in the mood to play anymore.

This deployment had suddenly got a lot more interesting. *Ram it, I'm RDP!*

Chapter Five

Big dog, little dog

It was obvious, after seeing his various dog impressions, that the Supply Officer on HMS Sheffield was literally barking, there was absolutely no doubt about it. But despite being as mad as the ship's cat he was otherwise harmless and in honesty, I think he fitted in well with most of the other officers on board. But if there had to be an award for the most mental Naval officer on the ship then no one deserved it more than the Executive Officer or 'XO'. The XO is the chap that Captain Jean-Luc Pickard calls 'Number One' while he is Star-Trekking on the Millennium Enterprise. He is the next chap down the pecking order from the Captain on the hierarchy ladder and our Executive Officer or to use his Jack-Speak slang name, 'The Jimmy' had a tendency to talk into his hat whilst he held it in front of his face. As if that was not disturbing enough on its own, the Jimmy appeared to call his hat 'Mother'. There are certain people within some jobs who simply just shouldn't be there. He qualified! Come to think of it, that was the vast majority of us. Let's face it you had to be missing something to work in our environment with the final step towards total sectional insanity surely being the jolly submariner. Now there's a bunch of sailors who have completely lost the plot. Just sit down with a beer and watch 'Das Boot' and you may begin to understand why these pale-skinned pink-eyed human beings are not playing with a full deck. "ALAAAARM!"

Naturally, nutters were not restricted to submarines or the officer's mess. I have already mentioned a young stoker aka 'Spike' who encountered a charming young lady in Barcelona complete with designer stubble and a larger than normal Adam's apple. Well, during one of our lengthier deployments on HMS Brazen the very same chap sent a gift to his girlfriend's parents. A definitive statement of his endearing love for their only daughter. The loopy little stoker went and taped two or three paper gash bags together, lay on the top and got a mate to draw around the outline of his body. He then drew on eyes, a mouth, a nose etc. Slightly 'pre-school' but not too bad so far. He then went on to remove eyelashes, pubic hair, head hair and toenail clippings and glued them all to the appropriate parts of the drawing.

He folded it up neatly and sent the parcel home. I would have loved to have seen their faces when they unwrapped that little love letter.

Another nut from HMS Brazen was Rick 'Fruity' Pascall. A man mountain and built like a brick privy, Fruity was usually to be found lifting something heavy in the 'hayloft' on board the Brazen, a small passageway annexe outside the Communications which was designated as the weights room. Fruity was training to earn himself a place on the Devonport Field Gun Crew and was working flat out to achieve it.

Something Naval ships do as a routine before sailing on any major deployment was undergo a fairly intense and thorough seven-week period of sea training called BOST or Basic Operation Sea Training. If you were unfortunate to be on a ship headed for the Middle-East then this was made all the worse as there was extra emphasis on nuclear, biological and chemical defence drills.

It is an absolute pain in the arse. Weekend leave is touch 'n' go if it happens at all, and the 'working' day starts around 05:00 hours with cleaning, scrubbing and preparation to various drills, exercises and inspections ending around 20:00 hours or later. For those who were Duty-Watch that meant ending around midnight or even running right the way through to 05:00 again the next day. This was more or less the daily routine for the duration of BOST. Large scale fire drills, pretend wars, *'oh bugger we're sinking'* exercises and along with all that the ship had to be kept in a state where you could eat your dinner off the floor in the shit house. Even the evenings gave us no respite. When alongside each evening at Portland the lads would run, and I do mean run off the ship the very second they got their pressed shirts, Levi jeans and Brut on. Just minutes after shore leave was granted the training staff would launch a fire exercise of such proportions that ships on adjacent berths would be roped in to provide additional fire fighting personnel. Any lads *trapped* on board would have to grab a hose and help out. There was nowhere to hide except the local pubs and only for those that escaped early enough. If you were half-way off the jetty when the fire exercise started you stood a good chance of being hauled back on board and digging out blind until it was over - usually a couple of hours later.

Not surprisingly some Matelots would go to great lengths to avoid BOST, and Fruity was no exception. After breaking his forearm fighting in the town a few weeks before BOST he was sent to a shore establishment for his broken bones to knit and repair. A quick medical just before the fun of BOST was due to begin revealed how the bones had mended and he would be allowed to return to the ship to muck in with the seven weeks of Sea Training.

"Good news Leader, your arm is fine," announced the Naval Doctor. "There will be no need to fit a new cast, a removable support should do the trick over the next couple of weeks and painkillers for the odd ache you may feel but all in all a good recovery."

"I don't think it's ready Doc, it still feels a little fragile," said the Walsall boy, "I don't think I can go back to the ship for a few weeks yet."

"Nonsense Leader, off you go, your arm is as good as new."

Fruity left the surgery and walked about forty feet from the building before finding a suitable wall and punching it as hard as he could!

Five minutes after leaving he strolled calmly back into the waiting room.

"Nurse I think I've broken me arm?"

What made him even more barking mad was that he would perform these stunts without the threat of BOST hanging over him. On another occasion after smashing his jaw in two or three places, again whilst scraping with the local gentry, Fruity was left with a wire contraption around the lower half of his boat race designed to keep his jaw virtually shut and aid a swift recovery. After wearing this device for a few days he got fed up with constantly sitting at a bar supping his ale through a straw. One evening the device and the restrictions it presented became too much for Fruity so he strolled home half-cut, found some wire cutters and sniped through the wires removing it from the working parts of his beer funnel. Job done, he then strolled back to the pub to continue where he left off.

Fighting with locals when in port was part of Fruity's day to day routine which infectiously rubbed off on the rest of us in 3R mess HMS Brazen without us even realising it.

A visit to Santander, Spain proved to be no different. When Fruity had been refused further beer in a local bar he dragged the barman over the top of the bar by the scruff of the neck. Fruity was quickly calmed down by a few lads from the mess and he agreed to bugger off somewhere and cool down for a while. He walked out leaving the rest of us sat in the bar eighty-five per cent rat-arsed and rising. A whole sixty-seconds must have passed before a shout of "Oi you fuckers!" was heard from outside.

There he was stood next to a row of neatly parked motorcycles, not mopeds but very expensive quality motorcycles. He placed both hands on to the fuel tank and started pushing them over one by one.

Bang! Bang! Crash!

He only managed to tip three or four of the machines over before he was hit hard by a wave of Spanish bikers. The bikers wanted blood and they had batons to prove it. A saloon-style cowboy punch up followed with locals battling with sailors, sailors punching anyone and more normal people diving for cover. Although Fruity's actions were not in the best interest of the rest of us we all had an obligation to get stuck in and help our misguided shipmate out of the pickle. In this particular bar in Santander brawling must've been fairly commonplace because without hesitation the barman started to throw out baseball bats to the customers, well the local ones anyway.

One of the local lads made the mistake of picking on a guy called 'Mossy', with his bat. Mossy was another man-mountain from 3R mess and one of Fruity's training partners. The first swing of the bat connected mid-way up Mossy's port thigh. Mossy leant to the left slightly. The second was a jab of the bats' end to his stomach and Mossy now bent forward, protecting the vital organs. The third and final blow was a direct hit to the left side of the head, again with the baseball bat.

Mossy crumpled sideways clutching his head with both hands and dropped to the deck – well for about three or four seconds at least.

The colour soon drained from the aspiring Babe Ruth's face as Mossy stood bolt upright in front of him now looking much taller and more intimidating than before. With a rapidly swelling face, cheekbone and modelling the latest in designer 'fucked up' ears Mossy looked down onto the cowering aggressor and gingerly rocked his head from side to side to check for injury or, maybe it was a warm-up.

"My turn," he said and took the bat.

Meanwhile elsewhere the fighting was in full swing. A few of us came to the conclusion after a few punches and swings that we were better off drifting away and we left. Actually, we legged it. We were seriously outnumbered and it seemed like the sensible 'survival' option. Jumping inside the nearest commercial wheelie bin I was given a shove and 'Cool Runnings' Matelot style commenced.

My run was halted halfway down the street by a rather nice Mercedes and by the time I'd climbed out of the bin all of the lads had overtaken me, all the lads but one that is.

Fat Clout, a young fair-haired and slightly rounded engineer from the mess, had not realised that we had all left and was using the roof of a nearby car as a trampoline.

"Fruity look! HA HA HA HA! Oh bollocks!"

Looking around him, Fat Clout quickly realised he was alone. Alone that is apart from a group of locals who weren't very impressed at his destructive antics. Fortunately for Fat at that moment the local constabulary arrived. After spending a night spent in a Spanish police cell Fat was escorted back to the ship at gunpoint for some strange reason and instructions passed to the Duty Officer of the Day that Fat should not be allowed ashore again.

Stories travel fast throughout a ship. Most people have heard of the saying, 'loose lips sink ships', well stories (or 'dits' as we like to call them) rumours and secrets all travel fast around a vessel like ours. There is no point in entrusting secrets to anyone whilst living on board ship, case and point, our young stoker friend with a flair for body drawings who after an encounter with a Spanish 'lady' in Barcelona decided to tell someone. That someone then told his mess-deck who then relayed the story to everyone on board by using the ships 'jungle drums'. It should be pretty obvious not to tell your mate's certain experiences you may encounter unless of course, you are either desperate for their advice or proud of what you have done, much like 'Rolf' our Aussie stoker who holidayed in Thailand.

Young 'Benny' Hill showed signs of promise for speaking without thinking. He was another baby engineer from 3R mess HMS Brazen. Benny decided to tell the mess about his rather worrying taxi trip from Dubai to Jebel Ali whilst we were there in 1991.

Benny was pretty pissed and as he was not long seventeen had skin and essence looks that were so far unblemished by beer, smokes and punch-ups. Benny fell fast asleep in the back of a cab and was woken by the taxi driver once they arrived at Jebel Ali dockyard however rather than shouting "Oi mate, you have arrived at your destination." The male driver had decided to wake young Benny with a kiss and a grope. Quite a long kiss and a good hard, can I search your pockets, grope. Benny leapt up and shot out of the taxi, legging it full flight back to the ship.

"Lads! Lads! Guess what just happened to me?" Screamed Benny as he thundered down the ladder into the mess-deck.

As he poured his heart out to the mess deck in the hope of finding a sympathetic ear he was instead greeted by laughter and criticism for not kicking the taxi drivers head in. How does the saying go? If you are looking for sympathy, it's between 'shit' and 'syphilis' in the dictionary. It certainly isn't found in a mess deck. I don't think poor Benny recovered.

The vast majority of the foreign taxi drivers weren't too bad but one or two tried to take the piss. When returning from a night out in Dubai with my mate, Dan we had been given one price when we got in the cab but by the time we got to the dockyard, it had trebled. I think the driver saw us as a couple of easy targets as we were both a few months short of 18 and he wrongly assumed too scared to argue. Oh, how wrong he was. I nicked his key's from the ignition and we spent the next twenty minutes playing 'piggy in the middle' until the price returned to what was originally quoted.

All in all local taxis did put up with an awful lot of shit from British sailors. I have lost count of the times I left 'go-faster vomit stripes' along the side of a cab. The sort that starts at the rear of the passenger window and gets wider the further to the back end of the car you get, a drunken version of Starsky and Hutch's 1974 Ford Torrino but instead of a white stripe also the side it was puke with diced carrot, chicken pieces and cider.

Royal Navy crews tend to think and act the same and I doubt whether much will ever happen to change that. After serving with Dan on HMS Brazen he went on to HMS Brilliant as home for his next sea draft where he was joined another veteran from the Brazen, Donk. Donk was a giant of a man and could devour two eighteen-inch pizza hut specials without so much as a stand-easy.

Whilst on a six month Adriatic deployment a British TV company decided to send a film crew along to document day to day 'life' on board a warship. This fly-on-the-wall look at goings-on was called 'HMS Brilliant' which was coincidentally the same name as the ship! A lot of imagination went into the title, didn't it?

Much of the filming centred around the 'larger than life', Leading Seaman 'Donk'. On a visit to Naples, Donk was performing his duties as a Quartermaster. This was a posh title given to the sentry who stood on the gangway greeting and challenging those who came on-board. Effectively, Donk was the 'Doorman'. Donk informed the viewers that a lad from the ship had been rushed to hospital after falling onto a metal railing. The railing was topped with a row of spikes running along the full length and it appeared that the young fella in question was trying to balance along the top and, losing his footing fell with one leg going either side. The resulting damage to the lad was eye-watering and inflicted significant injury to the 'A-hole'.

Somewhere between the time of the incident and Donk's account to the TV crew, a huge whopper was cooked up.

Dan revealed the truth about 'Arse-Gate' over a beer after he returned to the UK with a slightly different walk.

Matelots, like lads from the other armed forces, are often not content with inflicting pain on themselves or those they are fighting with but also like to injure, assault and generally abuse their mates. Dan was happily drinking away in a bar in Naples when someone crashed the cigarettes. Dan happily took one but needed a light so when someone sat on the opposite side of the table held up a lit zippo Dan rose from his seat to light up. At this point the twat sat next to him placed an open lock knife onto the seat and he held it there, pointy bit uppermost. The idea was apparently to give him a fright and make him jump a bit. Dan didn't know the plan however and, relieved to get his smoke lit, slammed back into his chair and onto the knife.

There are, in my opinion, only two things that should ever go up a bloke's ass. One - A thermometer and, two - Your finger when the toilet roll tears. Dan found a third.

Whilst on the subject of anal injuries it is only fair and appropriate that I mention the ultimate anal injury. I hope that any representatives from ROSPA issue leaflets without delay surrounding this next incident with advice on how to avoid it. Brace yourselves! If you thought Dans ass-stabbing was bad this one will really make you wince.

During my time on board HMS Illustrious, I had two bosses, both equally responsible for the section I worked on. One being Chief Petty Officer Max Holloway and the other Chief Petty Officer 'Taff' Vann. They couldn't have been more opposite but both were great bosses! Max was a tall muscle-bound silver-haired fox and former Portsmouth field gunner while Taff was a scrawny little Welsh fella who ran marathons for a past time when he was bored, which given the routine on the Illustrious was quite frequent.

Taff told me a cautionary tale of an unfortunate incident that had occurred to him shortly after joining the Navy. I am guessing that we are talking around the early eighties. If I had not heard it from the horse's mouth I seriously doubt I would have believed it but here goes.

Taff, who was appropriately serving on board HMS Cardiff at the time, had just been up for a dhoby and was returning to his mess-deck. The standard rig for this short venture was a towel wrapped firmly around the waist and a pair of flip-flops. He stepped on to the top of the ladder which led down to his mess-deck. After successfully negotiating the first couple of rungs he experienced what was commonly referred to as a 'flip-flop blow-out'. This occurred usually when climbing down the ladder on the way back into the mess-deck from the deck above and was believe it or not a common occurrence, a consequence of buying cheap flip-flops. The part of the strapping running through the wearers 'big' toe and 'second' toe would snap and the foot slide through the front of the flip-flop causing the wearer to slip on the rung of the ladder. No sailor worth his salt ever descends a ladder the correct 'health and safety approved way' i.e. facing it. They *always* walk down ladders in the same manner that they would descend a set of stairs at home, back facing the steps. A flip-flop blow-out would normally result in a fall of anywhere between ten to twenty feet and a large amount of pain and embarrassment and a 'kidney hatch' rash. On Taff's occasion, however, one of the on-duty flunkies had been furiously sweeping the mess-deck annexe before evening rounds. The dutyman had rested his wooden broom against the mess-deck ladder while he ran off to empty a gash bag.

Taff had a flip-flop blow-out, dropped down the ladder like a lump of finest Welsh Granite and straight on to the wooden broom handle. He completed the worlds first 'ass assisted pole vault'. The pain must have been fucking unbearable. The scream, akin to that of a murder victim, brought out many of his shipmates who didn't take long to realise the seriousness of the incident and after rolling about on the deck laughing made sure Taff was rushed to hospital. The broom handle had entered his back passage, travelling about five to seven inches before taking a sharp turn and entering the passage wall tearing tissues as it went and up into his body.

Poor Taff was about to enter a traumatic period of his life which would see a nurse shoving cotton wadding into the affected area daily while Taff lay helpless face down on a table. Several days later when he was eventually released from the Royal Naval hospital it was with a poo bag strapped to his stomach which Taff discovered proved to be quite a novelty.

As Taff could not work in any decent capacity he did most of his rest and repairing at home which coincidentally was also Cardiff. Some weeks after the incident HMS Cardiff sailed into Cardiff to visit the city and Taff thought he should take the opportunity the visit his shipmate's and let them know that he was healing well and bearing up under the difficult circumstances. Taff received the usual reception from the lads and within a matter of minutes after entering the mess-deck he found he was sat at the mess bar surrounded by beer tins. The drinking went on with yet more cans of beer stacking up as other members of the ship's company heard that he was visiting. Very soon a large pyramid of tins appeared on the bar in front of Taff where he perched on the top of a tall bar stool supping away while telling a story of how a few nights before he had enjoyed a dance with a gorgeous young maiden in a Cardiff night club with her blissfully unaware that he was doing a poo as they danced together in a romantic embrace. Oh, the joys of a colostomy bag.

The beer had been flowing for a good couple of hours and the lads were impressed with Taff's stamina as naturally he did not need to go rushing off to the loo for a wee after every other tin. The bag took care of that. What the bag couldn't handle though was the amount of gas which was being generated by all the beer the lads had given him. The pressure was too much for it to tolerate and it gave up. A large split appeared and the immediate and powerful stench not to mention the liquid leaking from the bag cleared the mess of all personnel faster than a hull breach. Taff squelched home.

Further weeks passed quickly and soon the day arrived when the bag would be removed giving Taff back the full functionality of his rusty bullet hole. He attended the local hospital where the deed was performed and then the scariest thing happened. It hadn't occurred to the poor bugger that he hadn't been using his chocolate starfish for a very, *very* long time. The nurse gave him some solution to drink and he was directed to the nearest toilet cubicle. Once within the small room, Taff took a seat and waited nervously.

He grunted, sweated a little, and then grunted some more. He groaned a little, then a bit more, and then he groaned a lot. With both hands gripping the sides of the pan he felt as though he was passing a bloody cricket ball! This turd could have had it's own bunk on board ship.

"F...U...C...KIN... 'ELL!"

How big could this turd possibly be? He pushed harder, sweat was pouring from his head as he threw out his arms, pressing against both walls of the cubicle.

"Are you OK in there Mr Vann?"

"Errr, yeah!"

The pain was excruciating. After some fifteen minutes of intense pain, the smallest of plops was heard down below. Taff breathed a sigh of relief. He had finally dropped the kids off at the pool. Taff felt as though that was enough for now, he certainly wasn't feeling up to more than that and stood up to examine the gorilla's finger which must now be causing a substantial hazard to shipping in the toilet pan beneath him. To his horror, on peering down he saw a hazelnut-sized green ball of very old excrement resembling an old clay marble which had been sat festering in his bowels since the accident some six months before.

Taff was sent on his way with a tube of KY lubricant and a rather fetching glass device which wouldn't look out of place on a shelf in Ann Summers. He was instructed to use the glass dildo twice a day to strengthen his anal muscles. At the time of this occurrence, homosexuality was illegal in HM Forces so it didn't come as much of a surprise when, after his first locker inspection he was marched up to the Regulators office and put before the Master-at-Arms.

He then spent the next hour trying to explain the presence of an anal dildo and KY jelly to the Jossman.

Taff told his story without even a glimmer of emotion on his face. I expect after that sort of ordeal there isn't much left that would make you frown or twitch anyway.

My other boss from the Illustrious, Max Holloway was, as I described earlier, the physical opposite of Taff.

Being an ex-field gunner for Portsmouth, Max once arranged a trip up to Earls Court, London to see the show and cheer on the field gun crews. We would have stacks of free beer in the hospitality tents set up for each of the three gun crews, Devonport, Portsmouth and the Fleet Air Arm.

I agreed to come along but was a little pissed off to find that as the new boy on the section I was being invited to come along as the duty driver. After loading the beige Ministry of Defence Leyland Sherpa with a few of Max's mates we left Plymouth bound for London. The journey up was completely uneventful, just some sea shanties and the normal pre-drinking banter most lads spew out as we charged up the M5 and M4. After arriving at Earls Court, London I dumped the wagon in the secure underground car park where I was satisfied it would be okay for the night. We all then walked off to get shit-faced in the hospitality tent of the field gun teams.

The field gun tournament was a side-line to the night of beer abuse and at about 04:00 hours we returned to the garage to find the Sherpa. Climbing into the driver's seat I turned the key whereby fuck all happened. Someone in the rear had left the interior lights on and the battery was well and truly flat.

With the assistance of my drunken pit-crew, I tried in vain to bump start the bloody thing but instead, the push resulted in a loud thud followed by an ear-piercing metallic scrape which running along the roof of the Sherpa. Then the penny dropped. When parking the Sherpa a few hours before we were fully laden with fat and thick-set Matelots, the body of the van sitting lower on the suspension as a result. Now, with just me sat inside, the wagon was higher and no longer fitted underneath the various ventilation ducts which were suspended from the roof of the car park. A large deep silver gouge appeared in the roof of the Sherpa running the full length, front to back.

To make things worse I was then dragged from the driver's seat by a pissed up Senior rate.

"I'll fucking do it!" he slurred.

Outranked I took my place behind the van with the others and pushed.

About forty feet later the Sherpa engine fired into life. Now having successfully restarted Apollo 13, Jim Lovell didn't fancy stopping. He was off through the car park and up the exit ramp only he didn't know where the light switches were and the Sherpa snaked around the outside car park area with the engine revving like crazy.

In doing this the driver attracted the attention of the four armed sentries posted to protect the site. We were in a time of high IRA activities and this pissed twat was driving around a sensitive site with no lights on. The sentries came to the ready and took aim. I don't remember exactly how long we were screaming at them but it felt like forever. My lungs hurt through yelling but eventually, the sentries realised that the melee was a result of alcohol, Matelots and a Pussers issue minibus. Shooting averted. No debrief required!

Chapter Six

Tigers

May the 22nd, 1995 and the next stop for HMS Sheffield was the Island paradise of Sri Lanka. A visit to Colombo, Sri Lanka's capital city was planned. Only a brief visit, a couple of days in which our 'British Defence Industry Promotional Road Show' could be conducted on the flight deck of the ship. That was, after all, the primary reason for this deployment. We were effectively a travelling sales team pitching a marquee and shouting, "BIG ISSUE!"

We were also going to take part in two VJ-Day parade and celebrations, Victory over Japan.

A few of the best looking handpicked sailors would have to march in 2 VJ-Day parades, one at Port Moresby, Papua New Guinea and another in Jakarta, Indonesia. The Jakarta event was going to be the biggest military parade in the area since the end of

World War 2 and was to celebrate the 50th anniversary of the Japanese surrender. Fifty Navies' would take part *including* the Japanese but our primary reason for the trip was still the defence sales show.

Columbo and once again we had been briefed on what to do and where to go by our friendly liaison team, but their presentation wasn't a patch on Shiner's Kuwait effort. It soon became apparent that the thing to buy ashore for returning to Blighty was fine bone china. By all accounts, Sri Lanka produces some of the finest bone china in the world. We spent the first 'working day' planning our *assaults* on the Columbo markets and changing our sterling to foreign currency in the ship's office accordingly.

There was a fly in the ointment though and it took the form of the Tamil Tigers. Since the early seventies the 'Liberation Tigers of Tamil Eelam' had been fighting a guerrilla campaign against the Armed Forces of Sri Lanka and also having pops at various political targets. Their recruits would receive rigorous training with the gift of a cyanide capsule being presented to them on their final passing out ceremony. Worn around the neck the capsule was used when avoiding live capture. The Tigers were known for their suicide attacks and even received financial help from as far away as Europe. They made the 'Peoples Front of Judea' look like something from a comedy sketch.

Recent peace talks had hit a stumbling block with the sinking of two Sri Lanka Naval vessels by the Tigers, coincidentally just before our little visit.

As a visiting Royal Navy warship, we were identified as a big target especially for the Tamil Tigers Naval Element, the 'Sea Tigers' who had control over the Northern and Eastern coastal areas of Sri Lanka.

To combat a threat from attack whilst alongside a Royal Navy ship sometimes conducts 'Operation Awkward'. I say sometimes because there has always been some form of threat to our 'sleek grey messenger of death' be it domestic terror groups, Greenpeace activists or a nutter with a potato peeler. Operation Awkward was the next step up. Therefore the threat from the Tigers was being taken a bit more seriously.

Shore leave was reduced to 50% instead of the customary 75%, so we can leave the harbour and float around just off the coast if necessary with only half the crew. This is a bummer if you happen to be out on the beer when the balloon goes up. It is a very strange feeling when sitting at a table in a beach bar supping beers, staring out to sea only to notice your ship sailing.

Other Operation Awkward measures include sounding our SONAR equipment constantly to upset any divers who might fancy a pop at the hull of the ship, an increased numbers of armed patrols around the upper decks and also using the ships CCTV system to monitor the dockyard comings and goings more closely. These cameras had the added benefit of thermal imaging and my first night in Colombo was spent on-duty as the operator of this camera. Apart from being told to be a little more vigilant, there was a surprising lack of practical advice for us when we went ashore. It was clear when a few guys and girls returned to the ship after a night out that relationships had started between some of the ship's company and a laugh was had watching the thermally enhanced images of couples going for it in some dark corner of the dockyard believing that they were out of sight. Another amusing sight was a Grand Prix of mopeds and forklift trucks charging around the dockyard, some weaving deliberately to warm the tyres and some weaving due to the mass amount of alcohol consumed by the driver. Strangely enough, when these vehicles crashed, which they nearly all did, the driver would be observed to look around briefly before making a dash towards the Sheffield, good to see that the ship's company weren't allowing the terrorist threat here ruin their fun nights out.

When it came to my turn to go out I made the unusually rare and out of character decision not to drink, I didn't even take the opportunity for a cultural visit to any fancy locations. I opted instead to run straight out and buy a set of fine bone china for my mum and arriving at a local china factory I found I was quickly lost for choice. The place was *heaving* with dinner sets and I was unable to see the wood for the trees. A vast factory outlet with boxes of precious china stacked up in every possible space, plates and teacups balanced precariously on display on the tops of the boxes. A Greek restaurant owner's playground, all that was missing was the Bull! Tug, another lad from my mess-deck was also there with the intention of picking up a nice china dinner set and both of us started to search for something to take home. The sheer heat of Sri Lanka meant that I was already reaching meltdown point but thankfully after about an hour of nervously walking around looking at various designs I found exactly what I wanted. It was a dainty tea set with elegant flowers subtly adorning the sides of each piece and gold leaf skilfully hand-painted around the rim and handles, the name of the set said it all, *'May Queen.'* The month of May and the term 'May Queen' being very significant to my Mum

With my set reassuringly boxed and padded by the attendant at the factory I made my way back to the dockyard along with Tug who being flash with the cash, decided to invest in two sets of China. We hadn't realised quite how long we had been out and also how far from the dockyard we were. The light was fading pretty quickly and things were going quite well and up to this point, we had not experienced any hostilities towards us foreigners. As we walked through the dockyard gates though, all that changed.

"Where are you going?" shouted an official at the dockyard gate.

"HMS Sheffield mate! British Navy!" I shouted back.

"Come here!" he yelled.

I assumed, as did Tug, that they were being extra vigilant and checking identification cards so we placed our boxes onto the floor and got our ID cards at the ready.

"Put dat away, I can see who you are!" he grunted.

With that, another two officials emerged from the gatehouse alerted presumably but their colleague's raised voice and articulate use of the English language. All three men were armed.

"What is in the boxes?" our new friend pointed.

"China!" we replied, in stereo.

"You taking it home?"

"Yeah, why?"

We were now becoming a little concerned.

"You must pay duty," he informed us.

"No mate, we pay duty in England, not here!" I corrected him.

"You must pay it here too!"

"Noooo, dut-tee in Eng-laaand, not Schri-lank-aaaa." I stood my ground.

"You pay money for duty or you will not get to your ship," he said.

I have been threatened several times before and know when to recognised good one. Unfortunately, this guy had two mates and an unnerving tick which meant he constantly reassured himself by touching the handle of the pistol around his waist every few seconds, that or it was a rehearsed method of intimidating foreign sailors. Tug and me were thinking along the same lines.

"Well, we ain't standing out 'ere in the dark to pay up," Tug said nodding his head towards to shitty concrete building contrasted next to the dockyard gate.

"OK, OK, come in," the guy replied and after a few words to his mates in the local lingo, he followed his two friends into the building.

We stood by the doorway and like a scene from the low budget crime drama, pulled the front door shut. As Tug held it closed I grabbed the nearest object which luckily happened to be a four-foot length of pipe and we slid it through the outer door handle.

"Fuck off pal!" Tug shouted through the door and grabbing our boxes of China we ran like hell through the dockyard. It was now dark and despite the small navigational errors amidst the large containers stacked in the dockyard we could see the foremast and gangway lights of HMS Sheffield and picked our way towards her. A few shouts were heard behind us but neither Tug nor I turned to see if we were being pursued. Running up onto the flight deck the Quartermaster noticed our haste, displaying a quizzing look.

"Don't ask," Tug said.

"I won't," replied the Quartermaster.

After dragging our heavy boxes the remaining few feet inside of the safety of the ship we sat in the large open flat and placing them gently on the deck. Opening them up and slowly we inspected every single piece. Miraculously despite the 500-metre speed marching not a single chip or break had occurred.

So far I was not impressed by Colombo.

Day two in Sri Lanka HMS Sheffield entertained a celebrity guest. A notice was placed on the board in 1-Lima flat asking for names of those who wished to have coffee with Arthur C. Clarke. Afterwards, the elderly supernatural author graced the ship with a visit. Matelots have a unique way of mixing with the rich and famous, usually without realising the true fame of their host. A mate of mine swears blind he was sat in a bar in Canada chatting away happily for ages to Alanis Morissette and only after she left did he suddenly realise why her face was so familiar.

Even my older brothers smiling mug found its way on the popular TV show 'Treasure Hunt' grinning from ear to ear as Anneka Rice wiggled her fit backside around the top deck of HMS Boxer looking for a pink card with her next clue on in 1987. *Matelots tut! They get everywhere!*

Chapter Seven

I am a British Sailor

The end of May saw us arriving in Bangkok, Thailand and an awful lot of the lads were, for one reason or another, looking forward to this part of the trip. For some, it was the high point of the entire seven months, the icing on the cake. Sailing around on the sea every night can play tricks with a man's minds while others relish the solitude, peace and escape. There isn't a lot to do each night at sea on a warship, sure there is a television conveniently attached to either a video recorder or a games console but all in all, evenings at sea are pretty boring. The idea of a stop in any port is something looked forward too with much enthusiasm but somewhere with a reputation such as Bangkok? Well, enough said.

Bangkok has a long history of vice even as far back as the 17th century when ships would anchor off-shore and women were ferried out to the sailors by boat. The traditional 'nightlife' we associate with Bangkok in modern times started to emerge around the late 1960s and early 1970s, coincidentally the time of the Vietnam war.

The ship's Medical Officer decided he should visit each mess-deck, including the Wrens and play an information video highlighting the problems that Jolly Jack (or Jill) Tar could encounter when playing with the local ladies. HIV and AIDS were the Medical Officer's main concerns. Although It would be out of line to say that Matelots are going to run straight to the nearest whore house but it would be fair to say that a few may do just that.

Evolution or mother nature has blessed man with two very special bodily organs. A brain and a 'gentleman sausage' but sadly only enough blood to work them one at a time. For this reason, the MO ensured his tape showed the downsides of an active Bangkok sex life. A lot of chaps were willing to laugh off the threat of genital warts, gonorrhoea or herpes so the Doc needed to show some harder hitting stuff. Extreme genital disfigurement might just do the trick!

The 'VD' video was played in each mess-deck with viewing compulsory. You could have heard a pin drop once the play button was hit. One poor bugger on the tape had a bell end which resembled a cricket ball, not just in size but also in colour. Stitching included. Another battered knob resembled a saxophone and to rub salt in they even named the condition after the musical instrument. Several other variations followed on our short documentary with each example becoming worse than the one before. Some oozed, some stretched the skin, some even looked like Sigourney Weaver should jump from behind a space hulk and shoot it with a laser-gun.

We watched dumbstruck, as the final victim was documented in front of the camera. The lost soul stood there naked. No penis evident, just a mass of pubic hair and what resembled an open axe wound. It looked like someone had cut the poor fella's tackle off with a blunt breadknife and hadn't even done him the courtesy of stitching him up. That's certainly what it looked like anyway. Whatever this bloke had caught had eaten away the entire length of his pecker and was now chewing away at the rest of his torso. I expect in time he eventually received the very best treatment available from the US government, but holy shit! If he had gone to visit one of our sick-bays he would have been given an Aspirin and a plaster.

This 'horror movie' was a government health film from the United States Military and was shown to troops before they headed off to fight in the Vietnam war.

Fortunately, I was now on a break from my normal duties in the Computer Room and a break from Brum.

As I was a leading rate or 'killick' the Weapons Engineering department would have to hand me over for a fortnight so I could sit in the ships 'HQ1' which shared a compartment with the Ships Control Centre, or SCC, and was located deep in the belly of the ship. This was quite a nice change for me as I could no longer be chased about and generally irritated by my twat of a boss. HQ1 duties involved sitting at a warning panel and watching over fire alarms or 'Minerva alarms'. Occasionally I would also be asked to blast out a quick information broadcast to the ship known as a 'pipe'. On the desk in front of me stood a telephone exchange panel. This was where all incoming calls came into the ship when alongside. Well almost all, the Captain got his own phone line of course. Rank has its privilege. The handy thing about this phone panel was that it gave me the chance to play a practical joke or two. Whilst bored at sea I would phone two mess-decks at the same time. Once both had answered I would patch the two calls together and listen in as the Chief's Mess and the Petty Officer's mess argued about who had phoned who. Small things like that amused me and helped break up the monotony.

The main perk about this particular job though was that on my days off I was my own boss, even when alongside in port. The duties alongside were deliberately divided up as fairly as possible. I was tasked to perform a quick HQ1 duty on the very first day at Thailand and the remaining three days were my own.

So day one in Thailand was an uneventful 'duty' day but day 2 was the start of fun time! Before leaving the mess-deck I grabbed hold of Bruce Willis as he had been Duty Leading Weapons Engineer for day one and therefore neither of us had yet seen the sites of Bangkok. Willis wasn't the sort of guy to throw on an Armani suit when he went out on the town. This was abundantly evident as he pulled on the only pair of jeans he had bought along for the entire seven-month deployment. Now, I can understand some people possessing lucky charms or keepsakes from loved ones back home but the reasons why Willis had decided to bring just one pair of jeans was beyond me. Sure, we didn't have a great deal of 'personal' storage space allocated to us on-board, a mere eighteen by thirty-six-inch locker wasn't in the same ballpark as a walk-in wardrobe but hey, this is a Royal Navy warship, not a Caribbean Love boat. Anyway, maybe they were his lucky jeans? Who am I to criticise fashion?

Crossing the gangway onto a foreign land is a very strange experience. Matelots enjoy the familiarity of their homes but find a new environment each time they open the door. The air not only smells different but also tastes different. Your home is a noisy one with generators, engine intakes, aerials buzzing, high-pressure air hissing, but home all the same and to step off onto a foreign dockyard in bizarre. You are sometimes hit by an extreme temperature change when leaving the ship as well, but we being made up mostly of Englishman we could cope easily with the mid-day sun. As a matter of fact in common with the mad dogs, it was probably our favourite time of the day.

Off we strolled but before even stepping from the gangway we were chased by the 'Bosun's Mate'.

"Oi lads, don't forget your taxi-chit!" he shouted.

"Our what?" we strained our ears.

"Your taxi-chit!" he repeated.

This was a new one on me. I trotted back up the gangway and approached the enthusiastic BM.

"What's a taxi chit?" I asked.

"It's a chit with some Thai shit written on it. Just hand it to a taxi driver when you need to get back to the ship 'cos I doubt if either of you speaks Thai"

Fair comment. Neither of us did, yet.

"Cheers mate."

I thanked him and walked back to Willis. Examining the paper I saw a mass of squiggles on one side with an English translation on the other.

'I am a British sailor, my ship is HMS Sheffield and is in the dockyard on jetty seven. Please take me there. Thank you.'

"Bloody 'ell they've thought of everything," Willis said, "a chit to get you home when you're pissed!"
"I think it may be more to do with the language barrier rather than the alcohol barrier," I suggested.
We had been given some hints about where to visit from the lads who had been out the night before and flagged down the nearest taxi.
"Nana Plaza," I told the driver as we climbed in.
After a quick fifteen minutes, we were dropped off outside and the first impression of this hotbed of bars and pole dancing girls was that it seemed a little tame. Mind you we were there at midday and like most places, night time is fun time.
The Plaza was made up of a large courtyard surrounded on three sides by three floors. The fourth side was open to the road. To the left was a set of stairs and to the right, an escalator which, I suspect, was the only thing in this place never to be turned on. Both of these external stairways led to a first-floor balcony which ran along the circumference of the three sides. The bottom floor appeared to be mostly bars, as did the first floor. The top floor looked like apartments. Bruce and me decided to stay put on the ground floor for now and walked to the far right-hand side of the Plaza where we found a place to sit and ordered our first bottle of beer. It wasn't long before a few locals focused their attention our way. First to approach was a small but smartly dressed bloke in his early twenties. He was a Thai 'Del-boy' with gelled hair and an impressive amount of gold jewellery which matched the rims of his *expensive* sunglasses.

"Hey man, you wan' buy watch?" he asked.

"No mate, I got watch."

"No like this, look!"

I was just about to administer a polite 'fuck off pill' when I saw what he was holding. Rolex and Tag copies but were bloody good ones complete with a smooth sweeping second hand and not a clunky tick-tock which we had been informed was the obvious first indication of a fake.

"How much do you want for them?" I asked albeit in a deliberately dismissive manner intended to show a lack of interest.

He suggested an amount in Thai Bahts which converted to about £15 for the classic looking Rolex Submariner and about £12 for any of the Tags and after a short haggle he ran off to get the watches we'd requested. A cheap digital would set me back a tenner so I thought I could get a couple of cheap Rolex instead to wear whilst I was here. While our new friend was away no doubt checking his stock room we found a couple of girls to chat with. Now for some reason I half expected a *"fucky-fucky ten dolla'!"* from these girls but received no such thing which threw me sideways. I certainly didn't intend to go out looking for any action so I could've happily told a *"fucky-fucky ten dolla'!"* girl to fucky-fucky off but after chatting with these girls for thirty minutes or so I was amazed how normal they appeared.

Both girls were dressed casually in jeans and T-shirts. The chatty one, who told me her name was stereotypically 'Suzi' though I severely doubt that was her real name, had been discussing babysitting arrangements for the others infant. Suzi told me that her friend had become pregnant by a tourist, quelle surprise, and she was now far more responsible as a result. She needed to get out and earn some money that evening. The girls would take turns to babysit the kids of all the others thus allowing the baby sitter a night off from the punters. A change is as good as a rest I suppose.

"You got a baby too?" I asked Suzi.

"No I am no stupid, I use pill and condom."

Suzi then pulled out a photo of her American boyfriend. He couldn't have been more than nineteen and she explained how he would visit her from the States and one day they would marry and she would move to the US with him. I started to think I had met a regular, normal girl in a regular, normal bar when she blurted, "You wan' fuck me?" instantly breaking my concentration.

"I wan' what?" I asked Suzi.

I'd even started to imitate the accent, for some bizarre reason a habit I developed and have tried unsuccessfully to shake ever since. Unconsciously I expect that it will make my English easier for them to understand.

"You wan' fuck me?" she repeated so casually it was as though she was asking me if I wanted a bag of crisps. No reference to '*ten dolla'!*'

She seemed unmoved when I told her I was staying here to drink my beer and wait for my watches.

"You will wan' fuck me later," she said, "don' go with any girl upstair I will fuck you *much* better, cheaper pri' too!"

I looked at Suzi for a short while and, questioning my manly-ness, wondered why I was more shocked than aroused by her offer when suddenly the watch man returned to rescue me from myself. True to his word he had bought me two Rolex copies and two Tag copies and yes, the Rolex watches both had the sweep hand. I had a good look over both and handed him some money.

"Tell your frens!" he said.

I bloody will.

A few beers later and we eventually wandered off to look at some sights but within moments predictably Bruce Willis and me jointly decided that we should head back to Nana Plaza as city centre Bangkok seemed both boring and busy. The Nana atmosphere of fun people, bars and beer had already become a more attractive place to hold out.

I am sure Bangkok is a beautiful city and Thailand a beautiful country but I now had started on the slippery downhill slope to alcoholism and simply didn't give a cultural shit. I just wanted more beer.

The daylight was fading and I knew that meant the best time to be at Nana. Fortunately this time we decided to visit for the first floor and not the ground floor. Maybe it was the abundance of people and sound of laughter and loud talking but a gut instinct told me that the ground floor should be avoided during the night, it was deserted compared to the first-floor bar but for a few 'business-like' looking local guys stood about with their arms folded. My gut instincts had served me very well in the past and I wasn't about to ignore them now. After strolling around a couple of the bars supping ales and admiring the endless numbers of Thai women in either lingerie, bikinis or 'Daisy-Duke' high-cut denim shorts we decided our local boozer for the duration would be the 'Hogs Breath'. It didn't seem quite as tacky as the other bars and the girls were more tastefully dressed. Also, there didn't seem to be as many German pensioners hanging around in the dark corners getting hand jobs from the girls. We had been joined by more lads from the ship who brought along with them a party atmosphere and in the words of that great Greek philosopher, Russ Abbott, "I love a party with happy atmosphere!"

The 'Hogs Breath' girls were fantastic but one, in particular, caught my eye. She was wearing a long denim skirt and a light brown top. I walked over and said hello. The girl introduced herself as Aell and she told me she was twenty-six. At a mere twenty-two, I was captivated by this 'older woman' for several reasons but mostly her no-fuss, girl-next-door, sweet to talk to, style. She possessed a broad friendly face with fantastically welcoming smile. Aell told me how she had previously been the property of a Swiss businessman. He had paid the equivalent of £125 for her 'release' and she had therefore lived with him whilst he conducted his business in Thailand. He had recently left Thailand and returned to Switzerland and to his normal Swiss life complete with Swiss friends and presumably Swiss family and Aell had no place in his Swiss life, so she went back to earning her money at a bar.

I was a little unsure if I had heard Aell correctly and she went on to elaborate. She told me it cost about £5 to buy a woman from the bar for the evening. That money then belonged to the establishment. What other price was then arranged between the girl and the client was a separate matter and the discretion of the girl. If a longer-term arrangement was required then a girls contract could be purchased from the bar for about £125. This meant that she no longer worked for the bar and was 'yours' instead. The girls weren't bothered as many of them saw it as a career. They were usually from the countryside and therefore farming families with not such much as two pennies to rub together. Their trip into the big city of Bangkok made them the primary breadwinner for the family and they would send money home on a regular basis. It was also a far better life if they found the right person to pay-off their contract for them.

Aell's *man* was only in Bangkok for about 6 years and she was at his 'beck and call' over that time. She would cook, clean and have sex with him. It was, according to Aell, customary for the male to be looked after by the woman and she would even wash and bathe him. Aell's man was gone and she needed to earn her living with someone else.

After chatting more with Aell and knocking back several of the 40p bottles of beers I wandered off to find the toilet. Here I found Bruce who was stood with his back towards me blocking my way into the small toilet cubicle. I thought he appeared to be having trouble standing as he was a little wobbly and using the door frame for support.

"Cheap beer but goes right through you, eh Bruce?" I said as I put my hand onto his shoulder dropping a hint that I wanted to pass by him for a piss.

"Alright Tony?" he replied in mild surprise.

I glanced in front of him and saw immediately that the toilet was occupied. A Thai girl about twenty years old was sat on the toilet. Her knickers around her ankles and skirt hitched up around her waist and she was blowing away on Bruce like a porn Queen.

"I'll be done in a bit mate if you want a go?" he said.

"You're alright mate, I only need a piss."

"I fucking love this place," he continued in his Lancashire drawl, "I only needed a piss too but she was already sat there."

Bruce had gone into the cubicle and on seeing the girl already in situ had unzipped himself. He told her to open her legs thinking it would be amusing to pee through the gap she made. The girl, on seeing Bruce's purple pump-action yoghurt rifle, leaned forward and swallowed it.

I still did need a piss however so I left the cubicle and went in the next bar to find the heads, no pun intended. On my return half an hour and a few beers later, Aell was sat in the same spot.

"I been waiting for you Toneee."

I had found some more Sheffield lads in the next bar and had decided to have a couple of beers with them. Aell hadn't moved a muscle.

"I like you, you don't have to buy me, just talk." She smiled.

I got the impression that at the grand age of twenty-six Aell was happier to sit and chill with someone normal rather than ply her trader. Aell explained how the atmosphere was different this evening.

"The girls are excited tonight," she told me, "we see lots and lots of old man, German man. They want strange things. They want to tie them and hit them sometime. One want to do that to me one time, I no let him. He got angry, he go."

Apparently, the girls were excited at the flood of fit, spritely and relatively young British lads which had suddenly invaded the bars. Their prime trade seemed largely to be old men with bizarre sexual tastes and many of those *old men* were evident as we sat around drinking but they kept themselves very much to themselves perhaps feeling a little intimidated by the groups of UK military personnel.

Aell grabbed a girl and said something to her in Thai. The girl nodded and walked away.

"She has gone to buy you a presen'." Aell said.

I couldn't wait!

The girl working behind the bar was getting quite a lot of attention. She was pretty cheerful and kept talking to Aell and was always courteous enough to chat in English so I could understand, even working to find the right words when needed.

"She is manager here," Aell told me, "she give best blow-job in Bangkok, that why she so pop-lar."

She didn't seem to be doing it now.

"She manager now, she no have time to go with man anymore," Aell said, "she will take one at the end of night I think."

The manageress was in her late twenties about five foot five in height and was a stunner. She had a cracking Demi Moore 'Ghost' haircut and wore a bright pink blazer with a black mini skirt. A little while later and Aell's friend returned with my present. Bar nibbles in the form of a packet of vacuum-packed beetles. Big fuckers too!

"You try," Aell suggested.

She could see I wasn't keen and breaking the packet open offered me one.

"Nah, I ain't eating that!" I said. "You dig out."

"I no eat, I on diet."

About 05:00 hours the following morning, after a blurred night of drinking cheap beer like it was my last day on earth, I made my way back to the ship using my 'all-important' taxi-chit. After a very short sleep, I woke to another rest-day from HQ1. Wow, this roster was gruelling! Around about midday, the lads started to drift into the mess from their various workplaces around the ship. The debriefing of the previous evening's activities commenced.

Whilst many of the lads had opted for Nana Plaza some had gone to Patpong and others Pattaya. While I spoke with high regard about the fun I had found in Nana, one poor 'skin and bone' Glaswegian lad from the dabbers mess, Thomo, had also visited Nana but, unlike me, had spent most of his time on the ground floor. He hated it! He had been there for about thirty minutes when a local man offered to show him and a couple of others 'the best sex show in Bangkok'. Thomo and his mates were ushered into a room which was lit with a very dim red lamp. The door was then promptly shut on them. After a few moments and with no evidence of the sex show a joint decision was reached to leave but as the lads went for the door a rather average-sized Thai male walked in accompanied by two others.

"You no leaving, you give us money!"

"Fuck off pal," Thomo replied in his best Glasgow hard man voice.

The male repeated his request only on this second request lifted his shirt and drew a pistol from the waist of his jeans. His accomplices drew knives from theirs. Thomo and his mates drew wallets from theirs.

Poor Thomo wasn't blessed with having the sharpest of minds.

As my big brother would say, "The wheel is spinning but the hamster's dead!"

There had been many previous incidents on board the Sheffield that would have made Thomo a prime contender for the Darwin Awards.

Thomo's two main nominations, however, would've been for the following, both of which occurred whilst we were in the Middle East. The first display of his stupidity was when asked to attend the flight deck on the 'hurry-up'. Once there the Chief Bosuns Mate instructed him to get kitted up in an anti-flash mask, overalls, fear-nought suit, a protective gunner's helmet, goggles and large fire fighting mittens. An 'expert' Royal Navy pilot had been placed on-board and in his possession was a large radio-controlled plane. This plane was launched by hand from the flight deck and the aim was for the gun crews on either of the bridge wings in their twin 30mm cannons or the lads manning the Port and Starboard 20mm cannons to shoot the plane down.

Thomo had been tasked with catching the petrol-powered plane complete with its hand dicing propeller on the front at the end of the exercise. Thomo was briefed that the small plane would fly above the flight deck and he would have to jump and catch it. For health and Safety reasons he was the only person allowed on the flight deck during the act. The fun with the plane went smoothly. No one managed a direct hit so with the exercise completed it was time to land the plane. A good sixty of us had gathered on the 'aft Seawolf launcher deck' overlooking the flight deck along with the Buffer and the plane operator. This vantage point afforded us a brilliant view of Thomo.

"Standby Tom!" shouted the Buffer. "Heads up matey, it's coming in!"

The operator dive-bombed Thomo who leapt onto the deck covering his head.

"FUCKING 'ELL!" he screamed.

"You nearly had it then mate, try again!" yelled the Buffer.

The plane circled before lining Thomo up for another go.

Whoooosh!

Thomo leapt towards the plane and very nearly caught it... with his head!

"Come on Thomo, put some effort in!" cried one of the spectators.

"This is ne fuckin easy ya know!" shouted Thomo.

Another two or three passes later and Thomo began to realise that he stood no chance what-so-ever of catching the bloody thing and when he looked up to find sixty Matelots in hysterics the penny finally dropped.

"Oh fucking har har!" he protested.

Now you would expect that to teach him a lesson, but not young Thomo. Within a week he was again in the hot seat. This time Thomo was tasked with being 'Splash Target Bosun.'

The splash target was a device made of wood and plastic towed along about two hundred yards behind the ship. The ship would then steam along at about ten to twelve knots which caused a course of water to flow through the internal channels within the target squirting a column straight on the top and into the air, looking a bit like a whale's blowhole on 'permanent squirt'. The target would then follow along behind the ship merrily until it was sunk by whatever aircraft had decided to take a pop at it. On this occasion, it was being used as a target for our own Lynx helicopter.

The Buffer decided that being a waterborne craft, the target should have a Bosun to steer it. Cue Thomo. He arrived on the quarter-deck enthusiastically sporting similar attire to what he had been instructed to wear in order to catch the radio-controlled plane the week before although this time he wore a hazardous duty life jacket as well. The task was simple, a bit like Thomo

"Right Thomo, once you are on the splash target you'll need to keep your head up or you will end up swallowing loads of water," explained the Buffer.

The correct position was demonstrated by a more experienced seaman climbing on to the Splash Target as it sat on the quarterdeck.

"Aye!" a very serious looking Thomo acknowledged.

"It's dead easy Thomo. Leaning left will steer you to Port and leaning right, to Starboard," the Buffer continued, "Smudge will be stood on the flight deck with a pair of RAS paddles which he will use to direct you! Keep an eye on where he's pointing. Have you got that Thomo?"

The RAS paddles resembled, for want of a better description, giant table tennis bats.

"Aye, no problem," Thomo was still keen.

"Right get used to the position and we will have a practice."

"Right'o Buffs."

Thomo climbed onto the target and settled in.

"This thing is quite tricky to sit on," he noted, "and there are no proper handles?"

"You'll do fine mate, just remember to duck when the budgie shoots at ya!" said one of Thomo's tormentors.

"Aye right, it is'ne' using real bullets is it?" asked Thomo, a shred of doubt appearing in his eyes.

"Yes mate real ones."

Clunk, the penny dropped again.

"You lot are fucking hilarious," Thomo resigned to further piss-taking.

I am willing to bet money that Thomo was a regular fog-patrol volunteer when going through basic training at HMS Raleigh. A simple task which involved patrolling the parade ground at night and if fog should close in, well you simply scooped some up with your plastic mug and brought it back to show the Duty Petty Officer who could see how thick the fog was and coincidentally how thick you were with it. Between this and Goldfish Duty which involved tapping on the tank to stop them falling asleep, lads discovered who was the most mentally challenged during seven weeks of basic training.

My second day off-duty in Bangkok and away I went once again to see the sights, with Bruce in tow. This time we wanted to sample some of the local grub but preferably not the sort that had six or eight legs. We headed in the rough direction of Nana Plaza again and found a cafe slash restaurant nearby. Although fast food and Maccy D's are great, it is a cultural 'must' to try some of the local cuisines once in a while. The cafe we found had plenty of local customers which is always encouraging when finding somewhere to eat. The waitress spoke some English and Bruce and me both ordered the same chicken dish, Cop-Kai. Well, that's what it sounded like. The food was heavenly and the beer was a fine local brew and very cold which was all that counted.

"We should fuck off Tony," Bruce announced mid mouthful.

"Not yet mate, I ain't finished me chicken," I wasn't going to be rushed.

"No, not like that," he continued, "fuck off for good, go AWOL."

I looked at Bruce and noticed he was wearing a serious expression. If he was a poker player, he was good at it.

"You are kidding?" I puzzled.

"Am I?" he *was* serious, "you could bugger off now into Thailand or even stay in Bangkok. Ain't no bastard gonna find ya."

We both sat in silence for a few minutes, chewing the spicy hot food and savouring the 'fresh from the freezer' bottles of local beer. I found it hard to disagree with Bruce, this was very nearly paradise. The atmosphere was fantastic and the people were fantastic. Why would you want to be anywhere else on the planet?

"Come on mate," I broke the golden silence, "let's get our asses to Nana."

Walking into the Plaza we were greeted by waves and cries from the balcony, "Hello Toneeee! Hello Bruce!"

You had to hand it to these girls, they kept a good lookout.

We took the stairs up to the first floor and planted ourselves outside of the Hogs Breath on some wooden chairs with an accompanying small service table. Aell came running out almost immediately with a bottle of beer for each of us.

"Here you go, drink," she insisted, "you look hot."

She dashed back inside only to return a short while later with cold flannels folded neatly on a tray. Taking a seat on my knee she began to dab one of the flannels across my forehead and around the back of my neck. The other she handed to a second girl who was now stood behind Bruce.

"You no have this sun in England?" she asked knowing full well the answer.

"Nope, just rain," I sighed, "lots and lots of rain."

"OK Tony, when it rain I think of you."

I thought I was dreaming, these girls were so eager to please. Bruce was still wearing his faithful and *only* pair of jeans and he was approaching the one month anniversary of wearing them without them seeing a laundry and one of the bar girls had picked up on this.

"Your clothes very dirty," the girl remarked.

"Can you wash 'em?" Bruce asked.

"Okay," she said, "take them off."

Without so much as a blink, Bruce took off everything but his pale blue boxer shorts, handing one pair of dirty stinking and beer-stained blue denim jeans and an equally filthy T-shirt to the girl. She then shouted commands in high pitched, high-speed Thai to someone inside the bar and a small elderly Yoda-like woman emerged, taking hold of the clothes before wandering off along the balcony and disappearing out of sight back into one of the bars.

After chatting with the girls for a while we started to pick up on a few useful Thai phrases. As Bruce no longer possessed pockets he decided to write these useful phrases onto his arm in black ink and in no time at all had his left arm covered with drunken scrawl resembling Egyptian hieroglyphics, only a little more random. The girls with him thought this was hilarious and started to write on him as well. After some time Bruce, with both arms looking like he had been in a fight with an OCD tattooist with a passion for algebra, strolled off to look for more cigarettes wearing nothing more than his boxer shorts. I stayed put and chatted with Aell. She was a good looking girl and very easy on the ears too though I was soon distracted by a long-legged and very tall Thai girl strolling past us. Followed by another and then another. I looked twice, something was odd. One had spoken a few words to Aell whilst walking past and, you guessed it the voice was a little deeper than expected.

"Ladyboys!" I blurted out like I'd just seen a pop star.

I knew this place was famous for Ladyboys but I had never seen one before. They were bloody convincing. Great arses and nice legs! Quite a novelty for a twenty-three-year-old Cornish boy.

"Fucky-fucky ten dollar!" I said in a deliberately deep voice. Aell immediately started to giggle and put her hand over my mouth.

"You no say that!" she laughed.

"Why not she, he, she can't hear me," I deepened my voice again, "I lurve you loooong time Jonny, I got special big hands for yooooo!"

Aell was struck with laughter and proceeded to tell her mate what I was saying, they both fell about. They didn't seem familiar with the British concept of taking the piss.

"You stop now, they get very angry if they hear."

Not wishing to get Aell into any trouble I stopped my piss-taking as she requested. I sat drinking more beer while Aell continued to re-supply fresh iced flannels for my roasting head. She then rather strangely, developed a fascination with my nose, or rather the bridge of my nose.

"It no fair, Thai people no have this," she said pointing to her nose.

She was unquestionably a *very* pretty girl with typical eastern look but she voiced her disappointment at this characteristic of some Oriental people. She was also angry that her hair was returning to its natural country girl colour, auburn. She routinely dyed her hair black as did most of her friends, to help them look that extra bit sassy. Aell then continued to tell me about her background and her childhood growing up on a small rice farm. Every few moments she would lean forward and sniff my head. This continued until my curiosity got the better of me and had to ask what stank so oddly about my swede. Apparently, I smelt like a baby. I took that to mean I smelt 'clean'. Another insight into the usual pub-goers the bar attracted maybe.

A short time later Bruce returned. I had no idea where he had been for his smokes but he had some. I told Bruce about the Ladyboys who wandered past and pointed to the bar 'DC10' where they had gone. For the next 40 minutes, we chugged back a few more stubbies of cold beer until Mistress Yoda returned with Bruce's clothes, clean and perfectly pressed like they were ready for an army kit muster.

"Cheers Love!" Bruce thanked her as though she had just passed him some peanuts from the bar before unfolding his crisp clean clothes to get dressed.

After a short while more lads appeared from the ship and as the afternoon wore on the beer flowed faster. We hung about the same general area as there seemed no rush to move on but eventually decided to visit a bar further around the floor for a change of scenery. Aell was worried that I wouldn't come back to see her so I gave her five quids worth of Bhats and told her that if someone tried to buy her, to give my money to the bar and then come and find me. Well, it was only a fiver.

We all walked to a bar a few doors along and each ordered a round of beers. At the equivalent of forty pence a bottle we could afford to be generous. Bruce was struck with the girl on the stage. She was technically a pole dancer but didn't do much dancing, more of an 'upright support' than a pole dancer. I think if she'd have tried to swing from the pole she'd have done herself some damage anyway. It wasn't at all secure and was wobbling about fairly precariously on the one bolt fastening it to the ceiling. Without provocation, Bruce reached out and grabbed the arm of a waitress as she walked past him collecting empty bottles.

"Hey, I like your jeans. Where d'you get them?" Bruce asked the waitress.

I think he was feeling the heat of the city, and that from the waitress was wearing a pair of cut-off's denim shorts.

"They no for sale," came the quick and absolute reply.

"Go and get me some, Love, I'll give you good price!"

The cut off Levi jeans worked well on her and Bruce wanted a pair for himself as the temperature was through the roof. She politely refused his request to 'source' some before walking away with her tray of empty bottles. A resigned Bruce had just taken another swig of his beer when the waitress re-appeared armed with a pair of large kitchen scissors. As Bruce stood at the bar with the rest of the lads the waitress squat down behind him and began to cut. First straight up from the bottom edge and around. After tailoring one leg to fit, she started on the other.

"There you go, now you got some too!" she said in delight.

Sure enough, Bruce now had a pair of cut off denim jeans only one leg, cut just above the knee, was a couple of inches shorter than the other which was cut just below. On top of that, the waitress had just cut up Bruce's *only* pair of jeans. Still, why should that bother him?

We floated from bar to bar finding a few lads from the mess in most until, after some debate, we headed towards DC10's, the bar in the far left where the Ladyboys all appeared to go. We strolled in and discovered, much to our surprise that it was almost empty. After getting in a round of drinks we sat once again taking in the sights and sounds. 3-Golfs mess Teddy Boy, Jim Brown was there and promptly started to spin the latest Thomo dit.

Matelots don't tell stories, they spin dits. I'm sure there will be some historical meaning behind the phrase as there tend to be historical meanings behind most thing Matelots do.

It turned out that poor Thomo while still bravely dealing with the effects of the previous night's robbery at gunpoint decided that the next afternoon he would spend safely drinking in a bar with a few more occupants. The display he was privy too on the stage was the infamous balloon popping act. For those who are not familiar with this, it is similar to the Ping-Pong ball act. For those still confused I shall elaborate.

A local girl had taken to the stage in the bar and performed a seductive striptease before sitting astride a bar stool, a few balloons were placed approximately ten feet away and using a small tube and a few darts placed in the holiest of holy's she began firing the darts one at a time using an impressive display of vaginal muscle control and air pressure. Deep breath in! She shot away at the balloons with the accuracy of a police marksman.

Phurft! POP!

Phuuurft! POP!

Phuurft! THUD!

"What the fuck was that?" cried Thomo rubbing his temple, "something hit me in me fuckin' heed?"

The sharpshooter jumped to her feet, leapt off the stage and ran straight over to slightly puzzled Thomo who was rubbing the pain and frown from his forehead.

"Me so sorry, me miss balloon," apologised the girl, "you okay though, no bleeding."

She reassured Thomo who didn't have the foggiest idea what had just happened and why everyone stood around him was in hysterics, even the dodgy old German's sat in their corners were smiling. Thomo had been oblivious to the balloon show and had just stood innocently with his back towards the stage. Unaware of why his mates were paying no attention to his latest story. He raised his bottle of Budweiser and took a long swig turning his head to glance around in the process. The turn of his head was timed to perfection and it intercepted the flight path of the Thai girl's fanny dart with the port side of his noggin.

Hearing that had us rolling about in stitches. I would have paid good money to see if she could repeat the performance though I doubt if Thomo would've been so keen.

We all had a good giggle, forgetting briefly that the bikini-clad girls sat on our laps were fella's. It wasn't hard to forget as their bodies were a close match to the girls usually found on the cover of 'Sports Illustrated'. In fact, their flaw was that they looked *too* good. Too much like flawless fitness models and not real everyday ladies. Where they hid their tackle was beyond me. The bikinis were tiny string efforts for the main part. I imagine a few strips of 'harry black maskers' were used to keep their peckers held back. It took me about two or three unconscious strokes of her back before I remembered the girl sat on my lap was a guy and I stopped immediately hoping no one had noticed. My ladyboy didn't seem to mind though. We all had a laugh and continued with the drinking, all of us but Davey Davidson. Davey was a very straight-laced bloke keen on promotion with an immaculate side parting in his hair and dress sense straight out a golfing catalogue. He currently had a broad-shouldered yellow bikini-clad lady on his lap and was getting very carried away with her. Surely Davey wasn't *that* pissed? He continued to go further with his lady and before long was having a good tuning the radio using the dials inside her bikini top, not the slightest bit deterred by the little slaps to his hand that she was dishing out every now and then.

We carried on chatting amongst ourselves but the conversation stopped mid-flow and all eyes turned to Davey who was now in a full lip lock with his young filly. We watched in silent disbelief as his hand went from her well-formed breast down her stomach and teased around the front of her bikini bottoms. Davey went rapidly into full grope mode and we all held our breaths, squinting our eyes in a primal attempt to hide our gazes. Then Davey froze! His hand stopped, his mouth petrified instantly before assuming the default gaping goldfish open position. Suddenly he jerked his head back ten inches and jumped off the stool sending his new friend flying onto her perfect ass.

"This one's got bollocks!" he squealed with a horrified tone to his voice.

"I know mate, they all have," laughed Bruce.

The girls were most offended at Davey's sudden change of behaviour and chased him out of the bar flailing their arms about but even though they were well practised in running with high heels they still weren't fast enough to catch him.

I made my way back to the Hogs Breath where I found Aell sat at the same table she was when I left. More than an hour had passed and she said she had been waiting for me to come back.

The evening went on and I soon reached the end of my second night in Bangkok and although there was no bell to mark last orders it was obvious when the staff were shutting up shop. Aell walked with me to the nearest 'burger' van serving unrecognisable Thai snacks and she purchased two bags of various appetisers from the lad behind the stall. We found a seat and Aell explained every single item of food, what it was and why it was healthy. I am unable to recall a single word she said due to a combination of fatigue and way too much beer. I just wanted to get my head down.

I returned to the ship at about 06:00 to avoid being adrift and went straight to my bunk where I crashed out. I woke roughly seven hours later to my last day in Bangkok. After grabbing lunch in the galley I found Bruce and we headed off to Nana, it felt as though we were commuting home after working in the dockyard just as we did in Devonport. The stories had flown around the ship about Davey and his Ladyboy along with Thomo with his close encounter of the fourth kind and we arranged times to meet up with other lads from the mess in our new local, Hogs Breath. Some of the lads were displaying loyalties to Patpong, another community of bars, scantily clad ladies and crap food, but I was happy where I was. We almost felt as though we were the hosts at the party. Andy Mathews came along with Bruce and me this time and he was intent on getting a genuine Thai massage. En-route to Nana we stumbled upon a genuine massage parlour and I took him in telling Bruce Willis that I would catch him up at Nana Plaza.

"Are you sure you're after a massage Andy?" I asked, "you sure you ain't looking for a shag instead?"

I don't think Andy M was going to admit to wanting a full monty. He was too conservative. I dropped him off in a parlour and said I would wait for him outside but I was instead offered a chair inside by the staff so I duly planted my arse in the corner. A small elderly woman and an equally small and elderly man strolled into the room which bore a striking resemblance to an operating theatre, all white and silver with uncomfortably bright lighting. The old man in his late early 70's walked straight towards me and shook my hand, in his left hand he held a black curly wig. I got the impression he thought I was Andy M's boss treating him to a work bonus or something. The small and frail elderly lady walked over to Andy and instructed him to get naked and lay face down on the operating table. He did this willingly possibly thinking the real masseur was on her way. The woman drew a see-through white curtain around the table similar to a privacy curtain in a hospital ward and covered Andy M's backside with a towel. She then got to work by starting on his shoulders, rubbing, chopping, squeezing and pulling. Andy submitted to his octogenarian masseur.

He hadn't been out with the lads here yet and I think he was hoping to experience something similar to what we had all been shouting about in the mess. I sat and smiled to myself. The old bloke was now sat next to me and began to chat away in pigeon English. He told me how he went across the river most evenings wearing his faithful black curly wig. He revealed how he dressed as a woman each evening then he laughed out loud like he had just told me the funniest joke in the Far East. I humoured him with smiles and the nodding motion of my head, raising my eyebrows although I was unable to make out most of what he was saying as his English got worse the more he laughed.

"Jesus, hurry up Andy!"

After a measly thirty minutes, Andy had his towel removed and was waved off the table.

"What did you think?" I asked, knowing that I would've felt seen off with the service.

"Very good, I feel very refreshed," he replied.

"Yeah but was it... you know?" I searched for an admission.

"Oh I wanted a genuine Thai massage," he nodded, "I feel I can get pissed now."

He lied like a cheap Chinese watch.

Pushing Andy M out the door I turned and gave the old couple a little wave and they both raised their hands in unison and nodded repeatedly with big grins in return, the old boy stood holding a manikin head which he used to display his black curly wig.

"Come on mate, I'll take you to Nana," I said and encouraged Andy further along the road.

I got to Nana and went immediately to the Hogs Breath where Aell was waiting. She ran up and threw her arms around me. "Toneeeee!" she cried, "I waiting for yoooo!"

Bruce was already well into his beer and was chatting away to an older western bloke. Andy M in the meantime wandered off after spying one of the Sheffield lads outside another bar. I joined Bruce with the western bloke. I noticed that this bloke, an American in his fifties, didn't have the usual crowd of girls around him. He didn't have hold of a beer just a retractable tape measure and a short carpenters pencil tucked behind his ear. He had collar-length grey hair an unkempt moustache and wore a black baseball cap tilted backwards on his head along with old jeans and a black short-sleeved shirt. In fact, he looked a lot like a handyman. After a short time a well dressed Thai lady of similar age to the Yank walked out and spoke to him, he replied in Thai and they both walked inside.

Curious, I asked Bruce who the Yank was. Bruce, who arms were already covered in more useful Thai phrases scrawled in biro.

"He owns the bar mate," Bruce divulged, "That Thai bird is his missus."

He was not permitted to work in Thailand, only to reside. So he was doing a few minor repairs to a neighbouring bar as a favour to the owner. He had come to be in Thailand after serving with the US Army in Vietnam but on returning to the US after the war was shocked by the hostile reception he had received from the American people that he left America almost immediately and had not returned since. Thailand was, in his opinion, not too dissimilar to Vietnam and after getting married to a local girl decided to raise a family here. He purchased the bar which he then gave to his wife as a present.

After a short while, the Yank returned and Bruce introduced me. He must've seen lots of western pissheads in his bar so I wasn't surprised when he disappeared again almost straight away to carry on with work elsewhere. His wife, however, stayed chatting with Aell for quite some time. She was wearing a large pair of red-framed glasses, a huge smile and seemed very friendly and chatty. When she left I took a seat at the same part of the balcony where I had spent most of my time the afternoon before. I felt it was rude to sit while the Landlady was present for some reason, almost like I was chatting with Thai Royalty.

Aell asked the waitress to bring me out a beer along with an iced flannel. Shortly after this another beer arrived, and another. Also, a plate of food was placed at my table and yes, another beer. I was a little bewildered as so far I had not paid for any of it. Aell then informed me that the boss and his wife were celebrating the marriage of their daughter to a local policeman. The food and the drinks were all on the house, but only to friends and I was considered, today at least, as a friend. I got up and made my way into the bar, if I was a friend and receiving this treatment then the least I could do was be sociable. I met the bride and groom, who was proudly wearing his best police uniform and found I got along quite well. My small town Cornish mind still struggling to comprehend how normal everyone seemed to be. We all shared a cognate agenda and sense of humour.

My final night was fairly subdued compared to the previous two. I spent what time I could just chatting to Aell and whatever shipmates drifted in off the street and I had no desire to leave the Hogs Breath. I felt like a local propping up the bar on my personal bar stool. It felt uncomfortably homely and the people I had met were friendly to the point of being 'close'. I don't mean the obvious girls who were out for some business but everyone I met gave the impression that they wanted to be your friend and welcome you in for a chat and a few drinks. As long as you were genuine with them, they loved you for it.

The very next morning it was 'Hands To Harbour Stations' and HMS Sheffield left Bangkok.

Chapter Eight

Demis Roussos

We sailed for Singapore and were kept occupied by the usual fire exercises, routine maintenance and drinking way in excess of our allocated 3 tins of beer in the evenings. This was to be the first of three visits to this enchanting and magical island referred to fondly as 'Singers'. We were stopping on this occasion for just a couple of days, a small taster for our second visit which would be for two weeks.

Berthing in the dockyard I was immediately aware of how spotlessly clean everything was. Our liaison speech before arriving warned us of the consequences of littering and chewing gum in public. I got the impression that things were strict here but I was wrong. The rules simply encouraged more respect of others. I had now finished my stint in HQ1 and was having to readapt to working for Brum again. We had put our differences behind us, most of them anyway and seemed to be getting along ok for the moment. We were near the halfway point of the deployment but it felt like longer. One side effect of the deployment so far however was that I was beginning to question my commitment to Abby. I had barely thought about her once over the last few days pining instead for far eastern bars and cold beer. Every time I thought of Abby I just recalled memories that made me frown rather than those that made me smile. In just over a two weeks she would be flying out to this very island for us to spend some time together. While the Sheffield was due to be resting at the trips half-way point the opportunity had cropped up for some of the crew to fly out their better halves for a luxury holiday.

This is the same for most Royal Navy ships on deployment with the rare exception being ships that go to a war zone for the obvious reasons. This holiday for the loved ones is usually far from cheap and I had to rustle up four grand to make it happen. To this day I am convinced the Supply Officer was working on commission from Kuoni Travel. I had never had a holiday abroad, sure I had been abroad many times with the Grey Funnel Line but that didn't count in my reckoning. I had been to well over thirty countries but never once had a stamp in my passport.

I was looking forward to seeing Abby again but concerned over the way my thoughts, longer-term were changing. Abby and I were due to marry the following summer and I wasn't feeling the same commitment to her I had felt when I left the UK. I had tasted some more fun aspects of life and I was wanting more. I would work something out no doubt, I'm sure I would get my feelings back on track before long but for now the tactic of putting my head in the sand as far as I could seemed to be the best policy.

The first night's shore leave in Singers saw me on duty as Duty LWEM, I had drawn the short straw but at least I managed to get off the ship albeit by forty feet to use one of the telephones in the dockyard. I threw my MasterCard into the phone slot and dialled home. It was great to hear the voices of my family at home in Padstow. I usually managed to call home when most people were in the house and I nattered away for half an hour before strolling back to the ship. A very quiet first night for me in Singapore.

I took most of the following day off and went ashore as soon as I got the steak and chips lunch down my throat. If the Army marches on its stomach then the Navy floats on its! I headed to Raffles Hotel along with the majority of the ship where we all started necking tumblers of their famous Singapore Sling.

Once we were all bored of the cocktails we started on the yards of ale. There wasn't an abundance of pubs to go to and we drifted instead to the shopping malls which were plentiful. I found a fairly expensive Sony car stereo which came with a ten disc CD auto-changer and remote joystick. This was hi-tech stuff for the '90s! I thought it would come in handy for my 1985 Audi Coupe which was currently sat in my brother's garage at home in Padstow so I forked out £240 in Singapore dollars. A similar stereo at home would have cost double so I well chuffed with the bargain. It was a toss-up between that and getting a posh watch but as my Bangkok 'Rolex' was working so well I saw no point in getting a new timepiece.

Most of us enjoy buying gifts to give to those at home on our return. I had bought two fake Rolex's and two fake Tag's which I decided to give one of each to my brothers. At least I didn't go totally overboard unlike Reggie Kray. Reggie, a killick Greenie like myself, had purchased fifteen 'Rolex' watches along with various other designer label watches to pass on to mates in his local when he returned to Blighty. More like Arthur Daley than Reggie Kray.

I made my way back to the ship where I dumped my newly acquired treasures in my locker. It was obvious that many lads were finding Singers a little on the tame side but after visiting Thailand most places on earth would be tame. The boys and girls didn't seem in any great hurry to get ashore and play and when we did finally muster enough lads together to launch a second assault we walked just up the road to what was formerly the 'Union Jack' club, a social club for mariners. I say formerly because like with most things it had been Americanised and had been renamed the 'Stars and Stripes' club or something. There were, however, no Americans in the 'Stars and Stripes', loads of Sheffield ship's company though, along with a few members of the local ex-pat rugby club, all throwing back ale and when we finally got kicked out we drifted back to the ship where our party continued thanks to the trusty beer fridge.

Each mess-deck on board has a beer fridge and to keep order of the fridge a beer bosun is appointed. He was responsible for keeping it topped up nightly and also for chasing money owed to the beer fridge. If a rating wanted a drink then they would simply reach into the fridge and remove one of their allocated beers, marking a tick in the beer book against their number.

This method worked surprisingly well. Despite Matelots being a general bunch of piss-heads we knew well the moral's of honesty and integrity especially regarding the beer fridge and the beer account almost always balanced perfectly.

To prevent us from being drunk all of the time, which no doubt would happen if we were given the chance, the fridge was padlocked with the key held by the HQ1 Watchkeeper. Times of opening were allocated to the fridge usually from 19:00 to 23:00 hours nightly. Along with this another method of control was employed, beer issue. Each sailor was allocated three cans of beer per night. Even this seemed excessive to our American friend during his little visit as they were allowed only one tin every forty days! As we knew a mere three tins of beer was plainly insufficient to get drunk and have a party on, therefore the beer bosun would hoard the stuff. The hierarchy turned a blind eye to this unless things got out of hand as it did with the 'ball and chain' affair on HMS Brave. The mere threat of a beer ban was enough to drag any rebellious sailors back into line. Most lads wouldn't bother drinking their nightly allowance so it was stored for times when we required a little more than usual, such as this one. Singapore was feeling somewhat of a letdown. I hadn't seen much of Bruce, none of the lads had. I'd given him my spare pair of jeans when we got here on day one since his had been cut to shreds by the waitress in Bangkok. Other than that I had barely seen him at all.

The following day I went to work as usual, I use the word *work* loosely of course. I was stood in the doorway of the ship's computer room with Brum and Phil Marshall, the Deputy Weapons Officer having a chat about something electrical. After a few minutes, a young Sub-Lieutenant approached us.

"Excuse me Sir, may I have a word?" said the young Subby.

"You may, Charles, fire away," replied the boss.

"Well, to be honest Sir I would rather discuss this matter in private," explained the Sub-Lieutenant Under Training or SLUT for short.

"Nonsense Charles, anything you say to me can be said in front of my lads."

"Well Sir, it *concerns* one of your lads," nervously he continued, "I was unable to sleep last night so at about 3 am I decided to go into the Wardroom and listen to the wireless or read."

The Wardroom was the name for the Officers Mess, like our mess-deck but far more civilised with real tables and real chairs along with a painting of Her Majesty Queen Elizabeth and Prince Philip majestically watching over the officers.

"And?" puzzled Phil so far unable to sense the reason for concern.

"Sir, one of your Leading Hands was *in* the wardroom," he cried, "the small skinny one who's always drunk."

Bruce!

"In the Wardroom?" asked Phil assuming him to be a late-night guest, "who with?"

"No one Sir, he was on his own. He was drinking a bottle of Bacardi with his feet up on a table!" he blurted on the borderline of tears, "and what's more Sir, he was playing *my* Demis Roussos tape!"

Phil, wearing his best poker face, tried desperately not to laugh.

"And what did you do?"

"Nothing Sir, I felt uncomfortable, so I left."

Unable to contain ourselves any longer we all burst into laughter. The young SLUT offended by the lack of respect offered by Brum and myself stormed off up the corridor to find some more toys to throw about.

To some, this may seem the actions of an 'oversensitive' junior officer but allow me to put this into context with a basic analogy. Mess-decks are our homes away from home, often for many months and are treated with according respect. Everyone knocks and waits at the door/hatch if they wish to speak to someone in another Mess. Any business is usually conducted outside of the door/hatch save for rare occasions where a person is invited inside usually for social reasons. Lt 'Shiner' Wright in our Mess Deck playing Uckers being the perfect example.

These rules are as ancient and as steadfast as the Ten Commandments and the two tablets upon which they are written. With Mess Deck etiquette so vital between sailors imagine then introducing the added complexity of 'rank' or 'rate'? With such strict rules between same rate mess-decks, it is no wonder that to gain entry to the Petty Officers Mess or the Chief Petty Officers Mess on a warship is near impossible for a rating from below deck. Now, multiply the mix of tradition and rank by ten and you start to understand the unwritten rules around entering not just any other Mess Deck, but the Wardroom, uninvited and unaccompanied and *then* pouring yourself some Whisky and popping some tunes on the stereo. Bruce had transgressed one of the holiest of commandments. He had, to return to an analogy, entered the home of a local dignity and helped himself to the wine cabinet while sifted though the Lady Mary's lingerie drawer for smalls.

He was rapidly becoming a legend!

Bruce seemed to wander off on his own in Singers and our final night was no different. Some of the lads reported a possible sighting of him drifting towards the north of the island with a lady in tow, sporting a left-arm plastered in Biro pen. We didn't bother to send out a search party, he was old enough to look after himself, so we opted instead to repeat the previous evening's performance and placed another dent in the beer fridge on our return after the nights run ashore to the 'Stars'. Singapore seemed a little tame and I think we were simply all too tired to go out and search hard for the nightlife.

The following day we were again ready to head out once more onto the blue wavy stuff and the same old familiar sailing routine got underway. Leave expired for all personnel at 0750 hours. HMS Sheffield was under 'Sailing Orders'.

At 08:00 hours Bruce had still not returned to the ship.

"Here we go again," I thought, Jebel Ali the sequel.

"Bruce's really in the shit this time," said Mick. "Twice adrift in one bloody trip!"

We all sat in the mess square knowing that our reluctance to get to our places of work on time would be completely overshadowed by Bruce's absence from the ship. We were not due to sail until 1400 hours but that wouldn't benefit Bruce at all. One minute late was taken just as seriously as one hour late. He was going to get a severest of bollockings for being adrift this time, even more so as we were under sailing orders which would automatically double any punishment he'd receive as a result of his shit timekeeping.

Zero nine-hundred came and went, then ten-hundred, then eleven. 'Operation Thimblehunt' had been unsuccessful along with the Jimmy's inch by inch search of Singapore dockyard no doubt checking under any lorry trailers as he went. At least this time the Jimmy knew what Bruce looked like. I had now been on the piss with Bruce a few times and I thought I knew his state of mind but I couldn't help but recall the words he'd spoken during our conversation in Thailand.

Surely he hadn't gone AWOL?

He certainly sounded pretty serious at the cafe in Bangkok but I didn't think for a minute he would really do it. He certainly appeared pretty distant and had kept himself to himself during this quick stop at Singers, if that *was* his game then he would be long gone.

Fucking hell Bruce, good luck mate!

'Special-Sea-Dutymen' closed to their harbour stations, 14:00 hours had eventually arrived and after closing the ship down to *'NBCD State 3 - Condition Yankee'* we were ready for the set sail. The Skipper was running everything ten minutes late just in case, by some miracle, Bruce should stroll down the jetty whistling and carrying a pint of milk we all knew that was wishful thinking. I believe if we had been sailing in the morning rather than mid-afternoon the Skipper would have held on even longer but as leave had expired seven hours ago Bruce had been allowed sufficient opportunity to make it back to the ship.

We left Singapore minus one crew member and headed out to sea, 3-Golf mess was under a cloud of subdued silence.

Our agenda over the next few days involved exercising with a foreign vessel that was a couple of hundred miles south. Cat and mouse games for a while testing our ability to hunt in a pack with our NATO Allies. The weather had closed in and this meant a very bumpy ride. To make matters worse, thanks to Bruce's disappearance we were running late and needed to steam at top speed to make this very important rendezvous. Despite the scary images of ships being tossed about on big waves I always enjoyed rough seas and large swells and got from them a kind of twisted pleasure. Each man's bunk was fitted with a seat belt style harness which could be drawn across the body in times of need, not too much of a problem if you slept on the bottom bunk as you were only twelve inches from the deck but if you were on the middle or even the top bunk, as I was, then the fall from bunk bed to the deck was considerably further.

Another twisted pleasure I derived from rough seas was the fun to be had at mealtimes. Anyone who has travelling on a larger cross channel ferry can probably recall a dining hall with fixed tables and chairs and the fun to be had trying to walk from the service counter to your table in rough weather. Exasperated somewhat by the tray you are trying to keep level and the plate of scran you have piled up to the gunwales with sausage, mashed spud and gravy. Your legs don't act how your mind intends and you resemble a career drunk trying to kick a rugby ball straight at a family barbecue. Well, firstly imagine that, the crazy Monty Python walk and the intense concentration, then the added complication of there being much less space to walk in, coupled with a ship moving a lot more violently than any cross channel ferry ever has. When you eventually find a seat at a table you are safe in the knowledge that, in common with the ferry, your table is fastened to the deck. While the table on the ferry is usually a permanent fixture, the table in a warship is not and is fastened temporarily to the deck with a cable of some sort, but fastened all the same. Your plate is held in place by a lovely sticky mat designed to stop it sliding about on the table and keeping your plate of scran, yours! Now, this is where the fun starts. The table is fixed and your plate will always remain 'stuck' in place on said table, however, in contrast to the ferry, your chair is not fixed. Not even *slightly*. The side effect of this is that at mealtimes when the ship hits a big wave everyone slides across the dining hall on their chairs clutching their Port and Starboard scran spanners with 'dear life'. Some sailors manage to hold on to their table for a short while before being collected unceremoniously by a twenty-stone Leading Seaman who is doing a 'log flume' in his own chair and slammed against the bulkhead in a game of chair Dodgems. When the ship settles briefly, it switches instantly to a game of musical chairs with everyone waddling hurriedly back to their table-spaces clutching their chairs against their arses. It is hilarious.

Another advantage with *very* rough sea was that unnecessary personnel were sometimes instructed to return to their Mess-Deck therefore reducing the chance of personnel injuring each other whilst running about the ship. More time to dwell on the solitude that months at sea brings.

Not all vessels were affected by the sea in the same way. Small ships were thrown everywhere almost constantly and should a cup of tea be served in a Mess with a large gap at the top of the cup it was fondly referred to as a 'small ship's wet'. The large gap reducing the chance of spillage when the ship leans or gets thrown about. Larger ships, therefore, remained less vulnerable to movement. Richie, my oppo from the Brave once had a guided tour of an American aircraft carrier, the 'USS Over-The-Top' and whilst being escorted around one of the recreation areas on-board came across a pool table.

"A pool table?" he puzzled, "Don't the balls fly around everywhere at sea?"

"Hell Boy, you seen the size this ship?" replied his southern state slurring US host, "This thang don't moooooove!"

Our *thang* certainly did move and all non-essential staff were told to get some shut-eye and keep out of the way to save getting a bump on the swede or a broken leg. Rough weather had it advantages.

Within a couple of hours of steaming Sheffield received a signal, message from Singapore Dockyard the details of which quickly filtered down to our Mess Deck rapidly, one advantage of having Radio Operators living with us in 3G. Bruce had returned to the dockyard about an hour after we had sailed. This presented the Captain with a small problem. There was no way he was going to turn the ship around to collect him, not for at least a week. We had a strict itinerary over the next few days and we were sticking to it. Fortunately for Bruce, but unfortunately for them, one of Her Majesty's submarines had just dropped into Singapore harbour to collect stores. Bruce was thrown on board as she was heading our way to join in the war games. She wouldn't be able to RV with us for at least five days but at least we would get our shipmate back. One problem, however, was that Bruce, being a skimmer, had never been on a submarine before and therefore had not undertaken the necessary training that went with such a vessel. He had not completed the tank at HMS Dolphin, Gosport. The tank, or to use its proper name, the 'Submarine Escape Training Tower' was a one hundred and twenty-foot tank of water from which aspiring submariners must 'escape from' during their training. A more serious issue was that he had not been medically tested to establish whether his body could cope with the changes in pressure, his ears may not pop properly resulting in damage to his hearing for example. As a consequence, the submarine he was thrown on was not allowed to submerge and instead had to bob along on the surface of the sea for five days experiencing one of the worst storms that the Indonesian waters could throw at it.

Normally submarines get off lightly in bad weather. They disappear below the waves for a fairly stable ride. They are not exactly designed for long distances on the surface and their tubular design tends to bob around like a cork. The crew were equally unprepared for this treatment and spent their five days being very seasick apart, that is from Bruce, who sat merrily in their Mess Deck and drinking their beer. The poor chap couldn't even work as part of the crew as there was no job for him on board. He was not popular with the submariners.

Meanwhile on board the Shiny Sheff we all found ways of amusing ourselves during the long evenings at sea when we were 'off' duty. Aside from a nightly staged exercise which varied in detail from a quick gash bag fire occupying some of the duty-watch fire to a larger fire in the ship's Galley for example, which took a little more effort to complete or even the joys of some minor flooding. Many of the lads had hobbies or past-times which they wouldn't have tried in a conventional evening at home. With no pub to go to and no option to go out to see friends or pop to the cinema, the crew were probably more well-read than folk at home in 'normal' life.

I had been spending some downtime on a design for our 3G deployment T-shirt and my artwork had been completed and finalised. It became the norm for Messes to have a trip T-shirt made up. I had been scribbling away at several designs and a final draft had been approved by the members of 3G. On the rear of the shirt was a hand-drawn map of the world with each visit for this trip marked by a red dot with a list of all the 3G mess members below. The front of the T-shirt saw a silhouette of HMS Sheffield launching an Exocet missile into the foreground on which was sat a Kangaroo wearing boxing gloves and hanging on to the front of the missile for dear life, a Koala bear.

The words across the front simply read, **'3G MESS - GROOVERS ON MANOEUVRES'**

We eventually met up with the submarine and Bruce returned to the comfort of the Sheffield much to the delight of the submarine crew.

"Come on mate, what happened then?" I got the first exclusive interview.

"I trapped off with some local bird di'n I," he started, "went back to her flat and spent all night boning it. She set her alarm clock for seven so I'd have forty-five minutes to get back on board."

"Well?" I waited for the 'but'.

"The alarm went off but I thought I'd have another ten minutes as I was only round the corner from the dockyard. So I went back to sleep and woke up again at two bloody thirty!"

It wasn't long before a pipe summoned Bruce to the Jimmy's cabin. He braced himself for a ton of bricks.

We took bets on the punishment Bruce was likely to receive but were all taken by surprise. The hard-line bollocking we expected didn't happen. Bruce got off extremely lightly although I am sure he would not have agreed. The Teflon coated, 'three badge' killick-oily got to hang on to his three good conduct badges but despite this, he returned to the Mess looking very angry. They had hit him where it would hurt the most.

"Five hundred pound fine," he protested, "and they stopped my beer for fourteen days!"

That was the bit that made him angry.

A sober Bruce would have to spend the next eight days floating around dry. After that, we would be back at Singapore for our fortnights visit and the beer stoppage wouldn't matter but for now, Bruce was hurting.

Sailing back into Singapore was a little more welcome this time. While most of the lads had holidays planned of some sort, Tug Wilson was off to Hong Kong to look up an old friend for instance, others had their loved ones flying out for a few days, myself included. Abby was due to land at Singapore's international airport after a flight lasting the best part of the day. She shared the flight over from the UK with others also flying out to meet their sailors. I had booked three nights in a five-star hotel in Singapore followed by a flight to Bali where we had a further nine nights booked at the five star Grand Hyatt in Bali, a stunning beachside hotel with numerous pools and bars and bars *in* pools.

I waited nervously at customs for her. I was apprehensive about the level of my commitment and it was weighing on my mind heavily. Abby was able to look right into my mind, I had known her since I was fifteen years old after we met on the harbour at Padstow. I was a bugger for chasing the girls that flocked to the town on their family summer holidays and along with two of my partners in crime managed to snare a healthy amount of holiday totty.

I suddenly saw her pushing her baggage trolley through the large glass arrivals doors at the airport and all of the thoughts weighing on my mind vanished. I gave her a huge hug and we were off.

Waving down a taxi we went straight to our hotel where I think it took us about five minutes of checking in before getting to try the bed out. The room was fantastic but then it was five-star accommodation and was costing me a packet. We ate out each night finding local restaurants nearby along the waterfront and watching some of the many street theatres performing to the huge crowds of tourists. Somehow Singapore was now a lively and wonderful place, something I hadn't noticed two weeks earlier. I guess a holiday is only as good as the company you are with. A visit to a Singapore bird sanctuary left us in a romantic and playful mood but a later visit to a crocodile park blew any idea of romance right out the water. It should've been called a crocodile skin farm. They were piles of sick looking crocs dragging themselves about when they found enough energy to move but I laughed when one of them nearly dragged the handler into the pen after he had looped its head with his lasso.

Ged'on ya mate, fight back!

We were doing the couple thing quite well. We decided to visit the Sentosa Water Park located at the South end of Singers. The park was located on another island and access was via a cable car system. Along with the fun in the park, I had the perk of watching Abby run around enjoying herself in her skimpy bikini. She was a gorgeous girl with long natural blonde hair that most girls tried to find in a bottle with a face and body that made men melt, encompassing pale ice blue eyes that could cut metal.

After three days of living it up in Singapore, we headed for the Indonesian island of Bali. I am not a keen flyer so grit my teeth and boarded a civil passenger plane for the first time in my life. I had flown in Chipmunk light aircraft, helicopters with the Navy and also a Viking glider but I wasn't keen on passenger jets and it showed. A newbie flyer I couldn't help but notice how the bloody wings were moving up and down. Shaking like a shitting dog, I felt a little more comfort in the knowledge that we were only a two or three-hour flight from Bali. I don't mind ships as I can swim and therefore have a chance should the one I am on sink but as for planes, I can't fly no matter how hard I flap my arms.

Bali was paradise and I understand the attraction for the masses which gather here. It is a little too far from the UK to be a cheap package holiday destination but the distance meant it was also too far for a convenient hop across the pond and therefore was ideal for keeping the chavs at bay. Our room in the Grand Hyatt was not in the main building but an apartment along the beach. Still five star of course. A balcony looked out onto the beach and almost directly below us a bar which sat on the very edge of the pool. We took our time over the next nine days. I didn't want them to end. We took long walks across the beach and ate each night at a different restaurant all of which were located directly on the beach near to a boardwalk which ran for miles across the top of the fantastic coastline. There was no end of tours on offer to us and we took up offers of a trip to the top of Bali's volcano, a visit to some theatres, rice fields and also a Monkey Temple. The highlight for me was witnessing the Tanar-Lot sunset. Tanar-Lot was a temple which had been constructed on a small island hundreds of years ago. It was easily accessible at low tide but, as the tours name suggests, at sunset it was simply incredible.

The holiday was over all too quickly and before I knew it Abby was walking through the same doors I had waited behind only twelve days previously. We had encountered a small amount of hassle when returning to Singapore from Bali as immigration puzzled over my passport stamps. They had worked out I was British but couldn't understand how I had no stamp for entering Singapore. After explaining to several different officials that I had arrived on a military ship they finally accepted my story. I waved farewell to Abby and wandered back to the Sheffield, my thoughts and feelings now completely messed up and all over the place.

At least once I got back on board the Sheffield I could jump back into my parallel reality and pretend life was all going to plan. I could stick my head back in the sand.

Chapter Nine

We Watched Disney

The Captain pointed the ship east in the direction of Brunei and opened the throttle. The ships enormous Rolls-Royce engines made a fantastic noise when given some welly and it was hypnotic to stand on the upper deck near an intake or a vent, even more so when there was a strong sea wind hammering away at your torso. I spent many a day (well at least one) wishing I had been a stoker in the engine room instead of fixing radar sets. The first night back at sea after Singapore resembled the night we had when we first left Plymouth some three and a half months before and we all got screaming drunk. 3G mess had now become the local hang out of the ship's dentist for some reason, a Lieutenant who bore a mild passing resemblance to a young, but a slightly public school-boy version of Tom Hanks. Nigel Somerset was much more at home with us than he was with the officers in the wardroom. I held the highest respect for most of the officers on board but it was also fair to say that some got right up my nose. Others, however, were much more down to earth and jumped at the chance to get to a lower deck Mess and spend time with the cannon fodder. Our Deputy Weapons Officer, Phil, was one of these officers as was Shiner but I don't think any officer spent as much time down our mess as Nigel and he was respected greatly for that, by us anyway.

The high standards and slight snobbery which are installed into the wardroom I believe was well-founded and drummed into the officers during their training at Britannia Royal Naval College Dartmouth. The Royal Navy always had with it heavy Royal connections.

Prince Charles made have been born in Buckingham Palace but he was made in the Royal Navy. Also 'made' in the RN was his younger brother, the Duke of York who saw service in the South Atlantic during the Falklands conflict as a Lynx pilot but Royal Privilege still didn't stop York treading on fingers, literally. A tale from Bernard Manning, who I'd known previously from HMS Illustrious and was now also a member of 3G mess HMS Sheffield, told how he had spent a considerable time stripping the polish from the deck of '1L flat' on board a ship on which the then Lieutenant HRH Prince Andrew was part of the crew.

This stripping and re-applying of 'ME7' deck polish was utterly pointless and took a huge amount of effort and time if it was to be done properly. I'm sure to this day it's the only purpose was to keep a sailor busy. You could rest assured that if it *wasn't* done properly then it would have to be re-stripped and the process started again from scratch. The unwritten rule which incidentally was also the polite and civil thing to do when encountering a corridor or flat which was receiving the ME7 treatment was to take a detour, obviously, and choose a new route. Almost everyone without exception would go the long way round to avoid stepping on a deck. It was even more obvious if the poor Matelot laying the polish was there on his or her knees evenly spreading their delicate artwork across the tiles with a solidifying rag. Everyone would take a detour apart from, that is, His Royal Highness Prince Andrew, Duke of York. He stormed right over Bernie's masterpiece without so much as an acknowledgement as to how bloody sorry he was. Big black skid marks from his rubber-soled shoes now covered the deck like Bruce's Biro forearm after a Thai language lesson. Another reason not to step on the wet polish was that it was very slippery! If HRH's hoofing great feet weren't problem enough the convoy of protection officers who accompanied him had to follow suit. Hi-ho, off we go again then. Strip - Scrub - Dry - Polish - Dry.

Prince Charles was far more down to earth. He had popped on board HMS Brazen whilst we were in the Gulf in 1990/1 to visit his old friend and our Skipper, Commander James C Rapp.

Charlie seemed a decent enough bloke and had commanded a ship or two in his time. I think the vast majority of the current British Royal family have attended Dartmouth at some time or another with the widely publicised exception being Price Edward who aimed a little *too* high on the physical endurance scale and had a stab at being a Royal Marine Officer only to later concede defeat.

I blame this Royal connection for the double standards throughout the Navy. I acknowledge the long traditions of the Senior Service but I also believe in modernisation and progress. Not too sure they are bedfellows but the Navy seemed to have the balance right *most* of the time. The double standards displayed by some officers often took a very serious form. An example is when acts of stupidity which may endanger life. The Stokers of HMS Brave discovered this with their ball and chain affair. Another blatantly obvious danger to safety was pissing around with any of the many breathing apparatus left at various locations all over the vessel. Stored in large red metal boxes about three feet in height and a foot and a half across the BASCCA equipment (Breathing Apparatus Self Contained Compressed Air) consisted of an oxygen cylinder and mask which would provide the wearer with approximately twenty-seven minutes of air enabling them to bravely attempt to extinguish any fires they were dealing with. It was worn by both the initial fire attack party and the fire support party on the top of their woolly 'Fearnought' suits. The twenty-seven minutes of air available was an estimate for an average person working under a degree of pressure and physical exertion, the real-time allowance I found to be more in the region of fifteen minutes depending on how fast your heart was beating as you fought to extinguish the inferno.

Should a Matelot be caught messing around with a BASCCA then the consequences would quite rightly be harsh, very harsh. My jaw dropped in disbelief one night as I watched two Lieutenants from a recent wardroom party playing kiss chase along the length of 1 deck, both wearing BASCCA. Anyone else would have been keelhauled. They farted around for a few minutes until they'd caught each other a few times then dumped the now 'undercharged' BASCCA back into their red metal stowage's before wandering back into the wardroom to no doubt laugh about it with their chums. *These* are the type of officers that got right up my fucking nose.

Fortunately, Lt. Nigel Somerset the dentist was a good lad and usually hung around the mess until the early hours. About four in the morning wasn't unheard of and I remember tempting him with yet another beer (there were ways to break into the beer fridge) but he politely declined as he felt he'd had enough. Besides that, he had surgery in five hours and was totally shit-faced. I lost my long-standing fear of dentists as a result of this. If Nigel can do it pissed then most dentists should be OK when sober.

A handful of days later and our arrival in Brunei saw the usual array of messages and events placed on the ships notice board. Lists were placed in the main communal areas looking for names of people willing to go on *this* trip, people who want to do *that* trip etc. Simply wait for the list to be posted detailing the trips and write your name on it as soon as you could. First come first serve. I usually shied away from placing my name on any of these lists as I had never taken a fancy to any of the activities on offer. This time, however, on offer was a 4x4 off-road experience in the jungle. I fancied a piece that! I loved the idea of taking a perfectly good car through a 'bitch of a ditch' and over 'the mother of all hills.' The added bonus was having at least a five-hour break from the Ship.

Brunei was looking good so far but it wasn't long before the ship's company noticed a major disadvantage with our berth, there wasn't one! The jetties here just weren't big enough to cope with our big fat frumpy 150-metre long frigate, therefore a timetable was also placed on our notice board detailing the times that we could expect a passenger, or 'PAS' boat to arrive and take us ashore. The last time I'd had to rely on a PAS boat was on the island of Montserrat in the West Indies whilst on a West Indies Guard Ship deployment in 1992. The island paradise had been hit hard by Hurricane Hugo that year and the jetty had been simply washed away. It seemed an unlucky place to live as four years after that, Montserrat's volcano got a shitty on and blew up half the island. Paradise lost!

I noted the times of our PAS boat service paying close attention to the fact that after 01:00hrs they stopped. A slight fly in the ointment for the beer monsters among us, although a far more serious problem for them being the lack of decent bars. In common with the Middle East, we were advised that the best places to find booze was the hotel bars however I was intent on avoiding the alcohol this visit. My thoughts with occupied by Abby and telling her that I couldn't go ahead with the lavish wedding she was dreaming of next year. It was just too soon and felt like we were both being rushed into it. I needed to keep a clear and rational head, something I had found difficulty in doing so far.

I felt that for now at least, the 4x4 expedition would be a welcome distraction and assist me in steering clear of the beer. The expedition started with promise and I found that I wasn't the only member of 3G to put their name on the list. Frank Ryder and Buck Rogers had also viewed the list adding their names to the bottom. We were ushered from the PAS boat and into three waiting 4x4 vehicles. Frank and me climbed into a Land Rover Defender 90, whilst Buck disappeared with some other lads inside of one of the two remaining wagon's, a big gnarly Toyota and a similarly bad-ass Nissan. All three vehicles and their occupants then headed off to find some jungle. After a while, the tarmac road we were travelling on turned to a track and then the track turned to a mud path, then back to a track and then a to mud path again. If it wasn't for the fact we were completed surrounded by thick Brunei jungle I would have been out and using Shanks's Pony to return to the ship. This was the routine for the next hour or so and it soon became pretty obvious that we were only going to be passengers in this expedition and not get a chance at driving. Somewhat despondent, Frank and I sat back into our seats and watched the view pass us by at twenty miles per hour. I began to wish I had been savvy enough to get my name on the other list that had appeared on the notice board which was an overnight stay in the jungle with the local militia. Hell, even the watching paint dry list was beginning to appeal. I sat and watched with shallow enthusiasm as we crept up some slightly steep inclines.

"I think I'll use second for this one," said our Ex-Pat Brit driver.

"OK if you think so," replied his wife.

Riveting.

A resting point emerged in the shape of a small village. To be more accurate is was barely even that and it resembled a cricket pitch with two or three static caravans at one end. We were allowed just enough time to steal a cup of tea from a flask and for one of the two Wrens who had come along to take a wee behind a bush. A quick look around the village and we were off again. Things became a little more interesting when another hour later the driver informed us that we were going to cross the border into Malaysia via an illegal river crossing. At last, my ears pricked up and the interest level rose. The illegal crossing was used frequently by the locals. We somehow found ourselves on a tarmac road surface again but only for another mile or so. I guess the road budget ran out because it stopped dead. Once again we were on a rough track but at least this track was not designed for motor vehicles and at long last the Land Rover started to get some action on the sort of terrain we had been expecting since we climbed in the back. The situation did get a little laughable however when we pulled in to the side of the track to give way to a Datsun Cherry heading in the same direction as ourselves, the 'taxi' bursting with local villagers hanging out of every window. The beaten old family hatchback tooted a pathetic sounding horn as it trundled past, the driver waving from the window like the Queen. We pulled back onto the track and continued.

"For some reason, we see a lot of Datsun's around here," the Landy driver informed us, "they are used as taxis by the locals to get them across the border."

Almost on cue, another Datsun taxi limped past purposefully. After some fairly testing tracks strewn with fairly substantial rocks and obstacles we eventually made it to our border crossing, a Datsun shell lay abandoned on its side nearby, beat-up and looking sorry for itself it had been stripped completely of any remaining useful parts. The driver parked the Landy somewhere 'off-piste' and leaving it, we clambered down a footpath and all managed to find a space on board three waiting wooden jungle gondolas. Our guide instructed the Gondolier to take us the 50 feet across the river and in a matter of minutes we had crossed the murky jungle river and entered Malaysia. Just why we had done this I don't know. We walked a further one hundred yards down a heavy jungle track before finding our second small village of the day.

There was more civilisation here than in the earlier village we had stopped at for our tea break. There appeared to more structure and planning. A main street and three-sided wooden shacks sat along its length on either side. The side facing the road was left open for all to see in. I joined a group from one of the other 4x4's sitting near the top of the street and was grateful when one of the lads revealed that their driver had packed a cooler box brimming with Fosters lager. It was heavenly. I sat for a while and took it all in. Frank gave me a nod and we strolled off down the road to explore the village. Towards the end of the row was a hut which must have been the local bar. A very basic serving area occupied the full length go the right-hand side with a couple of basic fridges behind it. Directly in the centre of the building was a large snooker table surrounded by locals. The players stopped briefly and all stood staring at Frank and me with their arms folded. Their glare was a cold as my beer so we walked on further to avoid stirring things up. A few children ran around the site. It was odd how, despite obvious poverty, all of the children we saw wore immaculate school uniforms and carried leather satchels. Not feeling the most welcome of guests Frank and I drifted back towards the others where we found them already packing up to leave after what was fifteen minutes at best.

"We must move on," our driver said, "it's only a short stay in case we get caught here."

I suppose we stood out a little more than the locals and would be quickly noticed by any passing authorities. Crossing the river again we were soon on our way in the 4x4's but only for a short thirty-minute bounce-about as the return trip to our ship would be made over water using the vast network of rivers in the area. We came to a larger town where we hung around until our ride appeared on the riverbank in the form of two large rigid inflatable boats each with a member of Brunei's armed forces sat at the helm.

Despite our tortoise paced drive through the Brunei jungle earlier it still took an hour on full *poooower* to get us back to the Sheffield via the boats. I was acutely aware of an additional soldier in each boat and when I asked why the heavy presence was told that it was for our own safety if the boat had developed a problem they would guide us through the jungle on foot for the remainder of the distance. It would've been a long walk and so I was bloody glad the boat kept going.

Returning to the Sheffield I settled into preparing myself for a night out. My attempt at avoiding the alcohol was about to fail as the highly charged adrenalin-filled day had given me back my carefree attitude. Throwing on a T-shirt, pair of jeans along with some sturdy boots I grabbed Bruce and caught the next available water taxi. I was feeling a little pissed off as we were not able to drive the Landy earlier so what the hell. Buck Rogers also decided to come along as he was of a similar frame of mind and we stormed off looking for the Brunei nightlife. A couple of hours later and a very long walk along some compacted mud roads and all we had managed to find was a hotel bar serving bottles of half respectable beer so we blagged a couple glasses and sat around the bar area. As we talked away among ourselves we were approached by a couple of very respectable looking ladies.

"Are you boys British sailors from the ship?" one asked.

"Yes love," replied Bruce.

"Thank God for that," she sighed, "we haven't been able to find anyone here to have any fun with yet!"

British nurses! Fan-fucking-tastic!

There are few occupations that share a similar dark sense of humour in this world. The Armed Forces, the Emergency Services which would include nurses and of course airline cabin crew! They all tend to seek each other out when socialising. The girls revealed how they had been based here working in the local hospitals as the NHS wages were so abysmal back home. They spent most nights confined to their rooms as the nightlife was non-existent with local women still expected to take the back seat in life. Independent women were not that evident here, or welcome. We took up the offer of wasting the hotel rooms mini-bar and I made myself at home sitting on the rooms double bed surrounded by nurses. When we killed the mini-bar in one room another one of the girls would run off and return with the contents of her mini-bar and when we had exhausted those we rang room service. I was then enlightened to the nurse's opinions and experiences of men's wedding tackle and tales of their sexual conquests, I couldn't help but feel a twinge or two of excitement, even more so when asked in a 'matter of fact' manner about my own turn on's and conquests. British nurses! Love 'em.

We eventually staggered from the nurse's hotel room and caught a taxi back to the dockyard. In contrast to our own dockyard, this one was one hundred per cent military. I did get the impression though that the authorities displayed a great deal of trust towards the local population as we walked into the dockyard unchallenged without even seeing any sentry or checkpoint. Standing on the pontoon near the location of the PAS boat pick up point, it suddenly occurred to me that we may be a little late. Glancing at my £15 Rolex Submariner I saw that we were about thirty minutes late and had missed the last boat of the night. The next PAS boat wasn't until 07:00 hours. We were stuck here.

"Bollocks!" I sounded my frustration. "Better take a look for somewhere to get our heads down."

After a little wandering about we soon found a small Brunei Navy Exocet patrol boat tied up alongside further down the jetty. Curiosity, and an amount of alcohol, got the better of me and I gingerly made my way up the gangway. On realising after a brief search inside that it was deserted I went back onto the upper deck to give the others the 'all clear'. After a few moments realising that our stomping feet were not alerting any hidden crew members sleeping within we all relaxed and took to strolling about the upper deck looking at the various fittings and fixtures she had.

"Shall we hotwire this fucker?" Bruce suggested.

I would've laughed but I knew instantly that if I agreed with him it would give Bruce the green light to try.

A thorough look round the vessel revealed plenty, we found the Operations Room packed with Radar equipment and fancy computers, the Bridge was interesting too and we even had a look around the Captain's cabin but after a while we all opted for the sensible option and got off. It would be one thing to be found sleeping in the dockyard but to be caught on board one of Brunei's obviously important Naval patrol boats would be a little bit more serious and I don't think the authorities would see the funny side.

Back on the jetty, I noticed that a small gathering of four or five lads from the ship were sat around looking a little lost and dazed. They had also been caught out by the PAS boat times and joined us as Brunei castaways as a result of their own shite timekeeping or similar reluctance to wave 'bye bye' to whatever pubs and clubs they had found. My weary booze head was beginning to kick in and I eventually crashed out on an Admiral's barge which we located moored near to the Exocet boat. It was fairly comfortable and out of the wind so it wasn't that long before I drifted off to sleep.

I was rudely awoken at about 06:45 hours the following morning by the sound of high pitched shouting like something from Tenko. It took me a short while to get my thoughts together enough to recall where I was and after a few more shouts nearby I thought I should pop my head up topside and see what the fuck was going on. I shook the remainder of the lads who had all found space to sleep on board the barge. The shouts I had been hearing were starting to sound more and more like commands and I noted that the language used was more Japanese POW camp than English. Taking to the nearby ladder I climbed from the barge and ascended two or three rungs, just enough to glance onto the jetty. The tide had gone out since getting my head down and the boat was significantly further down the wall than it was when we all clambered on a few hours before. A small parade of Brunei Sailors had fallen in for their morning divisions. There looked to be around eighty in total all stood to attention facing in my direction. At least four officers stood in front of the parade but luckily so far they kept facing their troop and hence had their backs toward me.
"Shit!"
I crept back down the ladder onto the barge. I delicately tip-toed across the barge and briefed the lads as to what was happening upstairs. I then took command of a stealth mission that any SAS platoon commander would have been proud of.

As the Brunei Navy stood at 'open order' for their inspections seven hung over Matelots clambered up the dockside ladder and emerged bedraggled onto the jetty from the Admiral's barge. We burped, we farted, we scratched our heads and arses, we tried unsuccessfully to make ourselves look smaller, shit some of us even managed a wave but all seven of us climbed on to the jetty and staggered, swayed and stumbled to our feet in front of the morning parade. In single file, we staggered past with not so much as a nod or remark from any of the Brunei drill instructors or inspecting officers. I think they were all a little dumbfounded.

"Cheers lads!" Bruce nodded a wink at the officer who been doing most of the yelling and we all went off to find our PAS boat.

Once back on the Sheffield we headed straight for the dining hall and tucked into a full cooked English breakfast to prep ourselves for a full duty day.

With Brunei being not the most captivating of visits with regard to nightlife and thrills we next headed for Manila, the capital city of the Philippines and hopes were high for a bit more excitement. We needed to cross northeast over the South China Sea so were technically in unfriendly waters and took appropriate steps. I got the impression that the Skipper wasn't overly bothered about the small matter of the Chinese Navy, as any attempt from them to take on British Warship would frankly be stupid. He was, however, concerned about the numerous groups of freelance pirates that frequented the area. These big grey war canoes do a sterling job of knocking out the opposition when they come in jet planes, missile attacks, other warships and submarines but have a distinct weakness from being bordered by mad Chinese pirates on smaller faster and craft with old rusty Russian automatic weapons. Admittedly, for any to try would be suicide but unless we were prepared it would take a short time for the crew to react effectively to combat any attempt. We don't routinely wander the corridors of the ship with weapons at the ready so needed to ensure we were prepared. Armed sentries were placed on the upper deck. We also deployed the most ingenious and hi-tech anti-pirate devices that the western world has ever known. A device of such cunning that it would be well at home in Q's next James Bond briefing alongside the laser watch and exploding condom.

"Now pay attention double-oh seven"

Using hefty pieces of Admiralty rope we tied the outer doors and hatches shut from the inside. The method struck me as being a bit low tech but was brilliantly effective. Although these precautions were applied on all doors to the ship they thankfully were not required and the transit from Brunei to the Philippines was an uneventful and boring crossing.

Entering the port at Manila the sense of excitement among the crew was obvious. After the buzz of Bangkok followed then by the somewhat tame and conservative visit to Brunei the lads needed some form of entertainment. Manila would be a safe bet considering the reputation of the city and population. We all needed decent bars and clubs where we could get rid of the frustration of being sat in the same grey box as thirty-six other blokes watching videos of 'Only Fools and Horses' over and over.

This is very likely the reason that the Navy tend to be a little on the boisterous side when visiting a foreign port. Long periods floating around at sea with sweet Fanny Adams can be damaging to our poor little minds! This problem isn't limited to the Brits or indeed the Navy. A friend of mine, a former US Marine, explained that as a prelude to combat his platoon was showed back to back war movies whilst sat off the coast of Libya many years ago. Good old 'USA takes on the world and saves the lives of nuns and orphans' style war movies loaded with violence, daft heroics and adoring women. The Marines sat and watched at least three war films a day for a week as part of their daily routine. The only problem being that after all that brainwashing they were ordered to stand down and the US warship carrying them turned about and headed back to the States. Their next port of call, the Canary Islands bore the brunt of this frustration and was ripped apart by several hundred 'wound up' US Marines. A collateral result of train hard, play hard.

Fortunately for the people of the Philippines 'Only Fools and Horses' did not have the same effect on us as the war films did on the Jarheads although some of us would take on the mantle of 'Trigger' during our visit here. The mood of the ship had changed and we were allowed shore leave almost as soon as we had finished berthing. Even the management just wanted to get on with the party. Everyone wanted to get ashore.

'LEAVE' was piped over the main broadcast and a tidal wave of 3G mess members swept across the gangway. Attracted by the sudden prospect of a mass of drunken customers a tattoo 'artist' magically appeared on the jetty and walking past him I stared in horror at the vast array of butchery equipment on display. Sporting my own selection of tattoo's I wasn't worried about the process but drew real concerns over his obvious lack of hygiene. His studio consisted of a small canvas tent open sided on one side with inks arranged on the table within. A single tattoo gun and no sign of any cleaning products. All of this in a country where the HIV risk was huge in comparison with Europe. The small frail elderly tattoo artist gave a smile and a wave as we passed in our mob and the words of the girl I spoke with when I first arrived at Bangkok resonated from the back of my mind.

"You will wan' fuck me later."

The lads were off on a mission with most favouring the bars over shops, markets and sightseeing. I'd decided that my first port of call needed to be a Barbershop and as luck would have it I found one nearby, and the added bonus was that it was right next to decent looking bar.

While I was in getting my locks chopped the others started on the booze. I sat in the chair and explained to the Barber that I wanted my head shaved assuming he would reach for electric clippers. Instead, he held up a cut-throat razor up to the mirror and smiled nodding.

"Fuck it," I thought, "When in Rome."

The icing on the cake was a flaming stick which was used to singe away any hairs that were taking root in my ears followed by a hot flannel over my head and a scalp massage. All this was performed for about two quid. After my self-indulgent pampering, I left my chair and strolled out on to the street. The bar that the lads had found was only fifty feet along the road and with my new bonce, I felt ready to start power drinking.

Entering the bar I immediately got the impression that we had found a local's only tavern rather than a well-trodden tourist destination. This was exactly the location I had pictured drinking myself silly in. The room was sparse with a few old tables and chairs placed along the left-hand side upon entering. A bar ran almost the length of the right-hand side behind which stood a small middle-aged local woman snapping off bottle tops and dishing out beer almost non-stop to the eight or more British sailors propping up the other side. Behind her stood a small stage area. I couldn't tell if this was a stage for topless girls or a local band. The beers on offer were all stubbies and understandably didn't last long once handed to the sailor of the receiving end. The barmaid was rushing around trying hard to keep up with the demand. I quickly found space down one end near to Bruce and Charlie Worker.

"Like the fucking haircut, Butch Coolidge!" said Chris referring to my bald head. Along with 'Only Fools and Horses', 'Pulp Fiction' had become the other deployment video for 3G mess. The film had not long been released and the mess had a copy that had been acquired in Dubai. The standard 'pirate' copy with shaky picture and an Arabic film company's logo printed in one corner for the whole duration of the movie.

Slight digression warning!

As a deployment movie, 'Pulp Fiction' was a dam sight more respectable than the HMS Brazen Operation Desert Storm deployment movie. Nothing better to guarantee Saddam Hussein a hot reception than Walt Disney's 'A Little Mermaid'.

The site of our resident Royal Marine, Del Hightower six foot and five inches of black boot-neck from four-two commando, sat in the corner of 3R Greenies mess HMS Brazen singing, "Down where it's wetter, down where it's better, under da sea" in time with a cartoon crab and other aquatic life forms, would leave Baghdad shaking.

The US Marines watched war films, we watched Disney.

Sat at the bar I took a long drink of my first beer in Manila. I was playing catch up with the others and immediately polishing it off asked for another. The barmaid passed one over the bar as urgently as I'd requested it.

"Tab, tab?" she said, making a writing motion with her left hand.

"No, I pay now," I replied taking some Ickies from my pocket.

I didn't want to drink on a slate although when I recall the last time I had done so it was good for my finances, or rather my brothers. Three years previously whilst sat in a bar in Bermuda during a stint as West Indies Guard ship on HMS Brazen, my big brother handed his MasterCard to the bar staff.

"Just for me and him," he instructed pointing me out to the bar staff.

We drank all night on his credit card safe in the knowledge that we wouldn't have to use up any of the local currency we'd bought. When, later that month, his credit card bill arrived the grand total taken by the night-club was a staggering fifty pence. The minuscule amount had been a pre-authorisation tester by the staff to ensure the card wasn't a duff one. They had either forgotten to place any of our drinks on to the card or the poor bugger at the other end of the bar with the diet coke got charged a couple of hundred dollars. We got shit-faced for fifty pence.

"Cheers Easy!"

If bar staff in Bermuda can make such a mistake in my favour then I wasn't prepared to risk the opposite thing happening in Manila. No thanks, I'll pay for my drinks as I get them.

Once again we found the locals friendly and although the bar was very much a welcoming place to sit we needed to find something more suitable for later in the evening, somewhere which packed a little more punch. The information board placed religiously in '1L' flat by the liaison staff during each foreign visit informed us that in Manilas case the place best avoided was the Makati district. Highlighting such areas to avoid on a map isn't a clever idea. It's like writing, 'Do not touch!' over a big red button on a control panel.

Makati was that big red button. The locals in the bar agreed that Makati would be the safest bet for us later but, for the meantime, we were staying put. A good three hours must've passed as we sat in the bar. The beer kept flowing and at the time I had no intentions of doing any site-seeing nor did I want to buy any historic *traditional* Philippine ornaments. I had no cultural fucks left to give, I just wanted beer and laughs.

The stage in the pub had given me crazy delusions of musical ability and whilst chatting to the barmaid about my natural accordion-playing ability (yes I was *that* drunk) a local bloke strolled up to Chris and started trying to sell him something. I ignored this bloke at first but when I heard him offer Chris a massage, my ears couldn't help but tune in. This bloke, although meaning well, was about to cause a riot.

"A fucking massage?" puzzled Chris, "do you think I'm into fella's or something?"

He stood and turned to face the male chest puffing out and arms lifting outwards from his body assuming the 'imaginary lat' position. We were half-cut and I knew it wouldn't take a great deal to get the St. Austell Slayer into full arm-swinging fight-club mode.

"No no Sir!" said the man offering his open hands forward to Chris, "A massage of your head, you look tired, it will wake you up. You drink better."

"He very good," chipped in the barmaid.

"Right, go on then skip," agreed Chris and he took to his seat, swivelling to face the bar.

The male masseur stood directly behind Chris and started to rub his head. Chris's face was a picture. As the masseur went about his business Chris's face was being subjected to prodding and pulling from all directions. Two minutes later and the masseur placed one hand on Chris' chin and one on the back of his head.

"Relax, relax," he instructed.

Twist.

Crack!

Chris' head was forced sharply to the left, the masseur swapped his hands over.

Twist.

Crack!

We had now *all* stopped drinking and were sat staring at Chris awaiting some form of violent nuclear reaction.

"Bloody 'ell," said Chris rolling his head in large slow circles, "That feels fukin' ace! You have a go Tone."

"You want?" asked the masseur looking at me.

I looked at Chris who appeared to be very content with his near neck breaking experience.

"Yeah go on then."

Leaving the small local bar we all clambered on board a couple of waiting brightly decorated Jeepney taxi's and instructed the drivers to take us to Makati. Bruce was already sporting his, now trademark, biro-pen riddled left arm. He had cooled off a little since the trouble in Singapore which had been evident in Brunei but then I think all of us cooled off a little there, we had no choice.

The Makati district appeared promising. Darkness had started to creep in and with that neon lights began to burst into life in a vast array of 'Get it here' signs designed to unconsciously trigger the primal beer lobe segment of the average British sailor's mind. The roads in and out were otherwise smooth and clutter-free. Not the great mass of people taking to foot, forcing their progress on the pavements and roads as we had witnessed in Bangkok. It gave the impression of a more socially responsible population, better manners. We abandoned the Jeepney at Makati, this big old Philippino workhorse looking to all extensive purposes like the love child of a Christmas tree, a limousine and a Jeep. I was transfixed by the mix of dusty roads and neon night club entrances. Bruce had demonstrated a good nose for clubs and bars so we followed him blindly in through the nearest doorway. I hesitated outside momentarily to read the clubs strict entry requirements rules printed on the wall.

'No T-shirts or shorts permitted.
No sandals or training shoes permitted.
No torn jeans permitted.
No abusive language.
All knives and firearms to be left with door staff.'

Fair enough, beats Newquay's 'No jeans and trainers' I suppose. I entered Mogambo.

Having not eaten since leaving the ship at midday my stomach was beginning to complain. Bruce was also up for a bite to eat so we asked for the menu along with our beer. My thoughts returning to my quest for a curry that would match 'Wai Kui' in Wadebridge.

"Do you do curries?" I asked the barmaid.

She stood on a platform behind the bar which was raised about 2 feet higher than the floor on our side. This meant that when I was seated I was eye level with her crutch and ass. Whether this was a deliberate marketing ploy I'll never know but it worked! She had a rather slinky figure covered only by a short black dress.

"Chicken and meat," she replied.

"I'll have a meat one love," interrupted Bruce.

"What do *you* want?" she asked me.

"Yeah, meat one please," I replied.

"OK," she smiled.

She looked pretty edible herself. Here I go again, a walking bloody hormone. The very tasty dish returned fairly quickly and she had our curries with her. Each with a neatly moulded pile of perfectly boiled rice placed on the side of the plate. Bruce devoured his, but I took my time as I had my connoisseur head on although it was starting to pick arguments with the drunk one. I was massively impressed. A very close contender for the crown. While we ate the other lads informed us that they were going further up the road. Agreeing to catch them up later we ordered more beer and I began chatting up our barmaid. A very well-spoken girl with nearly perfect English she told of how she came from a small Manila family who lived here in the city. Unlike the Bangkok girls, she did not bear the responsibility of being the sole breadwinner, her family were urban orientated with a cousin driving his own Taxi. I noticed a distinct difference between the girls here and the girls of Bangkok. The Philippine girls looked far more modern, more western and less rustic. Both were equally stunning with the Thai girls possessing a raw beauty and I found myself subconsciously comparing their qualities trying to establish which would cope better in the UK.

The Bangkok girls would make a better wife, but the Philippine girls looked as though they would make better lovers, although I felt the Philippine girls appeared more independent and would therefore leave once they had heard all my jokes. I found this trip was rapidly turning me into a male chauvinist and my idea of the perfect family unit had retarded by fifty years or so.

After finishing the curry then downing a couple more bottles I grabbed Bruce and headed off to catch up with the others. A thorough search at least three bars including a bottle in each we eventually located them in one called 'Bottoms'. Whilst Mogambo was a 'bar' bar, Bottoms struck me as a 'club' bar. It was a little cramped inside but possessed numerous dark corners. A small stage at the far end carried five or six girls each dressed in high cut camouflage shorts and little camo tops tied at the front. They performed sexy wiggles in time with the modern dance tracks. The sudden influx of young British men seemed to have invigorated them a bit and the dancing was purposely seductive. This place had already attracted a lot of lads and the Petty Officers mess had also discovered Bottoms firmly establishing themselves in a club. I cracked on with the beer and, performing a headcount discovered that almost all of the customers were Sheffield ships company. I then spied Frank Ryder sat on the floor at one end of the stage signing autographs. I had already noticed that a lot of the girls in those other bars had square HMS Sheffield Australasia '95 stickers stuck to their stomachs or on their chests though I hadn't paid much attention at the time. It soon became apparent that Frank was the culprit and was, in fact, signing autographs. He had brought a huge pile of these stickers out with him and the girls must've thought he was some form of superstar as they were flocking around him asking for him to sign them. Most ships carry a stockpile of 'zap' stickers, small ships crests that find their way onto the walls of numerous bar around the world but Sheffield had to go one better and had a 'deployment' sticker created.

We carried on with drinking and laughing with the girls and had what I can only describe as a normal night out chatting sensibly to everyone there but pretty soon the time caught us. Grabbing a Taxi with Chris, Bruce and Buck I sat back and closed my eyes.

I woke to the squealing of brakes and followed the others out of the cab to find we weren't back at the ship. It was three o'clock in the morning and Chris had instructed the driver to take us back to the small local bar which we had first found when we came ashore the day before. I followed the others in through the unlocked door but found little sign of life. Chris had however and he shook the peacefully sleeping barmaid who was lying across some chairs in a far corner, I had no idea whether she was expecting us or she slept there every night.

"Oi come on girl, get the beers going," Chris demanded.

The barmaid stood rubbing her eyes and yawning.

"OK I get other girl too," she said and she walked off through a small doorway at the back of the room. She returned after a couple of minutes with another sleepy-looking barmaid and between them started to serve us drinks. I politely managed another two or three bottles before bidding farewell and left the others to it opting instead for a taxi back to the ship.

I was beginning to get used to the lack of sleep when alongside making up for it when out at sea. Brum was now well aware that, because of my redundancy on return to the UK, I didn't give a toss anymore and I took full advantage of that. I woke about 07:00 after only a short power nap and still feeling the effects of the drink. I had no intention on using the early start to get to work bright-eyed and bushy-tailed but needed the early start so I could get a full cooked breakfast from the galley. The Royal Navy chefs are nothing short of world-class and their breakfast has to be top of the list, for me anyway. After filling my stomach I returned to the mess. Chris was back on board as, surprisingly, was Bruce who'd already started on a bottle of Bacardi that he had smuggled on past the Quartermaster. Chris wasn't looking too pleased with himself and went straight to his bunk. Bruce meanwhile was pretty much incoherent and talking gibberish in his 'cut off' jeans. I left the mess and went up to the office to check in with Brum and Fez. Brum was now almost as laid back as the rest of us and I was beginning to get on with him a little more. A short debrief from Fez revealed how one Petty Officer had gone home with a local girl. He was considered such a special guest that the family allowed him to sleep on their *only* bed. The other occupants of the family home were turfed on to the floor. The Petty Officer in question was fed and watered before leaving to return to the ship this morning for work. He was understandably humbled by the whole experience and couldn't bring himself to even attempt shagging the twenty-year-old girl that he'd originally gone home with.

It was about 11:00 hours and I had successfully managed to go another day without breaking into a sweat. I now had to pass some time waiting for shore leave to be piped.

Today's routine on board was designated as a Saturday routine. This meant that the working hours were from 08:00 hours until midday, after that time we were left to our own devices which usually meant getting ashore as quickly as possible. A Sunday routine meant working 08:00 hours to 10:00 hours with a daily routine being 08:00 hours to 16:00 hours. The most welcome had to be 'Lazy Sunday' where no one except the Duty watch was required to 'turn-to'.

Each day in the Philippines, as with most of our overseas visits, would be a Saturday. In exchange for these generous days in foreign ports, the Jimmy would often recover the lost days at sea. Many weekends out on the wavy stuff were declared Daily routines and it wasn't uncommon to go for several days without being granted a Sunday.

Entering the mess-deck I found the Port mess square in complete darkness. The Eagles Greatest Hits was being played at a comfortable volume. I walked into the dark void and realised it was empty apart from Bruce. He was sat in the far corner of the mess square, his head lowered and face covered with the peak of a red baseball cap. His head and upper body were wobbling almost in time with the music. The near-empty Bacardi bottle sat in front of him on the small round table.

"Bruce?" I said.

No reply.

"Bruce!"

I was acknowledged with a feeble wave and immediately after heard a knock from the hatch entrance above 3G. Looking up I saw a Wren Steward.

"Is LWEM Willis down there?" She asked.

"Yeah."

"Oh good, I've got his ice," she chirped and descended our ladder.

"Ice?" I asked as she got to the bottom of our ladder.

"Bruce phoned the wardroom a minute ago, he asked me to bring down some ice to go with his Bacardi."

In her arm, she carried an ice bucket packed with crushed ice straight from the wardroom and walked brazenly past me and into the mess square. She placed the bucket on the table next to Bruce's Bacardi and left offering me a little farewell smile. I looked back at Bruce who was digging some ice out and dropping it into his glass.

"Who's turned the bloody lights off?"

I then heard Chris behind me who had risen from the dead was scratching his head. He looked into the mess square and saw Bruce sat down. Chris took a sharp detour and sat in the fully lit Starboard mess square instead joining Jim Brown and Lord Lucan who were already there.

"What the fuck is that on your arm?" Jim asked discretely.

"It's a bloody tattoo," replied Chris.

After leaving the bar the early hours of this morning Chris had returned to the ship and found Peter Daley sat in the tattoo tent on the jetty getting his arm vandalised. Chris thought this was a clever idea and waited in line for his spontaneous artwork. He regretted it the second he got back across the gangway. The whole affair had been watched from the ship from the 'Officer of the Day' who's concerns over HIV were brought to the attention of Chris and Peter as they walked on board. The OOD also informed the Captain and Medical Officer. Chris had never been that happy with the tattoo already occupying his upper arm and opted for a cover-up. He asked for a tattoo of St George sat triumphantly on the back of a Dragon, instead he got a Peter Daley look-a-like sat on top of a giant Easter egg. I think the tattoo artist must've drawn his influence from the previous customer, Peter who had also opted for a cover-up and was left with a tattoo of equally bad quality. Both lads were immediately summonsed for HIV tests.

Shore leave came quickly and we all found ourselves sat once again in our new local bar. There were far more Sheffield ships company on this occasion and I again turned down the offer of a tab behind the bar. After an afternoon wasted in the bar, we once again headed to Makati and got into a similar routine as the previous day. I had another curry from Mogambo and continued to chat up the same barmaid. I was a little more friendly with Mai by now, and she kept chatting with me every spare moment she got. I was armed with my video camera this time and wanted to get some footage of the lovely Bottom girls so I explained to Mai that I'd be back later for another drink and I left to pop down the road. Entering Bottoms I found Tug with one of the ships gunners, Gary. Both of the 3G reprobates were sat on a high table at the edge of the bar. Gary had an older and not so pretty, local lady with him. I was told that she was the Mamasan. Mamasan was in charge of the girls. She could fix you up with who you wanted but she could also ensure you are thrown from the club. She kept order and the girls on the stage did what she asked. As Gary was with her he decided to take on the mantle of Papasan, but only for the night. I later discovered that the previous night, Mamasan had arranged for Gary to have a jacuzzi with two of the stage girls, all in their birthday suits, but as Gary entered the water and felt the first girls hand on his nether regions he fell fast asleep and missed the wank of a lifetime. I gave my video camera to one of the girls on the stage to play with and went off to get myself a beer. Some three or more hours later I retrieved my camcorder from the dancing girls and strolled back to see Mai. Being so drunk I was no longer able to keep track of who had gone where and I had lost Bruce earlier in the evening but on returning to Mogambo found him outside talking to the doormen.

There are three certainties in life. One is death. The second, sex with a nurse and the third is Bruce narrowly avoiding an experience with the first two. The doormen were armed and Bruce was getting on with them like a house on fire but it occurred to me when one drew his revolver that maybe he was getting on a little too well. The doorman handed his firearm to Bruce. I was pissed but not *that* pissed.

"Bruce, what you doing mate?" I shouted.

"Alright Tony," he replied with a smile, "playing Russian-Roulette with these fella's."

The four doormen stood surrounding an unsteady Bruce laughing away amongst themselves at their crazy new English friend.

FUCK!

Bruce placed the muzzle of the revolver to his temple and fingered the trigger. I froze completely.

CLICK!

"Gun don't fucking work mate!" he complained.

I breathed momentarily before watching Bruce complete a pissed examination at the business end of the revolver before placing it again to his head.

CLICK!

"Piece of shit!" he moaned.

I grabbed the doorman.

"Get that fucking gun off him!" I growled.

"It ok, we take bullet out," he laughed, "we no tell your friend though, he craaaaaaaaaaaaazy!"

I watched bewildered as Bruce tried everything from shaking the gun to shouting at it.

"When you're done mate I'm in here."

I walked past Bruce and entered Mogambo.

The following day I once again avoided doing any work on board and went ashore just after midday this time armed with my trusty accordion. I had promised some of my new friends in Bottoms that I would bring it out along with promising the barmaid in our new local. As I felt half pissed all of the time and didn't mind making a complete twat of myself. Entering our local for our last visit I was accompanied by the usual suspects. Buck Rogers, Bruce and Chris were there along with two or three others from the mess. I chatted for a short while to a couple of American tourists who were intrigued by the 120 bass accordion I was carrying before hauling it onto my chest for a blast. I took a seat on the stage behind the bar and knocked out a couple of tunes to warm my fingers up before commencing my party favourite, 'The Irish Rover'. Chris joined me on stage and obliged with singing and he was shortly joined by the two Yanks. A few more hits singles and several rowdy beer bonding shouting sessions and it was time to depart the local bar for the last time. We had certainly had a good run in the bar and it had felt like home for three days but there was suddenly a problem. We had drunk in the bar each afternoon and returned there about three o'clock each morning waking the staff from their sleep for nightcaps. While I was always keen to pay as I drank most of the other lads had taken full advantage of the slate on offer. We were all about to walk out the bar for the last time and made no secret of this so when the barman came over and prevented us from leaving I was a little surprised. He demanded that the slate was met. It came to the equivalent of about £180 and I watched the lads scratching around for the money. They were searching in their pockets and their wallets. Bruce was even looking in his bloody shoes. Strangely no one had a spare note.

"Ok I take this!" said the barman pointing to my accordion.

"You can fuck right off pal!" I snarled.

I puffed out my chest and grew four inches in height. I was on my moral high ground with the knowledge that I had met my personal beer bill but I don't think the barman gave a shit.

"Come on lads, dig deep," Chris said.

Buck Rogers strolled up to my right side, "Give me your accordion Tone, they'll have to kill me for it."

I slipped the straps of my squeezebox onto Buck's shoulders and he left the bar and stood on the pavement outside flagging for cabs. It was suddenly obvious that no one would be able to make the bar bill. *Come on Wilton, think!*

Suddenly I had a light bulb moment.

"Oi!" I got the attention of the barman. "I will give you my watch, but only as security until I come back to pay the bill in a couple hours."

The barman thought hard for a second.

"Let me see your watch?" he queried, clearly unsure.

I held my wrist up and showed him my super-smart sweep hand fake Rolex Submariner watch.

"I get manager," he said and shouted something at the barmaid stood behind him.

As we waited Buck shouted to us through the door that two Taxis were now waiting with engines running for the getaway. The barmaid returned accompanied by a rather stout chap. Some foreign lingo was exchanged between him and the barman and the stout bloke reached for my wrist.

His attempt to take my wrist was met by a sharp slap like I was scolding a naughty kid.

"Hey, you can look but not touch," I growled now displaying a clenched right fist, "this is my fucking Rolex and I will give it to you as security but when I come back to pay the bill I will collect my watch. If there is so much as a scratch on it when I get it back I will fucking murder you!"

The boss man looked at the fake sat on my wrist. I stubbornly refused to let him touch it. I hoped that the convincing sweep hand along my obvious possessiveness and aggression surrounding my watch would help with the illusion that my Rolex was the genuine article.

A wise man once told me if you can't be right, be wrong at the top of your voice. I was at the top of my voice

It worked a treat. The boss nodded in agreement and I slipped the Rolex from my wrist. He immediately started to examine it. I knew that it was a quality copy and would hold him for a while but still needed to distract his attention from looking at it too much while we were all still in his bar.

"Oi Chief! I will be back in four hours and there had better not be a scratch on it!"

I gave him my best Paddington Bear 'hard stare' which in all honesty wasn't that convincing. We left the bar walking calmly but with urgency as though we had just robbed a bank and climbed into the two getaway cabs, Buck sitting vigilantly with my accordion on his lap.

"Well done Tone," Congratulated Chris.

"Yeah, well done mate," said Bruce now fighting with his shoelaces.

We charged back to the ship for some scan and to get dressed up for our final night in Makati. I reached into my locker and pulled out my second fake Rolex watch.

Chapter Ten

Crossing the Line

We were in for a fairly long stint and sea until our next stop, Port Moresby in Papua New Guinea. It was nearly August and we were about 5 months into the trip. Although we had done the lions share of the deployment an unhealthy mix of mental fatigue and boredom was starting to kick in. Boredom due to the repetition of long weeks at sea and being restricted heavily on everyday life. This meant that solitary and sometimes surreal thoughts and fantasies would creep into a person's mind. If left festering, these thoughts could be destructive and depressive. In my case, I found thoughts of Abby occupied my mind constantly as we sailed again through the South China Sea. I was too much a coward to tell her of the problems I was having with marriage when I had my chance in Bali. My feelings towards her were never an issue but I was now also having way too much fun as an effectively single bloke. Not fun in terms of sexual conquests or getting smashed on the beer at every opportunity but fun in the form of simple freedom. Ironic that a situation where many of my freedoms had become restricted by being part of the crew on a warship on deployment yet this deployment and this environment highlighted just how much I was enjoying the little snippets of freedom that I was getting when ashore with my mates, ironic how these snippets had become so impactive that I was doubting my commitment to a girl I had loved for years. I became averse to the thought of having to conform or be answerable to another person. I did not feel I wanted any of that 'being a husband' stuff, not yet anyway. The destructive parallel universe of a Naval deployment got the better of me and I sat in the mess one evening and wrote her a letter, an apology for letting her down and I hoped that she wouldn't hate me too much. I was ashamed of my shortfall and I wasn't very proud of myself. The letter left the ship with the next mail.

To get to Papua New Guinea we had to cross an infamous imaginary line on the globe. Not just any old line but a line that maritime legends are made of. Yes, we had to cross the equator. Zero degrees. By plane, car, horseback or even on foot this is a novelty but in a ship, this is a whole different and a rather significant event. An extremely important and necessary ceremony must be performed by the ship's company in order to secure our safe passage. We would need to pay homage to King Neptune, God of the sea. I was vaguely aware of the routine. Slowly a list was compiled of the equator virgins, sailors who had never 'crossed the line' before. It was obvious that the author of the 3G list must reside somewhere within the mess deck but the 'snitches' identity was a mystery. Should his secret be discovered he would be ripped limb from limb and left to die in the hot desert sun. Ok, maybe not but he would be given a good kick-in at least. 'Crossing the line' was the most Majestic and important of ceremonies to undertake and one of the oldest in maritime history. A ceremony practised by sailors the world over. The snitch would provide a list of names to the Sea Bears, the servants of Neptune. They would then send this list to Neptune's barber and secret police who on the day of the crossing would hunt out every name and ensure they paid homage to Neptune.

A couple of days before the crossing Bernie Manning came to meet me in the Computer room.

"Tony who do you know who's not crossed the line yet?" he asked.

"Dunno mate?" I put on my best puzzled innocent face.

I wasn't going to mention my name and assumed that Bernie already had it down and he was double bluffing me.

"Only I've got a few down, the obvious ones like," he disclosed his research, "I didn't know whether you knew if any of the killicks were virgins or not?"

My paranoia felt him digging although the rational side of my brain couldn't.

"No mate, I can't help you. I think most have been across," I continued with my Oscar-winning performance, "there aren't any fresh Killicks to speak of."

Bernie sighed and walked out. I still couldn't fathom out what he was thinking or detect if my name was on his snitch list or not.

Later that evening after my routine work was sorted I dusted off the squeezebox for a prearranged meeting. My limited flare with the piano accordion had not gone unnoticed. My makeshift practice hall on those lonely nights at sea was the Computer Room where I worked. It was also where I hid my accordion under the desk from prying eyes. When I was giving it the beans I was well within earshot of any personnel wandering about on 1 deck. A few days previously I had been approached by the Petty Officers mess to provide the entertainment for their 'Sundowners'. As the name suggests involves being privileged to the most fantastic sunset afforded to sailors. Not a single piece of land can be seen on the horizon. Nothing but flat, calm, open and unobstructed sea. It is a glorious and humbling site. The Petty Officers had invited the Ships Captain, Commander Simon Gillespie RN, along with other members of the Wardroom to a gathering on the Aft Seawolf Launcher deck. Beer and other drinks were on offer as well as a little light music.

I was that 'light music' but forgot to point out to the Petty Officers that I wasn't actually any good, having an accordion repertoire as long as a McDonald's menu and only really any good when half drunk and surrounded by other accordionists in a similar state.

My first challenge was getting to the Launcher Deck. The Sheffield was a Batch II Type 22 frigate which meant it had a higher helicopter hanger and this was where I was required to climb as the Seawolf launcher was perched peacefully right on the top of it. I made my way some 25 feet up the bolt upright vertical ladder desperately hoping my accordion would stay strapped to my shoulder and onto the launcher deck where I was met by Windy Miller. I knew Windy from the Illustrious where he was a killick. He was promoted to Petty Officer just before joining the Sheffield.

"Tony, help yourself to beer mate," Windy gave me the green light to drink as much as I could with those choice poetic words.

He then pointed me in the direction of a stool which he had brought up and placed, conveniently for me, right next to the beer. Once I was seated and the first tin had been cracked I received my briefing.

"Just knock some tunes out Tone," he continued, "about thirty seconds before sunset I will call everyone to attention..."

"Ok?" I puzzled.

"...Then God Save The Queen," Windy dropped the bombshell.

When he told me last week that I would be playing the national anthem as the skipper and his mates stood to attention on the ass end I thought he was taking the piss. I felt a little dumped in at the deep but couldn't argue I wasn't made aware and so quickly destroyed beer number one and starting an assault on beer number two before the first empty tin hit the bottom of the gash bag.

As it happened I only managed three tunes and five tins before Windy yelled everyone to order.

"Captain Sir, Gentlemen, members of the Wardroom and Petty Officers mess!"

Queen Victoria had apparently declared at some point in history that Naval Officers were not gentlemen!

"Please stand to attention and face aft, sunset."

That was my cue. The accordion produces one of the finest sounds in music however I feel that certain songs work better than others. A Reel, a Slip Jig or a Slow Air for instance. *'God Save The Queen'* didn't quite work and was comparable to Coldplay on Bagpipes. I hit the right notes and think I played a grand job considering my limitations but I couldn't help feeling the drum roll would have enhanced things at the start. The fun bit was dragging the last note out for as long as possible, in a manner which would make Brian May proud after a Queen concert, and watching everyone stood to attention perfectly still waiting for me to finish. A cough and hard stare in my direction from Windy and I closed the box. I didn't want to bite the hand that fed me and he was providing the beer after all.

With that task now behind me I felt far more relaxed and got stuck into my catalogue of drunken pubs tunes. The beer was certainly helping my fingers loosen up. I play better if I'm relaxed and beer helps me to relax. Windy and the Petty Officers mess were suitably happy with my performance so far on the Seawolf deck and so I was invited to the PO's mess after the formality of sundowners was over.

The Navy is responsible for creating some serious beer monsters. Some of the drink monsters stay sober long enough to complete the necessary promotion process and leave the lower deck to find their way to the Petty Officers mess where they join other piss-heads. Pure breed pedigree beer monsters and to add more fuel to the fire, they had wines and spirits too!

As I entered the mess the condition of entry was explained to me. You keep playing and your glass will never be empty. I didn't need telling twice, I was handed a pint of lager and from that point never saw the glass drop below a half-full.

I spun off my hits over and over falling from my seat countless times saved from injury by my 120 bass Italian airbag. By the end of the night I couldn't hit a single key without striking three others and my delicate tinkles on the ivory instead resembled a concussed boxer's desperate haymaker attempts at holding on to his championship belt. To make matters worse I'd lost the power of speech. At about midnight I was released from my commitment and, discarding the accordion to the safekeeping of the Petty Officers, fell down the ladder into 3G mess the deck below. Picking myself up I stumbled in through the doorway of the port mess square. Using the bulkhead for support I began speaking utter shite.

"I've been in the PO's mess."

"Right-o Tone."

"I'm fucked."

"We can see that Tone."

"Night lads."

"Night Tone."

The next day was a daily routine. I was taking every possible opportunity to spend time on the upper deck as the weather was scorching hot and were just off the equator. You could fry an egg on the deck. As my responsibilities consisted of internal computer equipment there wasn't a lot that can be done outside in the sun. The only real thing we had up there was the 1007 radar but at sea that was needed for navigation. So I spent the majority of my time loafing around finding Bruce for a coffee fix. The day passed without incident with the monotony being momentarily broken by a quick 'man overboard' exercise.

These appear to be a bit of fun for the lads involved and involved throwing a large heavyweight orange dummy over the side of the ship.

FOR EXERCISE, FOR EXERCISE!
MAN OVERBOARD, MAN OVERBOARD!

The sea boat crew would close up to their posts preparing to launch their Rigid Inflatable Boat or RIB. The 'Swimmer of the Watch' would arrive on the upper deck wearing a diving drysuit that he had just spent the last 60 seconds squeezing into. Whilst all this went on the Officer of the Watch (OOW) would steer the ship through a large figure of eight the purpose of which was to return the ship to virtually the same spot where the 'man' fell overboard or at least the spot where someone first noticed and raised the alarm. I did hear that once the Commanding Officer of HMS Brave decided one day to give his OOW the shock of his life and walked from the Bridge only to return five minutes later wearing a dry suit.

"You have the ship Lieutenant. Man Overboard," he declared confidently.

On that note, he walked out onto the bridge wing, took a quick look over the side and jumped. Now *that* is faith in your crew and wins the gold medal in the 'Mad Captain' competition which in previous years had been won by the Commanding Officer of Ark Royal who used to water ski behind his Aircraft Carrier.

That evening saw the reading of Neptune's Warrants. We waited in the mess deck for our host's to arrive. The Sea Bears, aka the Chief Petty Officers mess, were not to be made welcome. The Sea Bears were not guests in the mess and would not request permission to come down into *our* space. They were coming to do Neptune's dirty work and tradition dictated they must receive a hostile reception accordingly. The lads downed several beers before the Bears arrival and when the time came we put on the war faces.

Clank! Clank! Clank!

The metallic clanking of many pairs of heavy booted feet descending into our mess along with the high pitched squeal of hands sliding down the aluminium handrail. They entered our annexe.

"Turn the music off!" the first Sea Bear demanded.

Dressed top to toe in thermal furry suits and decorated anti-flash hoods they didn't only sound but even *looked* Grizzly.

"Fuck off!" blasted a defiant reply.

"I said turn that fucking music off!" repeated the Bear.

"Turn it off a minute Taff," Richie instructed Taff Elliot who was sat nearest the stereo.

"D'ya hear there," presumably the head Sea Bear announced, "your presence is required on the flight deck of Her Majesty's Ship Sheffield tomorrow at noon when the said vessel will pass over the equator. As this is the domain of King Nep..."

The Chief Sea Bear didn't have time to finish when Taff shoved his way past him forcing the Sea Bear to put out a hand for support.

"You fucking mortal, show more respect!" demanded a second Sea Bear from the annexe.

"Up yours you fat twat." Taff retaliated.

At no other time would such insubordination be tolerated but we were crossing the line and these guys weren't Chief Petty Officers, not tonight anyway.

The Sea Bear grabbed Taff around the throat and Taff launched a series of punches into the Sea Bears face. More lads rose from their seats and jumped in to help

Taff and were met by further Sea Bears from the annexe. These Sea Bears pushed against the wall of lads attempting to evict them. All tumbled inwards and the pile collapsed onto the mess floor knocking our table, teapot, several cups of tea and tins of beer onto the deck. Three of the Bears took offence at Taff's attitude and all piled in. The remaining Bears and 3G lads who weren't involved in the fighting reached in to pull the Bears from on top of Taff, he was getting a decent pasting. The fighting Bears resembled the Chief Stoker, The Chief Gunner and one even resembled Brum. It was Brum Bear which appeared to be most unhappy. It may be due to him receiving most of the lad's attention which took the form of various blows to the head and torso. The Sea Bears were eventually beaten back and retreated up the ladder and on with their route, battered and bleeding they still hadn't been to the Wardroom or the PO's mess. The Wardroom would no doubt be a walk in the park, maybe receiving some heckling, a bit of *'Rar Rar'* and some *'Oh I say that's not cricket!'* but the PO's mess would likely offer a similar welcome to the one they got with us.

The next day was a Lazy Sunday routine. That meant a day off apart from the duty-watch. I went and grabbed brunch at 10:00 hours. As the Sea Bears had been rudely interrupted the night before they unable to read the list of those paying homage and I was still unaware if my name had been included in the snitch list or not.

At 11:55 all available personnel gathered on the flight deck. There were two hundred and seventy-ish people on board this warship and at least eighty per cent were stood on the flight deck. We were all wearing shorts and T-shirts with some of the wiser lads choosing to wear a little sunblock or sun hats. It was hot. We were as close to the sun as it was possible to get while on planet Earth. My trainers were melting to the deck where I stood. My feet were feeling the induction of heat through the soles and I found myself shifting weight from left foot to right to relieve the heat. Judging by what the Captain wore he had never crossed the line either. He had the standard-issue white tropic shorts and short-sleeved shirt but his shoulder tabs had been replaced with some rather large cardboard epaulettes sporting the three gold rings to signify his rank of Commander in the Royal Navy. He stood at the aft end of the flight deck and looked as apprehensive as I felt.

The ceremony commenced to the sound of a bugle and the aircraft hangar doors slowly lifted revealing clouds of thick foul-smelling smoke, the canisters reserved for fire exercises had been activated and placed in the entrance. From behind this smoke emerged King Neptune's Bugler followed by several members of his secret police complete with homemade police uniforms, plastic squeaky truncheons at the ready. The electric motor of the green helicopter trolley sprung into life and it crawled from the hanger parting the smoke to reveal the man himself, King Neptune who's willowy and slender frame, mature in years and sporting a long grey matted beard looked suspiciously similar to the Chief Ops. Neptune emerged from the smoke like rock star royalty on a world tour. On Neptune's left-hand side sat his favourite mermaid sporting a blonde afro and with coconut shells covering the modesty of her hairy chest. The helicopter trolley crept forward at its maximum speed of one mile an hour before suffering mechanical failure and stopping dead. As the ship's company laughed at their performance Neptune and his mermaid rose regally from the foam cushion on the trolley and approached the Captain. The secret police advanced in a wide protective circle surrounding the King stopping every two or three footsteps to strike an onlooker with a plastic squeaky truncheon.

"Be Humble!" one bellowed. "Be humble before King Neptune."

Several of the ship's company dropped onto one knee to show our respect but this position was painful to maintain as the deck was scorching hot and the flesh of knee sizzled and burnt. Neptune halted alongside the Captain before then turning to face him. It was obvious who was in charge today.

"We have never met, you and I," he roared at the Skipper, "but I understand you are wishing to cross my domain?"

Neptune then began to spin off a long and traditional sounding poem from ye olde days welcoming the Shiny Sheff and her crew. He presented the Captain with a starfish medallion and then ordered him to the barber's chair. The centre of the flight deck had been taken over by an elaborately constructed stage. A large fabric walled swimming pool stood on the port side of the flight deck and wallowing around within were the Sea Bears dressed in the same green furry suits as the night before with dyed brown anti-flash hoods the top corners of which were tied to give them little bear ears on their heads. The pool was directly next to a raised stage upon which was found Neptune's Barber, Neptune's Doctor complete with a long white coat, Neptune's mermaid and of course Neptune himself perched on his throne. The mermaid lay at his feet stomach bloated by the years of ale investment. The Barber and Doctor stood either side of a hinged seat. The hinge being at the rear meant it could be flipped backwards ejecting the occupant into the pool where the Sea Bears waited. Finally stood just off the front starboard corner of the stage was Neptune's Clerk wearing a splendid barrister's wig.

As the Captain took his seat the Clerk began to speak.

"Captain Simon Maxwell Gillespie," I wondered whose snitch list the Skipper had been on, "you are charged with leaving the ship without an adult in charge, for returning on board without a newspaper, milk or the oggies and for distracting the Chief Petty Officers mess whilst on the golf course by letting your mobile phone ring and not taking the customary two-stroke penalty."

While this charge was read out the Doctor administered the foulest biscuit ever cooked up by the chefs, stuffing the cookie into the skipper's shocked gaping gob. About the size of a large thick cookie, it was a mix of hot chilli pepper, soap powder and other nasties designed to make you gag, the Doctor held his hand over the patient ensuring the biscuit was chewed and not spat onto the deck. The Barber meanwhile used a wide paintbrush to slap a thick green liquid over the head and face of the Captain before picking up a two-foot cardboard cut-throat razor and shaving him.

"Sire, to the Bears!" cried the Clerk and the Captains two tormentors tipped the seat by the two handles on either side catapulting the skipper backwards off the chair and headfirst into the pool of saltwater whereupon the four Sea Bears commenced to punch him several times dragging him back into the pool as he tried to escape. After thirty seconds of this treatment, the Captain was launched bodily from the pool and on to the hot metal surface of the flight deck. With the utmost decorum, Commander Simon Maxwell Gillespie stood up and picking up a rather soggy red baseball cap took his place with the onlookers. He had paid homage.

"Wren OM Guildford!" shouted the Clerk.

Gilly walked forward. The poor girl had a reputation of not being the sharpest tool in the box, she knelt before Neptune.

"Kiss the mermaid!" she was ordered.

She walked onto the stage and was immediately lip-locked by the twenty stone mermaid before being told to take her place on the seat.

"Wren OM Guildford, you are charged with being very vacant and suggesting to your messmates that the ship cut short the visit to Port Moresby by two days and add those two days onto the Papua New Guinea visit."

The flight deck erupted in laughter.

"Sire, to the Bears!"

As with the Captain before her, she was ceremoniously shaved and force-fed her biscuit before being thrown backwards for the Sea Bears to play with.

The victims lined up as their names were called from their respective mess snitch lists. When the Deputy Weapons Officer Phil Gascoigne was called to pay homage he was charged with constantly falling asleep in the Chief's mess after drinking their beer. More victims were summonsed and their charges read aloud.

It soon became Taff Elliot's turn and I expected him to get a real hammering considering the performance in the mess the night before.

"Radio Operator Elliot, you are charged with claiming to have a rod of steel in Bangkok and also for claiming that your hair loss was due to the Malaria Monday tablets," More laughter followed with a degree of apprehension evident.

"Sire, to the Bears!"

Taff was dumped into the pool. If the Sea Bears wanted revenge that would have to work for it. He was only a little over five foot five and certainly wasn't a big man but he fought hard nearly throwing a couple of the Bears out over the edge of the pool. After a minute or two of beating he was thrown from the side and after picking himself up off the deck strolled back to us grinning from ear to ear.

"Ha fucking ha!" he laughed, "I pissed in their fucking pool!"

"Thanks mate," said a disgruntled Mick Bridger, "not all of us have been in yet."

Others were subjected to the ordeal and charged accordingly. Jim Brown for idolising Elvis Presley, Mick Bridger who, as president of the HMS Sheffield rugby club, used an identical boring speech after every match played against our host countries. Even young Robbie Robertson was hammered. Robbie was our mess baby who despite being twenty-four years old didn't look a day over fourteen. He was charged with supporting Norwich City and spinning nothing but HMS Raleigh basic training dits.

Peter Daley's charge was failing to hold on to his rate as he had temporarily being promoted to Petty Officer, and for needing an HIV test following the stupid tattoo he had opted for in Manila.

All of these charges had been skilfully composed with the assistance from each mess deck's snitch. I accidentally dropped a young Wren Engineer in it when asked by Bernie for any stories. She had been put on my section for a few weeks nearer the start of our deployment and one of the basic tasks I had asked her to perform was to clean an electronic circuit board. I watched in utter amazement when she returned to the Computer room with a bucket of steaming hot soapy water and a sponge to perform the task.

Things ticked along nicely with numerous victims being dragged up and charged until there was a brief interruption. Halfway through the proceedings, King Neptune found himself being pelted with rotten fruit from the heavens. I turned and saw at least four or five lads stood on the relative safety of the aft Seawolf launcher deck each wearing a paper bag over his head with eye holes cut out. They did manage to throw a fair amount of fruit before the secret police clicked into action and, after pushing through the crowd gathered on the flight deck, gave chase blowing their whistles. With some of the police now missing from the flight deck, a small fight broke out among the remaining bobbies and three lads who were held in their custody behind a rope barrier awaiting their court appearance. Frantic whistleblowing followed and the police who had chased the fruit bombers returned swiftly to assist their colleagues. A minute or two later the good-humoured disorder was squashed and the ceremony was able to continue.

Lieutenant Commander 'Big Dog - Little Dog' was up next.

The clerk spoke.

"Sire, there are no charges to read for this mortal. There is in fact a totally different crime outstanding against him and the punishment had been predetermined."

With that announcement, the doctor reached across with a strip of 'harry black' masking tape and with one single perfect 8-inch piece held firmly at either end, taped his gob shut.

"Sire, to the Bears!"

The Supply Officer got a good beating, big doggy style. The play was getting rougher and my name had still not been called out. I was getting a little anxious.

Eventually, our snitch, Bernie Manning, was summonsed. He bravely walked over to the stage and knelt before Neptune, his confidence bolstered in the knowledge that he had been the Bear's 'pet' in the preceding arrangements. As soon as he was on the floor he was ambushed by some of the lads from our mess. His bare back was whipped with the wet T-shirts until the police stepped forward to regain order. Sitting comfortably in the Barber's chair he was charged with being a rat on his mates and sent to the Bears with cries of '*Wanker!*' ringing in his ears. The Sea Bears took hold of Bernie and, like a vicar cradling a small child at baptism, very gentle lowered him into the pool. They raised and lowered their pet a few times to the jeers of the watching ship's company much to the amusement of Bernie who gave the two-finger salute to his fan club in the cheap seats. Then on the blow of a whistle, they dropped him hard into the pool and beat him as they did the others before spewing him onto the flight deck

Nobody escaped paying homage, the Chief's mess who were running the show even grassed their own equator nozzers up to King Neptune. The Wardroom gave up their equator virgins. Nobody escaped - except for me!

The ceremony eventually drew to a close and I was relieved that I had not been grabbed at any point by Neptune's police but, to be honest, also a little disappointed. I knew the opportunity was never likely to arise again but at least I'd had a grandstand viewing though I wouldn't have been as nervous if I'd known Bernie had wrongly assumed I'd crossed the line already.

As the ship was enjoying a Lazy Sunday routine the atmosphere on board was very relaxed. It is a fact of life that many Matelots can be a little on the vain side and certain parts of the ship were allocated for the topping up of vitamin-D, aka sunbathing when the opportunity presented itself. The tranquil and scenic roof of the ship's bridge was reserved for the officers whilst us mortals from below decks were allowed onto the forward and after launcher decks and any spaces we could find on the fo'c's'le. The forward launcher deck was tricky because of the mass of dedicated joggers who, despite being well into the trip and beyond the 'new year's resolution' style honeymoon period of the trip, still routinely stomped around the upper deck each and every day. I didn't feel the need for either jogging or sunbathing. The latter because my scalp had suffered so much exposure to the midday equator sun that the shower I had a while afterwards felt like acid rain on my head.

The last time I suffered sunburn like that was in Santander when my back erupted in huge blisters, amazingly I found a tidy Spanish girl who was happy to rub sun cream into it. I don't think it helped my back much but it sure felt good and was ample compensation for my stupidity. As for jogging, well I simply couldn't be arsed.

Crossing the line had presented the chance to allow everyone a breather. It was the 2nd of August and while we had the majority of the deployment behind us we still had good old Oz to look forward too. To add more excitement to our idyllic lazy Sunday were informed that the evening meal would be a flight deck barbeque and that meant music, burgers and beer. Lots and lots of beer. It was one thing to get ashore and drink beer until it leaked from your ears but a different experience altogether to sit with your beer on the ass end on the ship with half a chicken and a slab of steak surrounded by your mates and a vast expanse of ocean. While I diligently fought my way through the mountain of grub I had amassed on my paper plate I quietly watched the sun slowly drop out of sight below the horizon. As the natural light faded additional 'party' lighting rigged around the flight deck took over and with a full belly I polished off a few more beers with my mates.

Chapter Eleven

I Know the Tampax Song

A few weeks earlier, about halfway into the deployment, a few lucky random names were selected to perform the duties of Ceremonial Guard in the forthcoming 50th Anniversary of 'Victory over Japan' or 'VJ' day. A parade was planned for Indonesia; a gathering of Navies from fifty countries all marching through the streets of the capital city, Jakarta. To avoid making total twats of ourselves we were to have a trial run in Port Moresby, our next stop. Before leaving Devonport each member of the ship's company had to ensure they had their full complement of tropical rig. Our working tropics, as they were known, consisted simply of blue shorts for working, white shorts for the evening and Jesus style sandals. Our 'ceremonial' tropics uniform were a little fancier and consisted of the white suit and shoes that many women like to imagine are worn every day by the sailor carrying them off into the sunset, the one that strippers or village people wannabes tend to wear. Our ice-cream suit as it was fondly known.

The bell-bottoms we had on our normal blue ceremonial rig, or Number 1's were bad enough but the flares on the tropical suit were fucking huge. A strong gust of wind would have even the heaviest Matelot parasailing instantly. What made it worse was that as ceremonial guard we had to tuck them into white gaiters shackling our shiny drill boots and march a few miles wearing it all in a city that wasn't much below the line of the equator we had recently crossed. Another problem with the ice-cream suit was that being ceremonial, it had not evolved much since the beginning of the 20th century. We still needed to tie a black piece of 'silk' around the neck and thread it through a Lanyard which itself was tied in a very specific way. The silk having already been folded several times before being twisted and sewed end to end. If you think it sounds a bit complicated you should try wearing it.

On the 8th of August, we arrived at Port Moresby, Papua New Guinea stories circulated rapidly, thanks mainly to the research of our liaison team, of cannibalism. Now consigned to the history books we had been assured that the practice was unsurprisingly outlawed and now limited to a few tribes that were hidden up in the mountains. Nevertheless, it still left us a little nervous about getting pissed up with the locals. Our first day alongside saw us marching up and down the jetty all morning practising for the big parade. Thankfully I wasn't the only lad picked out of our mess to be part of the ceremonial guard. A few others were too, including Tug Wilson and Jack Daniels, a killick Comms Tech. We were dragged from our normal duties, which I was gutted about as Brum had some tedious cleaning task planned, and formed up on the jetty with SA80 rifles. We stood smartly to attention before running through a few rifle drills. One downside of the SA80 was that it was a little awkward to carry for any great length of time resulting in some lactic acid and the Officer directed to take command of our rabble had to ensure that every eight minutes he gave an order for us to 'Change Arms'. This meant simply, we swapped the rifle from our left side to our right and vice versa. This was practised on the move as we were going to be marching for about five miles through the streets of Jakarta. Tomorrow we would be doing likewise in Port Moresby but only for half the distance. A good opportunity to brush off the cobwebs. About an hour of shouting, poking, prodding and swearing passed and the Gunnery Instructor (GI) started to see some form of order and co-ordination from us. Matelots aren't generally very good at marching, we don't throw our knees up in the air like the Army seem to enjoy so much or even stand still for long periods if we can possibly help it. Most of us are usually too hung-over to stay perfectly still on our feet even if we wanted to. All the same, the GI was beginning to smile and as a reward for our efforts, we were allowed a breather and a drink, of water.

"Right lads, you are not permitted to get wankered tonight," the GI bellowed, "and if any of you little bastards fall over on parade you had better be fucking dead because by the time I have finished with you, you will wish you were!"

GI's only have two volumes, off and fucking loud.

"Right enjoy yourselves tonight. See you bright and breezy tomorrow morning, Tropics, belts and gaiters 07:00 by the armoury to collect weapons."

That evening I fully intended to stay clear of the beer. Not because of pride or a desire to impress the GI but because I knew I'd feel like utter shite if I overdid the booze and had to do the whole march holding back a stomach of chunder or without the ability to fart with confidence. I opted for a night out with Tug and we walked off from the flight deck hoping to hail the next available taxi along with another one of our 3G reprobates Gary, a fellow Cornishman. A cab pulled up to us almost straight away. The grinning driver looked the spitting image of Jimi Hendrix but his teeth were almost entirely red, blood red! Either this bloke had a serious gum problem or he had just had his mate around for dinner. Suddenly the thoughts of cannibals leapt to the front of my mind. He smiled at us through his window, his teeth looking sharper the longer I stared at them. Reservedly we jumped in the car. After nervously travelling about two miles we got to our requested destination and started decamping from the taxi but as we did so Gary, as blunt as ever, could resist the urge to ask if the driver had recently eaten his mate.

"I have not eaten my friend, why?" he puzzled.

"Your teeth are covered in blood mate," Gary pointed out.

"Ha! Not blood, fruit!"

The driver reached into a side pocket on his door and lifted a bag of berries to Gary.

"Here you try," he offered the bag to Gary.

"Cheers mate."

Gary took a small handful of berries from the white paper bag and we bid farewell to our man-eating taxi driver.

"Right let's not piss the locals off anyway," Tug suggested. Those teeth still looked pretty bloody sharp.

It was only a short stroll along the main street before we found a respectable air-conditioned bar which had within it a comfortable mix of the upper end of society along with a good measure of westerners. We sat and enjoyed good conversation with those we met. The sober head was a new experience for me and for a while I felt like an important executive who was dropping into Papua New Guinea on business rather than a British sailor looking to have a clear head the next morning.

What a refreshing change.

The following day we mustered outside of the ship's armoury as requested, all stood around in our ice-cream suits looking like professional sailors. The SA80 rifles were dished out along with the white webbing belts and gaiters we would be wearing. We walked up onto the flight deck trying desperately not to damage the fragile shell of our highly polished mirror finished black toe caps of our parade boots and were directed to a waiting coach. Nobody at all looked hung-over which was encouraging, well except for the young officer who was to be shouting the orders but I think he was suffering from nerves rather than a headache though. We were driven for a couple of miles by another 'man-eating' Jimmy Hendrix before being dumped in a car park close to the area we had been only the night before. Once we were all off the coach we fell into our respective predetermined spots, put on our war faces and marched off down the road. A band provided by the local police force marched along behind us and the whole parade went pretty well with no major fuck ups. The Officer in Charge made a small error in one of his commands but we were well rehearsed and nobody let it show. It was a warm welcome with what appeared to be hundreds of cheering onlookers some even waving the Union flag. With a couple of miles of marching done it was back to the ship for tea and medals.

"Well done lads, you looked shit hot!" said the GI.

He would know. It was his job to hang back and watch our performance.

Later that evening, back on the Sheffield we made the local news. And thanks to Petty Officer Jack Hatty's ability to tune the SRE/TV equipment into a local network for a change we were able to watch ourselves on the mess television marching down the main street of Port Moresby I felt a small sense of pride and to top it all I'd kept my step for the entire 5 seconds the camera was on me. I was now hoping that I could pull it off again in Jakarta.

A week later, the 14th of August and it was time to find out. HMS Sheffield sailed smoothly into the cool blue waters off of the Indonesian capital. There was undoubtedly an abundance of World Navy's present at Jakarta and this was obvious as we steamed towards with not only warships dotted all about but also pleasure cruisers and sight-seeing boats carrying tourists out to get a glimpse of these fabulous sleek grey vessels. I'd imagine the awesome sight of seeing such a fleet was sufficient to bring out the ship-spotter in hundreds of people. Certainly a, 'once in a lifetime' event for many. Pulling alongside we appeared to act more like an attraction at a village fete rather than a warship in port. Marquees were scattered throughout the dockyard with display stands and fast food stalls. A large marquee tent was erected on Sheffield's flight deck and company representatives from various sectors of the British defence industry who had flown to Jakarta especially, came on board to occupy their stalls within the tent.

I had again been lumbered with being on-duty the first night in and was quietly grateful. Due to being on-duty and on board, I was not allowed to drink alcohol, a blessing in the circumstances. Most of the duty watch could drink only their allotted 3 tins but as Duty 'Leading Weapons Engineer' I was second 'in charge' of a team known as the SPO or 'Ships Protection Organisation' under the control of the Duty Petty Officer. In the event of an armed threat, we would draw weapons and take three personnel each flushing each compartment within the ship thereby locating and neutralising the intruder. Well, in theory anyway. If the threat was external then we would close to various well-protected cover positions on the upper deck hopefully scaring the buggers away with covering gunfire, shouting and flashing our private parts. In addition to ourselves, both the Quartermaster and Bosun's Mate were armed with either SA80's or Browning 9mm pistols. They would however always remain on or near the gangway protecting the access from the jetty. For this necessity to bear arms I was not permitted to drink on duty, a sensible precaution really.

The day after we arrived and pitched up we were whisked away for our parade, again in a large coach but a somewhat more luxurious one this time. I boarded the coach taking care once again not to scuff or chip the polish on my parade boots and found a seat next to Tug. The energy surrounding this parade was far greater than the smaller-scale parade we had performed in Papua New Guinea. This was a ma-hoo-sive event. The 50th anniversary of 'Victory in Europe' day had been huge in Europe and for the similar reasons 'Victory over Japan' day would be huge here. Pulling up at the coach park the driver was directed to our parking spot by fluorescent traffic marshals, a spot which was in an allocated bay next to countless other identical coaches. As well as the large scale ceremonial kicks we would get from this parade we were advised to bring our white tropic shoes with us. On completion of the parade, those who so desired were allowed to go out on a rig-run into Jakarta. The only thing better than going out for a beer in a foreign port is going out for a beer in a foreign port in full whites complete with medals and 'Old Spice' aftershave.

We formed up right next to a similar looking guard from the Royal Australian Navy. Every five platoons there was a marching band which entertaining the onlookers but also helped to keep us all in step. Mid-August in Indonesia and it was no surprise that the heat was already starting to hit us and the young Lieutenant in charge allowed us to relax our headwear while we waited. He stood in front of us grinding his teeth nervously whilst the GI went to speak with his Australian counterpart.

These events are timed to perfection and the British Armed Forces taking the biscuit. At 10:55 we were told to replace our headgear and stand 'properly at ease'.

"HMS SHEFFIELD SHIPS COMPANY!" shouted the young Lieutenant. We instantly drew in our stomachs, stuck out our chests and grew two inches in height.

"HMS SHEFFIELD SHIPS COMPANY HO!"

We snapped to attention, the pride immediately obvious in the smash of metal Blakeys against the hard ground of the car park. The Aussie contingent next door did likewise as did the representatives from other countries. There were all manner of nations present, the Dutch, the Yanks, even the Japanese. We turned to our right and awaited the 'off' from our young Lieutenant. Somewhere down towards the start of the huge line of trained professionals an order was given to 'Quick March' and the faint sounds of a brass band was heard. It was only a minute before a second band sprang to life slightly nearer our location and we could see in the distance other squads marching off in time with the music. The procession was so big that several military brass bands were needed to keep us all in step. We were fortunate in the respect that directly behind us was a band which had already filled us with confidence during their brief tune-up. Within moments we were being prepped to go. A parade officer walked past our Lieutenant and gave him the nod.

"HMS SHEFFIELD BY THE CENTRE QUICK MARCH!" He bellowed.

That was more like it. He was shouting like he meant it. The band started to blast out a tune the instant our leading foot made its first strike onto the road in front. I am not the type to get overly enthusiastic about shiny boots and sharp creases but the few hairs that still grew on the back of my neck stood up and I felt the pride in each and every footstep we put down. We were celebrating the liberation of the Far East and Pacific from the Japanese fifty years before but it felt as though we had just liberated them personally the day before. We were cheered from the second we entered the streets. To my amusement, I noticed that the same hospitality was not afforded to the Australians who, marching just in front of us, were receiving quite a cold reception from the huge crowds lining the pavements and roadsides. I restricted my chuckles to mental ones but focused on the difference in the shouts from the crowd as their cries went from "boooooooo!" to "Hooray!" as they were passed by firstly the Aussies and then ourselves. The marching very soon became effortless; I was enjoying it so much that I paid no attention to the mileage we had begun to notch up. Several 'change arms' were yelled and we performed them without effort or fault. Quite some into the march we passed a Dias which required us to 'eyes right' and salute the dignitary within.

The band kept our feet in step, our arms swinging and our busting with pride until, about an hour later, we returned to our original assembly point and marched up to the same spot from which we had stepped off from just two hours before. The sore head where my cap had been perched and my aching feet seemed a very small price to pay for the phenomenal welcoming we had all just received from the locals. We were stood at ease and the young Lieutenant's face broke to afford a huge smile to himself, he deserved it.

"Well done lads!" he said.

Under any other circumstances I would've paid no attention to his remark but I felt this was a compliment well deserved. One of the lads shouted back.

"Well done to you, Sir!" the anonymous voice declared.

Mutterings of approval swept across the squad of Matelots. Well done indeed Sir.

"Sheffield Ship's Company, stand at ease, stand easy." Called the young officer. "I'll find out what's happening, hang fire here for a second."

He then strolled off with a new sense of authority to speak to the GI who was already getting a quick debrief from parade officials. I turned to look at Tug and raised my eyebrows to indicate my lack of knowledge as to what was going to happen next. We all seemed equally unsure. A minute later the young officer returned with the GI.

"Well done boys and girls," congratulated the GI, "fucking good effort. The Captain saw you and says he was fucking proud of you!"

I smiled contentedly like a little boy who just impressed Mum and Dad at sports day.

"He also says that anyone who wants to stay ashore now and get pissed can do so, just make sure that all kit that you want taking back to the ship goes onto the coach."

We didn't need to hear that twice. We were snapped quickly back to attention and then dismissed by the young Lieutenant.

"Once I've counted the weapons onto the coach you can all bugger off!" added the GI.

I swapped my drills boots for the white tropical shoes I had put on the coach earlier and ditched my webbing and gaiters. My shoes felt like ice-cool slippers, they were bloody heavenly. Tug, Jack Daniels and me all headed straight off in the direction of the town centre where we knew a party was already underway. A rig-run in paradise, medals included. Matelot paradise.

Our first port of call in the quest for ale was the Hard Rock Cafe and it was heaving. Most punters were foreign service personnel but also hundreds of locals. Getting a seat at a table for a meal was impossible so with no further excuse needed we opted for rapidly drinking as many bottles of beer as possible. It wasn't long before we were chatting up local girls aided by our new found friend, Petty Officer Marine Engineer George Something-or-other, Royal Australian Navy.

George was a decent bloke with a similar agenda to ourselves, get drunk and laughing as much as possible. He had been marching in the parade just ahead of ourselves, hence the reason he was also still in his rig. I did notice a medal pinned to his jacket which looked like it needed landing lights and it's own control room.

"That's some medal George?" I asked already fuelled by several Budweisers.

"Yes mate," replied George.

Silence

"Go on then?" I hinted.

"Oh I was awarded it," he replied.

"No shit Sherlock, how?"

I appreciate some people don't like blowing their own trumpet but I was keen to find out the story behind the medal.

"The ship I was on a few years back had an engine room fire so I pulled a lad out and dragged 'im up a ladder," we raised our eyebrows, "then I went back for a couple more."

"D'ya get hurt?" asked Tug.

"Just a few burns," said George and proceeded to undress discreetly showing a mass of scar tissue on his abdomen.

"It goes up me chest," he continued, "and down me arms and legs."

He then pulled up a trouser leg to show more scar tissue followed by the sleeve on his jacket to show yet more.

We all examined the burns briefly.

"Want another beer?" I said.

"My turn mate," replied George, "I'll get the round in."

With that, he walked off to the bar.

The Afternoon was going well and we were slowly joined by more lads from the ship only they hadn't taken advantage of the chance to wear rig and it was obvious that some were regretting it. The uniform drew folk in like lemmings to a cliff edge. We were getting drinks bought for us, arms wrapped over us and constant kisses on the cheeks, even from the ladies! Frank Ryder had joined us among others and he had bought his new toy along, a laser key-ring which projected a small red dot brightly onto any object within a 2000 mile range. These are fucking annoying little toys that I have since learnt to hate but at that time they were new technology and therefore a bit of a novelty. Frank found a suitable spot and proceeded to project the 'laser' onto the chest of any lovely ladies within eyeshot. The effect was an anti-climax and he soon realised that girls just got pissed off with the annoying little red dot waving from side to side over their boobs so taking the key-ring from Frank, decided instead to direct it onto a group of geeky looking blokes in the far corner of the cafe who were all sat peacefully around a table enjoying a meal. I scored a direct hit on one bloke's forehead and within in a split second and a sharp alert from his friend sat opposite the fella dived from the chair and onto the floor next to his table. We began to piss ourselves laughing, all but Frank who had turned his back on us to chat up some local talent. The unamused geek stared towards us and after dusting himself down began to take very large footsteps towards us.

"Bugger!" I thought, "Frank have this back mate."

I thrust the key-ring back into Franks hand moments before the geek arrived with us. I am well aware of how distance can play tricks with the eyes but it wasn't until the geek stood directly in front of us I realised how big the fucker was. As broad as he was tall I was beginning to think I had just upset Dolph Lundgren.

"Who has the laser?" he spoke to us in English backed with a thick German accent.

"I do mate!" smiled Frank waving the key-ring in his face blissfully unaware of why Dolph was so interested in it. Dolph promptly grabbed Frank around the throat.

"The last time I had one of these pointed at me it had a rifle on the end of it," Dolph snarled. "Watch where you aim it!"

"Sorry mate, I didn't realise, I didn't think, I..."

"You people don't think!" barked Dolph and released Frank from the grip of his shovel sized fist before storming back to his friends who were watching sternly from the corner.

"What the fuck was that about?" asked Frank.

"Dunno?" I said to Frank trying desperately to contain the laughter.

"I'd put that key-ring away if I were you," advised Aussie George.

"Yeah, good idea," Frank agreed, still in looking bewildered.

As the day wore on Tug, Jack and me decided to have a wander about, or rather a stagger about. It's great when you find somewhere nice to booze away the hours but it still nice to explore a little. We soon found Jakarta's Planet Hollywood. I am not sure of the history of Planet Hollywood restaurants and know as much as the next man, if not less but I think three Hollywood giants decided to start a chain of fast-food style restaurants in various exotic locations around the globe which, luckily for us, included Jakarta. Again there was a large queue for those wishing to sit for a meal but if you were only after something to drink then it was easy to walk straight in without having to hang about. Having never visited a 'Planet Hollywood' I was quickly captivated by the vast array of big movie artefacts that adorned the walls and ceilings. Almost directly above me was a full size naked Sylvester Stallone crouched inside a clear tube with just a triangular piece of black plastic covering his gentleman sausage. A plaque informed me how it was a futuristic prison cell from the movie 'Demolition Man'. I examined all sorts of movie memorabilia in this Aladdin's cave. We sat side by side at the bar and pulled a cocktail menu across to see what was on offer. Maybe it was due to our slightly off-sober state but I misread the menu. I ordered a large cocktail as did Tug and Jack. After knocking back a glass of blue screen wash I was handed a rather nifty free shot glass with Planet Hollywood Jakarta on it.

"Cheers mate!" I smiled, "Can I have three more of those blue things?"

I don't know what was in them but they hit me square in the face and started to ramble on about writing to Arnold Schwarzenegger to tell him what amazing staff he was employing and how good his cocktails were.

After yet more blue things we left Plant Hollywood and headed back to the Hard Rock Cafe via McDonald's. It became apparent when we got there that it had become the focal point for most of the visiting Navies including yet more lads from the Sheffield. George the Aussie was still there looking far worse for wear than ourselves. After some time chatting to a mix of locals, tourists, businessmen and fellow Matelots, I found I was receiving quite a bit of attention from a local Indonesian girl who looked every bit like Pocahontas. I have no idea why she had singled me out but I wasn't complaining.

Carpe diem. I introduced myself.

"I am Fatty," she said in cracking English.

"Is that a nickname?" I asked.

"No nickname, my name is Fatty," said Fatty.

She wore a black and white striped top with a white mini skirt and her arse was bloody fantastic, in fact, all of her was. After a bit of chit chat, Fatty told me she was twenty-four years old.

Things started to look up and she went on to explain that she loved England and loved English men especially us brave sailors. She was also studying English with the intention of living there one day and so, in a public-spirited and culturally considerate way the lads and I took the opportunity to help with her lesson by teaching her a few words of 'Jack-Speak'.

"I surely must be in with a shot with this one?" I turned and said to Tug whilst Fatty was off buying *us* some drinks.

"She looks pretty keen on ya Tone." Tug replied.

Contrary to the stereotype I wasn't looking to shag my way around the globe but she had caught my eye and ignited a little interest.

Fatty returned with bottles of Bud for us. I noticed that the one I had bought for her was still untouched and she had opted to get herself a coke as a substitute.

"Cheers Easy!" Tug said grabbing a bottle from Fatty.

"You haven't touched your Bud?" I pointed out.

"I don't drink alcohol," she replied passing me the bottle, "you drink it."

"Why not?" I asked.

"I am good catholic girl," Fatty said proudly, her chest swelling and posture improving much in the same way ours did when called to attention at the start of the day's parade. "I don't drink, I don't smoke, I don't swear!"

Tiny alarm bells started to ring in the back of my head but were drowned out by Tugs sudden and rather blunt interruption.

"Do you fuck?" Tug asked as discreetly as a Geordie Bricklayer in 1980's Düsseldorf.

"You are sooooo funny!" She looked at Tug burst into laughter then struck me playfully on the arm. "I do when I am in love."

After a very hurried executive meeting with Tug whilst Fatty was being distracted by Jack and his intellectual conversation about bird watching I decided to keep hold of Fatty a while longer. She had, after all, bought a round of drinks and seemed to be a bit of a ladette and who knows she might even decide by the end of the night that she loved me just enough to make it worthwhile.

As the evening wore on however it soon became apparent that wasn't going to happen and despite her commendable sweetness, I had become bored of her so to ditch Fatty I told her that I needed to return to the ship. This also gave me a chance to drop my brothers present back in my locker which I had found somewhere between Planet Hollywood and the Hard Rock Cafe. I had thoughtfully found him a fully working intricately carved blow-pipe complete with darts. Something I knew would come in very handy in deepest Cornwall. Fatty walked with me back to the ship after a promise of a look around which I had foolishly made to her a couple of hours before when I thought I was in with half a chance. She had become a limpet. The tour consisted very quickly of the upper deck followed by our mess deck. I cracked open a beer from the fridge and offered her one but as expected she politely refused. I sat with her for a while in the mess square while some of the lads found her sweetness equally amusing. Then after finishing my beer I ushered her up to the flight deck where a taxi-moped was waiting to whisk her away. I watched with thoughts of what could have been as her perfect ass squatted tantalisingly onto the back of the moped. As the small machine revved up and pulled away she looked back, waved and me and shouted the few words of Jack speak I had taught her.

"Cheers Easy, I know the Tampax Song!" she yelled as the moped disappeared off along the jetty.

I turned to walk back to the mess.

"You found a fucking loopy one there Tone." Said the Quartermaster.

"Tell me about it." I chuckled.

I ran down the mess to load up on some well-priced cans of McEwans Red Death and within half an hour was back in Hard Rock Cafe with the lads.

The rest of the night went in a drunken blur and soon we were all back on board sleeping like babies in our pits.

Waking the next morning with a sore head, sore feet and sore wallet I cast the usual weary eye around my surroundings and was immediately drawn to an unusual white fluffy object sat on top of Bruce's bed across the other side of the gulch and just three feet from my own. I partially squinted my hung-over beer goggles in an attempt to focus. Bruce wasn't in his bed, just this fluffy thing which turned its head and looked right at me.

"Cluck!" It said, then blinked.

Strolling into the mess with my deployment mug I chucked a spoonful of coffee into the bottom and climbed the mess ladder. The idea of a deployment mug was to go the full seven months without washing it. I never managed the feat as it always got so filthy that so many chunks of debris would float to the top that I would gag. After drawing some water from the boiler in the small annexe aft of the Senior Rates dining hall I prepared to drop back down into 3G but was stopped by one of the killick Dabbers who had been on duty overnight.

"Did Bruce get his chicken?"

"Yeah, thanks," I replied.

"Tell him when you see him that we had to let his Donkey go."

"Yeah, will do," I nodded and walked carefully down the ladder.

Settling down to enjoy my morning coffee I spotted a large potted plant perched in the corner of the mess directly under the wall phone. It definitely wasn't there yesterday. I settled in to enjoy my brew. After a short stint of Indonesian television, a sober Mick Bridger climbed down the ladder. He had been the Duty LWEM and had just completed his set of morning rounds.

"What's the score with the chicken?" I asked all ears.

"Bruce dropped into HQ1 about two o'clock this morning and asked whether the duty watch fancied some chicken," Mick said, "Dobbo said 'yes' expecting a KFC but Bruce threw in a live chicken."

It was only polite that when some lads were out for a night on the beer they would if they remembered, try to bring some fast food back for either the HQ1 watchkeeper or the Quartermaster on the gangway. The offer of chicken from Bruce left the HQ1 lad expecting something edible and cooked with a bit of chilli sauce and garlic. Instead, he got a live chicken complete with feathers and beak. Not wishing to offend Bruce too much he discreetly dropped it back into 3G about half an hour later where it was placed on Bruce's pit awaiting his return only, as usual, Bruce slept in the mess square. He was one of the few who could get away with it as anyone else would fall victim to a head shave or the Duty Banksy complete with felt tip permanent marker.

Bruce hadn't forgotten the Quartermaster on the flight deck either, he bought him back a kebab in the guise of a live donkey which Bruce tied to the end of the gangway after the Quartermaster had firmly refused to let Bruce bring it on board. To help decorate the mess square, Bruce also brought back a large potted plant and a Witches broomstick to help with cleaning up. He'd been busy.

An hour passed during which I grabbed a full English breakfast from the galley, I allowed myself the treat as I never usually made it out of bed in time to catch breakfast. Bruce eventually appeared along with the post for the morning among which was a large box addressed to Jim Brown.

"What you gonna do with the chicken Bruce?" Mick asked.

"Your donkey has been let go mate," I added, "the QM asked me to pass the message on."

"Ungrateful bastards! I paid five fucking dollars for that donkey." Bruce moaned.

"Where'd you get it?" Mick asked, "a donkey shop?"

"Nah, some old bloke was walking along the main road with it last night, I asked him if he knew where I could get some big eats and waved five dollars at him, so he gave me the bloody donkey," Bruce explained.

"And you had to take it I suppose?" said Mick.

"Did he give you the chicken as well?" I asked.

"Already had the chicken," Bruce said, "picked that up earlier."

I was happy with that explanation, I mean who wouldn't want a ships chicken on board their frigate.

"What about the house plant and the broom mate?" I continued.

"Found them, they're gizzits," Bruce said and he took a seat in the corner lighting his tab. With that, Jim Brown plodded down the ladder in the traditional naval battle dress of towel and flip-flops having been up top for his morning dhoby.

"Oh you fucking beauty!" he spotted the box waiting with his name on it. "Looks like the T-shirts are here."

The remainder of the morning went on as normal with an early end to the working day again. Once the majority of the lads were gathered in the one place Jim broke open the box containing the deployment T-shirts. The drawing on the front was almost a spitting image of the cartoon design I had done and the rough guide to what was required on the back had been tidied up considerably and looked first-rate. Jim dished out the appropriate number to each member of the mess. I'd ordered a couple for myself, after all, it is always handy to have a spare. After stashing them away in my locker I threw on my civvies for another night out in Jakarta. We took the opportunity to release the chicken back into the wild as the hierarchy would undoubtedly get a little annoyed with it. I mean some people have no sense of humour. Some debate had taken place as to whether we could bribe one of the chefs into making a curry for Bruce with it but we didn't think he would appreciate it as he'd originally wanted *Ethel* as a pet.

Besides that, the next stop was going to be Darwin and knowing Bruce he would probably bring back a bloody Kangaroo. We were going to need the space.

Chapter Twelve

Jeans and Strippers

During our transit from Indonesia to Australia, we were briefed on something called Exercise Kangaroo '95 or K95 for short. I must hand it to the team of highly paid and no doubt high ranking people that think of these names, K95!

As a foreign force, we were to take the role of a hostile foe and we were therefore known by the colour Orange for some bizarre reason, maybe Red conjured up too many recent memories. We were assured that although the exercise was being conducted on land, sea and air any involvement for ourselves would be restricted to sea operations and would have no effect on our 'freedom' when ashore.

Life seemed to be rather peaceful in 3G during the steam from Jakarta to Oz. The mess seemed to be far more relaxed than at any other time during the deployment so far. I think the prospect of an Australian visit was a big plus, not forgetting that we were getting into the final stages of our deployment. 3G had over time grown reputation of being a rowdy mess deck. Before I'd arrived on board a story was doing the rounds that it was the only mess on board to 'close the hatch' in protest at something. Usually involving quality of life issues it was a risky practice which in Navy terms would not be that far from a mini-mutiny and would involve, much as the name suggests, closing the main hatch to the mess and telling everyone to fuck off!

One evening, during our passage to Oz we found had the usual set of evening rounds with the Officer of the Day but this time he was accompanied on his route by the Jossman of Joss for short. A fair-ish bloke but as head of discipline on board still had his rule book to play by, he had spotted our potted palm plant and asked about the story behind it. I wonder to this day whether he had been tipped off to our mini Eden project.

"Sorry lads, it'll have to go," he frowned sympathetically. "you could have anything crawling around in that."

He had a point but also broke the news to us that the witch's broom, another one of Bruce's spoils, would have to go as well. It was made of shitty bits of twigs and could have as much wildlife in it as the plant.

"No time like the present, throw it off the ass end or something," he added, "just ditch it quickly."

Within moments of evening scran finishing, we had assembled a 'plant ditching detail' on the flight deck. Dressed in our evening whites and now sporting our new deployment '3G Mess Groovers on Manoeuvres' T-shirts we formed a ceremonial group complete with beer. After posing for a quick photo we formed a line on the flight deck. The first item to get float tested was the broom which I had the task of disposing of. I marched to the guard rail at the aft end of the flight deck holding the broom as though it were my SA80 rifle from the parade a few days previously and with a long blast from one of the lads on his bosun's pipe I did a 'Carry On Sergeant' general salute and sent it flying skywards off the back end and into the churning black wake behind us. The plant was next and was thrown, complete with clay pot by two lads into the great depths of the Indian Ocean to join its mate. We all saluted before returning to 3G to get pissed.

We charged about off the North coast of Australia for a while engaged in games with the Aussie Navy before eventually coming alongside in Darwin. We sadly didn't get chance to drag any Aussie Matelots on board and write them off. Sure it would have been a riot if we had.

There is a fantastic sense of competition between Australia and the Brits in almost everything we do together and although this mainly applies to sport it nearly always turns into drinking at some stage. I recall how a few years before whilst on HMS Brazen an Aussie ship dropped some of their lads over while we floated around in the Middle East. Two of them came down to 3R mess just for a couple of hours, one of the two fell from the ladder as we passed them back to their rigid inflatable boat which had been sent to collect them. He missed the boat and went for a swim. While they were with us the poor lads were getting beer thrown at them from all angles with the only instruction being "drink it!"

During these long deployments, living in cramped quarters you become fairly tolerant of some habits and idiosyncrasies of your messmates. Bruce had many positive attributes which everyone found entertaining but one thing that was a little less enduring was his general untidiness, Bruce's inability to pick things up. He was a little messy but usually, items of clothing would be directed back to his pit where it would sit for a short while before being shoved into his locker. We now decided however that on this occasion enough was enough, partly because he was messy and we were getting fed up and partly because we were going to have a laugh so Richie set out to sabotage Bruce's jeans, or rather the jeans I'd given him in place of the ones that were destroyed in Thailand by Edwina Scissorhands the Bangkok waitress. He had left his self-walking jeans floating around the mess for a couple of days so Richie decided to hide them shortly after leaving Jakarta to teach Bruce to tidy up.

On the 23rd of August, we arrived at Darwin in the Northern Territory, berthing at Stokes Hill Wharf. This visit presented a greater than average rush of lads trying to get ashore. What made matter worse was that just before leave was piped two girls, a blonde and a brunette sporting very high cut Daisy Duke shorts and tiny bikini tops had clip-clopped up the gangway and handed the Quartermaster a bunch of flyers for their strip show which would start that very afternoon. Imagine the coincidence, what are the chances?

Bruce was furiously looking around the mess squares for his jeans but refused to ask anyone for help locating them. Whether he thought he'd mislaid them or twigged to the fact that they had been hidden I don't know. I also don't know what made him look in the small ice compartment of the beer fridge but that's exactly where he found them now made into a solid block of ice, frozen like a long lost iceman having already spent some a few days in the sub-zero temperature. He didn't have a hope in hell of thawing them out in time so he did what all switched on members of the Royal Navy would do, he improvised.

At just after midday a bunch of British sailors from 3G mess, HMS Sheffield strolled along the concrete jetty towards Darwin City centre. It was bloody hot so we were all dressed accordingly except of course for Bruce who wore the latest in designer naval issue Nos 8's working trousers. On his head, instead of a sun hat, he wore something which closely resembled a pair of frozen black Levi 501 jeans. The ice had made them very inflexible but he had been able to crack and bend them enough to purchase on his cranium and was letting the hot August Northern Territory sun thaw them out. Obviously, they were closer to the sun if they were on his head!

We all bimbled along the jetty discussing what to buy the loved ones at home and whether the mix of beer and hospitality would be any good. About halfway along but despite firing a few questions in his direction, Bruce had gone uncharacteristically silent. Looking around to see why the rude little shit was ignoring us we spotted him about fifty feet behind and flat out on his back like a starfish. A few seconds passed of us all laughing before we realised that he wasn't pissing about and we walked back along the jetty to pick him up. It wasn't rocket science to see the cause of the collapse. Bruce's head was absolutely ice cold. The jeans he had placed on his head to thaw out had numbed his brain enough for him to lose consciousness and keel over. Within a couple of minutes of sitting him up and rubbing his head, Bruce began to speak.

"Fucking hell that was weird," he said timidly.

"Can you walk mate?" asked Tug.

"Yep," replied Bruce.

"Right," Tug said, "carry your bloody jeans from now on and don't put 'em on your head!"

In a change to my usual routine my first intention was to buy some pressies for family at home and along with a few others strolled around looking at a variety of Aussie gifts from Koala bears to boomerangs. In one shop I found a nifty looking bush hat for my brother and thought it would go nicely with the blowpipe I had found him in Jakarta. As we had done a little walking, a splattering of shopping and in line with tradition I started feeling a little peckish and was about to leave our latest gift shop to find some food when the shopkeeper became overly keen on keeping us all inside.

"Have a good look round guys and see what else you may fancy," she insisted.

"I'm done thanks!" said one of the Dabbers.

"You mustn't go yet!" her pleas hiding a hint of desperation.

I think it was safe to say we were all a little puzzled by her enthusiasm but all became clear when another customer strolled over.

"She called the cops on ya!" he explained.

"She bloody what?" replied the Dabber.

"There's a reward for the capture orange forces," he enlightened us, "look!"

He pointed to a poster displayed behind her desk.

Sure enough, a small A4 poster displayed behind the counter explained to locals that should they come into contact with any orange hostiles they should contact the local police or army on the hotline number printed on the poster.

After thirty seconds of protesting it occurred to us that we would better of moving on so we all left the shop.

The Aussie hosts were taking this game very seriously but the poster had failed to point out that only orange hostiles in combat gear and holding machine guns were actually playing on dry land. I smugly walked off with Bruce and Tug to find a cafe where I tucked into a nice cultural plate of 'sweet and sour' crocodile.

With presents for family at home taken care of, it was time to pay a visit to the club that the two scantily clad girls had been advertising when the ship arrived. A short taxi trip later during which the driver explained that the venue in question didn't open during the day as he mused at our urgency to get there.

"Oh they're open!" he said in surprise as he pulled up outside, "Must be 'cos of you fellas"

"Yeah, you think?" I replied.

On the pavement outside was a billboard which informed us the time of the next strip.

"Only half-hour to wait mate," Bruce pointed out, "Enough time to get a couple beers down our necks."

The sign specifically welcomed the British sailors from HMS Sheffield. Clearly, the club was cashing in on our arrival and who could blame them, the small ground-floor club was packed to the gunwales with sailors from the Sheffield. Most, like me, still had their souvenirs with them. Walking over to bar I was greeted by one off the girls who had been at the gangway earlier in the day handing out the flyers. It was the small brunette and she was wearing only a tiny white thong bikini bottom and a pair of sandals. I got the distinct impression that she had been to visit the plastic surgeon as her tits defied gravity and although perfectly rounded looked totally out of place as though stuck to the front of her chest with glue resembling Homer Simpson's eyeballs much to my amusement, still I wouldn't have kicked her out of bed for eating biscuits.

I bought a couple of beers from her and walked back to sit with a few of the 3G lads and some of the Senior Rates who had also found the temptation of the strip club too much to resist on this pleasant Aussie afternoon. After forty-five minutes of gassing a few of the lads began to mumble and gripe.

"The fuckers have done it again ain't they?" one of the Chiefs moaned.

"Done what?" I asked.

Brum was hovering about, "What time was written on the board outside for the next stripper Tone?" he puzzled.

"Three o'clock," I replied.

"Pop outside and look again will ya?" asked Brum, "it said two fucking thirty when we came in."

Sure enough, the sign had been altered again and now stated that the show started at three-thirty.

After some further complaining about how the staff were keeping us in here to buy more beers, which in all honesty is what any switched-on bar manager would have done, we all decided to give it to the new time of three-thirty in case she came out to play. If we didn't have any joy then, well, complaints to the barmaid would likely follow from a few frustrated Matelots who undoubtedly would then sit back down with freshly charged beer glasses and wait for the four o'clock show instead. Great tactic Miss or Mister Bar Manager!

At three-thirty, as though the added tension and protests of the lads had become uncomfortable for the staff, the music was changed and the volume turned up. The lads who had witnessed the earlier show all stared in the direction of a long staircase to the left of the small dance floor.

"It was the brunette last time," Brum leant forward to explain, "the blonde was behind the bar serving topless.

I'm hoping they've swapped and it's her turn to get the kit off."

"Here we fucking go boys!" another Chief nudged us into paying attention before lifting up a camcorder to his eye socket.

Sure enough, the blonde who had accompanied the brunette to the ship earlier strolled quite gracefully down the curved staircase to the left of the dance floor. She wore a pinstripe business trouser suit and carried a briefcase pretending to talk on a chunky Motorola flip phone as she walked.

"A multitasker eh?" I elbowed Brum, "wink-wink, nudge-nudge!"

She then proceeded to throw the briefcase and the mobile phone to the side of the dance floor and began peeling off parts of her suit in time with Jon Bon Jovi. She did the usual stripper thing and dragged one of her audience, a rather shocked but 'giddy as a schoolboy' Petty Officer, onto the dance floor and began to rub her now near-naked body against him like a dog on heat. She stood in front of him and bent over pushing her ass back into his groin before turning around and rubbing her face into his gentleman area, all the usual stripper moves. We all started to envy the lucky git and even more so when she got him down on the floor laid on his back. She undid the flies and belt buckle of her victim but instead of exposing any part of him she stood back up and walked around coming to a standstill with a foot placed either side of his head. She then slowly removed the final part of her clothing, her white knickers before squatting down stopping herself just a couple of inches over the guys face but alas only afforded her victim a quick glimpse of her ailerons before standing up again to give her audience the 'dumb office blonde' look. Our hostess then dropped forward onto her hands and positioned herself above him in a sixty-nine.

Just as we were beginning to think what a lucky fucker the Petty Officer was she began to smash her pelvis down onto his face. All but the most masochistic hard-on's quickly disappeared. She was using her camel's toe or rather her camel's hoof to pummel the crap out of the poor guy's face. There would have been less venom if she'd have just caught him shagging her sister. The lad was just starting to overcome the shock of it all when, as quickly as she started, she stood up. The blonde bitch then bowed to us and gathered her clothing up before fucking off up the same flight of stairs she'd come down from a few minutes before. The young Petty Officer got up looking a little worse for wear, his nose now flat and leaking a fair bit of blood. He staggered slowly back to his messmates who were laughing their heads off at his misfortune.

"What the fuck did you do, stick your tongue in her box or what?" one asked.

"I didn't *do* anything!" he mumbled, spraying blood over his 'I love Darwin' T-shirt, "but if I'd have known she was going to do that I'd have fucking bitten it."

Looking around I noticed that our naked blonde friend had left her mobile phone on the floor of the club and strolled over to pick it up. It didn't take long for me to realise that the dial tone meant it is was fully working.

"Here mate!" I caught the attention of the young Petty Officer, "your new girlfriend has left her mobile behind."

A few eyebrows raised.

"Zero zero four four for the UK isn't it?" I asked.

"Fucking right it is!" He said and taking the phone he walked to a corner of the club to make his call.

This was still a fairly decent place to drink the first few beers of the day and we hung around for a while longer. Long enough to see about five or six different chaps take advantage of the free UK phone line and regardless of the time difference ring their family, their mates, their neighbours and their neighbour's mates. Pretty much anyone and everyone they could think of. He who laughs last laughs longest.

It didn't seem long until the brunette was stripping and the blonde serving. It had been another hour but time was flying faster as more beer flowed. Once content that we had seen enough of both girls Bruce, Tug and myself strolled back towards the main street. We had spotted a more traditional looking pub and wanted to investigate in further.

We soon discovered that Darwin had a fairly small hub to it and found this very warming. We soon reached the traditional pub we had seen earlier and I even liked the name, the Victoria Inn. The atmosphere within was friendly and welcoming, a welcome change to what we had just experienced and it wasn't long before more lads joined us. I couldn't resist the temptation and strolled over to a couple of girls who were sat on their own at the far end of the pub. I was feeling brave and had already assumed that I would get blown out by such gorgeous healthy looking stunners so figured there was nothing to lose. I started to chat with the pretty redhead because she had smiled at me as I had walked over which I felt was a good signal.

"Do you live around here?" I found blatantly obvious questions flowed easiest when faced with totty nerves.

"Yeah, you with the British warship?" she asked the even more obvious.

"Yeah, trying to find some good clubs and pubs," I answered.

"Well, stick around and I will see if I can help you out."

"Tony." I introduced myself and held out my hand.

"Jo," she replied and taking my hand leant forward and kissed me on the cheek.

"I guess you want a drink then?" I pointed back to the bar.

This was rapidly turning in to the 'Obvious Olympics'.

"Yes please," she replied and gave me a huge smile and a slow wink.

Either she saw an easy drink coming or I was actually in luck. I certainly got the impression it was the later as no sooner had I finished my beer Jo was up on her feet and she bought me another. This ruled out the easy drink theory in my reckoning.

This got even better when half an hour later, after a quick-fire question and answer session about the UK, Buck Rogers strolled over and tried to slope in. Jo reached under the table and took hold of my hand, giving it a squeeze.

"Tony, I have to go home and change before I can go out tonight, want to come back with me?" Fuck me! She was looking like a gold medal contender!

I didn't need asking twice and leaving the 'Vic Bar' jumped in a cab outside. She had a very slim body but retained a lovely shape in all the vital areas and I was certainly looking forward to getting a better look. Her red hair hung halfway down her back and was slightly curled. A freckled face held a pair of sapphire blue eyes and my thoughts were racing towards a strip show of my own. She certainly wasn't backwards in coming forwards. Arriving at her house a short cab right later, I took a seat in the living room on the sofa and Jo sat down next to me. Then to my absolute horror shortly after starting a conversation about the benefits of skin to skin massages the front door swung open and the biggest man-mountain ever strolled in blocking out half the sunlight as he did so. It was Dolph's Australian cousin.

"Hiya mate!" he said.

"Fuck!" I thought.

"Paul, this is Tony from the British warship." Jo introduced us and I suddenly felt like I was now in a set of Candid Neighbours.

"G'day Tony!" He bellowed, stretching out his hand for a handshake which I had no intention of refusing for fear of causing offence and also painfully aware he would then figure out how shite my grip strength was in comparison to his own and therefore how easily he would be able to kick ten shades of shit out of me.

"I'm Jo's housemate, I'm in the Air Force. You here for K95 I guess?"

"Yeah," I replied half expecting to get dragged from the house by *friendly* forces.

"Don't worry he's not my boyfriend," Jo added.

"Thank fuck for that," I laughed.

Jo then strolled upstairs to get changed and Paul walked off to the kitchen.

"You want a Beer Tony?" He shouted from the hole he had made in the brick wall as he walked through it.

"Yeah, cheers." I breathed a massive sigh of relief. It would have been rude to say no!

"It's not me you wanna worry about mate," he offered out a tin of beer to me as he walked past, "Jo ain't had a shag for bloody ages. She keeps moaning about how fucking horny she gets."

I nodded and tried to give the impression that I wasn't a little shocked by his forwardness on behalf of his housemate.

"She is gonna eat you alive pal," Paul smiled then looking at his watch threw the remains of his tinny down his neck, "Fuck, I'd better get ready myself."

With that, Paul disappeared upstairs as well. I looked around at the decor for a while and watched the television. All sorts of scenarios, some pleasant and some downright fucking awful, were running through my slightly pickled but rapidly sobering head but I didn't want to jump to conclusions too soon after all Jo was pretty stunning. She walked back into the living room wearing just a towel wrapped around chest, her hair wet from the shower she'd just had.

"I've just phoned my girlfriend and she wants to know if you've got a sailor she can have?" Jo said.

"I can think of several," I didn't want to disappoint the girl.

"She is going to be a while getting ready, if I give you my car can you go back and find one?"

No sooner had she said that her phone rung. Jo's mate informed her that she was on her way over in the next ten minutes so therefore she asked if I would take them both on board the ship. I happily agreed and finished off my beer. Jo then went off to the kitchen and made both of us a coffee to drink while we waited for her mate. She handed me the mug then sat down next to me on the sofa, we played a short game of tonsil tennis for a while and I took my chances slipping a hand up inside her loosening towel.

"Better finish dressing, she'll be here in a minute," she chirped and jumped up from the sofa.

"Fuck!" I thought, "Nearly."

Jo came back downstairs ten minutes later wearing a very short summer dress which did little to cover the creases under her arse. Her body looked good enough to eat. We chatted for a bit and once her mate arrived she threw me her car keys.

"You drive sailor," she winked.

I took both girls back to the Sheffield with a bit of navigation advice and after signing the girls on board they sat their near-perfect asses in the mess square as I took my turn to chuck on something fresh. Jo's mate was every bit as stunning as she was but with black curly hair and an even greater allergy to clothing.

After a half-hour of nattering with some of the lads in the mess, Jo asked if I was ready to go. I'd been ready for a while but was simply enjoying watching my Aussie maid and the attention she was getting, after all, she was there as *my* guest. Once back at the car Jo's mate enlightened us how she hadn't seen any blokes in the mess that she fancied and on top of that she was now on a downer as she had recently been dumped. A quick chat was had between the girls during which Jo's mate told her that she wanted to go home. Jo navigated me back to her house and we dumped both her mate and the car outside. Before leaving the Sheffield I had arranged to catch up with some of the lads later on in the Victoria so Jo and me headed straight there.

"Tony, will you do me a favour?" she asked.

"Course?" I said, curious to know what was coming next.

"My nails are too long to push the buttons on the cash machine," she waved her hands at me, "if I give you my pin code will you get some cash out for me?'

Was this girl for real?

"Sure." I agreed.

"Tony?"

"Yes love?"

"I've got no pockets, can you hold on to my bank card?"

"Sure." I willingly offered my services between pinching myself to ascertain if this was a dream or not.

She was a very trusting girl. Jo had told me when we first met that she worked as a cashier in a local bank so I thought she should've known better. Good for her that I trusted myself.

We walked hand in hand to the cashpoint and I drew fifty dollars from Jo's account as she watched. I drew another one hundred dollars for myself but this time from my account, as the hundred I had drawn out earlier that day had now gone on fluffy Kangaroos, Koalas and some beers in a strip club. Following her wishes I put her fifty in my back pocket along with her cashpoint card then we strolled a few yards up the road and entered the Victoria for more of the amber nectar.

The bar was rammed, there were loads of folk, a good mix of locals with lads from the Sheffield including Bruce. We started on beers and quickly graduated to straight whiskies. Jo was sat on my lap at the bar. Her short summer dress barely covered her dignity when she stood so I took the easy opportunity to have another feel of her amazing backside. I quickly found my way round to the front of her thong and began to have a play tracing the frilly edge of the fabric surrounding her modesty, she didn't object in fact judging by the response she was enjoying it. We were all taking in turns buying the rounds and the night seemed to be going pretty well. Jo appeared to be in her element but after an hour or so she was wandering off and flirting with any bloke that entered the bar. I thought she was too good to be true so undeterred I continued knocking back the alcohol with Bruce. Alcohol was now taking lead. The light had faded outside and the bar was filling rapidly with nightlife.

I was never very good with whisky and was now borderline shit-faced!

"Coming to Herbies then?" Bruce asked.

He had grown as bored of the Victoria as I had. It was a cracking pub but two hours continuously there was enough for the moment.

"Yep, will do. I'll just find my little mate and give her card back," I let him know.

She was now spending no time with me and my ego had been sent crashing back to earth as a result. I strolled off to find the little lady with a group of lads in the far end of the bar.

"Ere maid," I caught Jo's attention with the traditional Cornish mating call, "I'm going to someplace called Herbies, have your card back!"

"Oh Tony!" she protested, "I want you to stay here with me."

"I'm off to Herbies, you can come to if you want you know," I said, pointing out the bleedin' obvious, which was so abundant in our opening theme it seemed quite appropriate for our end credits. We were now playing a slightly different version of the game.

"I don't want to go there!" her deeply frowning face and crossed arms clearly showing her disapproval of my plans.

"Well stay here then," I said plainly.

"I don't want to stay here without you."

"Okay so come with me then."

"No, I want us *both* to stay here."

For the life of me, I couldn't work out what she was thinking. She wouldn't come to Herbies and would only stay in the Victoria if I was there with her. The alcohol was now firmly established in my bloodstream by this point and it was fair to say I was now more than a little pissed off with her.

"You don't want to go Herbies, but you don't want to stay here unless I'm here, even though you ain't spoken to me in the last half hour?" I quizzed.

"Yeah!" she agreed with me, nodding.

Bruce was eager to get going.

"Right come with me then!" I took her arm.

"I'm not going to Herbies!" she protested.

"I know you're not," I agreed. "Back in a minute Bruce."

Jo trotted along behind me struggling to keep up in her high heels as I strode purposefully from the bar. I walked over to the main road which happened to have a taxi rank complete with a single taxi waiting and called to the driver.

"You free mate?"

"Yeah," he replied putting down his newspaper.

I opened the rear door and pointed to the seat. Jo sat inside.

"Where'd you live Jo?"

She blurted out her address behind an oddly disappointed expression.

"How much to go there mate?"

"That'll be ten dollars." Replied the driver.

I handed him a tenner and pushed Jo's door shut firmly getting my last glimpse of those long slender legs. She promptly wound down her window and stared up at me with what I can only describe as puppy eyes.

"Aren't you coming with me?" She looked confused.

"Nope."

"Well do you want my phone number then?"

"Nope. See ya!"

I stepped back and watched the taxi pull away, perform a U-turn and drive off down the road.

I spun around and performed a pissed power walk back to the Victoria bar to find Bruce.

Finding Herbies was a turning out to be a bit of a struggle but Bruce assured me that we were going in the right direction. He had been told how to get there by some friendly locals in the bar. After a mile, the ten-minute walk to the club seemed to be going a little astray so we looked around to get some idea where we were and perhaps some fresh directions from some locals. The only life to be seen was a cop car with one occupant. The stereotypical obvious choice for directions, for the time or for the best places to buy doughnuts.

"'Scuse me mate!' I approached the driver's open window.

The Aussie cop turned to take a look.

"I'm trying to find Herbies night club mate, do you know where it is?"

I figured mate was a formal title in Darwin as everyone seemed to use.

The cop replied in a familiar accent, broad Brummie, "It's just down the road, only a couple of hundred yards behind those buildings on the right-hand side."

"I ain't from Brum!" I complained, assuming he was taking the piss out of me, defending my Cornish twang.

"I know, you sound like you're from the West Country or something. *I'm* from Brum." He replied.

"Bloody 'ell! How long you been out here then?" I asked.

"Emigrated about nineteen years ago."

I had to admire him, the entire English cricket team somehow managed to develop strong Aussie accents each time they are interviewed on TV whilst on tour in Oz after only having being there for a few days. Just earlier in the same day I'd popped into a cafe for a sobering coffee, the waitress sounded as Aussie as Charlene Minogue only to then informed me that she was a Brit who had flown out from London to find work only a fortnight before. What is it about the Aussie accent that makes everyone try to imitate it after just a day in the bloody country?

At last, someone had kept a firm hold of their heritage. After nineteen years living in the Northern Territory, the Brummie cop still sounded just like Jasper Carrot. Hats off to the guy.

Bruce strolled over and Brummie cop went on to give a very abbreviated account as to why he and his family moved to Australia before we were rudely interrupted by a car in the main road which performed a fucking good hand brake turn and then continued the display by offering our law enforcement friend some doughnuts, rear-wheel-drive style.

"You gonna let him get away with that?" I said.

"No I'm not mate. Take care guys, see you later."

Bosting!

A mere two hundred yards later we were at Herbie's. It wasn't a night club it was a shack but a very large shack that sold beer by the bucket load. Bruce and me were happy but even though I was very pissed I realised instantly why it might not have been Jo's cup of tea. The inside didn't disappoint, to me it felt like heaven. It reeked atmosphere and although there was hardly anyone there it still felt full of life. We soon found two homegrown Northern Territory girls who were actually mother and daughter. I nearly pissed myself when I found out the daughter was called Kylie but there the similarity with Miss Minogue ended. She was a good-sized girl with plenty of cushion for the pushin', who drew her talent for drinking from her mum and boy could they both drink. I, on the other hand, was beginning to have trouble standing upright. I had been knocking back copious amounts of beer like never before on any part of the trip and to top it I was following each drink with a whisky chaser.

Then the obvious happened. Bang! I was out like a light.

As I started to come round, as full consciousness slowly crept back I felt something cold and wet against my right ear. A sharp hiss of air followed, then a tongue on my cheek. Opening my left eye in an attempt to protect the right from whatever was seducing me I saw the culprit to be some grotty mongrel dog. I felt a little on the hot side and noticed a huge amount of patchwork covered duvets on top of me, my immediate fears of being starkers lasted a micro-second as I felt for my jeans and guessed I was fully clothed but still needed confirmation which I did by affording a quick glance underneath the covers. I sat up to see a second scruffy Heinz 57 dog sat at my feet quietly watching me as though it expected to pull out a bag of dog treats at any moment. A swift look around told me that I was in the back of a camper van of some sort. There are times when I have woken not knowing exactly where I was or how I got there but this was at the top of the list for being a head fuck.

I tried to stand only to strike my head on the roof of the van but after a quick rub realised I wasn't in any pain and had just been shocked by the sudden jolt. Just a protective reaction of mine which wasn't needed as the booze was working as an anaesthetic for everything. The view through the windows was darkness one side and neon lights on the other. A good dose of thumping bass in a dull but constant rhythmic pattern was breaking into the van through the flawless German seams in the body panelling. Crawling over the made-up bed I found an escape handle on the door and gave it a tug. The sliding door opened with ease and I stepped out onto a pavement. It then took me about five minutes to get the door to shut on the Volkswagen. Both dogs seemed to appreciate my difficulty and remained contentedly inside watching my performance.

Whoooosh......... Clank!
Whoooosh......... Clank!
Whoooosh......... Clank!
"Fucking thing!"
Whooooosh....... CLUNK!
"Got it you bollocks shit twaty arsehole monkey fuck!"

Now I was out of the van I needed to establish where I was and how the fuck I got there. I noticed that the camper van was parked almost directly outside a set of doors to a bar.

Ah good! The answer must lie within the bar. Lieutenant Columbo, eat your heart out!

I staggered in with no trouble, receiving a smile from the suited pretty brunette hostess on the door and it took me less than a minute to find Bruce sat on a table with his arms around Kylie, on his left side, and her mum on the right. Mystery solved.

"Toneeeeeeeeey!" He greeted in his best Thai accent.
"How ya feeling Tony?" Asked Kylie.
"Need a drink," I said. "Your door's a bugger to shut."
"You gotta slam it real hard." She replied.

I got the distinct impression she said that to lots of guys.

"We bunged you in there to let ya sleep for a bit." Chirped up mother.

"Cheers maid, how long was I out?" I asked, dreading the answer.

"Only ten or twenty minutes mate."

"Felt like longer," I said relieved.

Refreshed and recharged I got the drinks in.

It felt like an eternity before I started the wander back to the Sheffield. I firmly believe that Matelots have an uncanny ability to find their way back to their ship wherever they end up. The professional term for such a feat is called the 'Beer Compass'. Bruce also possessed this skill but I feel the clock on his runs a few hours behind everybody else's.

I was slaughtered but sobered up a little when I gained sight off the ship in the distance, the orange lights on her foremast once again guiding me home. I managed to find the start of the jetty and along with it, Brummie cop leaning against his patrol car.

"Hey alright Brum!" I called.

"Alright there Cornish!" Said Jasper Carrot, "You looked like you've had a good night! Where've ya been?"

"I have no idea but I did meet Kylie although she's put on a little weight." I chuckled.

"I prefer Danni myself." He laughed.

"Did you catch up with matey boy in that car?" I asked.

"Yeah, good shout there mate," he smiled, "he was wanted for questioning about a rape some time ago, we've been after him a few weeks now."

"Really? Well, I'm glad I could help." I gave a thumbs up and strolled onto the jetty.

"You be good now, or if you can't be good at least try not to get caught eh?" Brummie cop added.

"Cheers mate, take it easy."

I staggered back along the jetty to the ship, found my pit and went to sleep.

My head was banging severely when I woke about four hours later. Day two in Darwin and I'd missed breakfast by miles. Delicately walking into the mess square I was informed that Bruce had been in and already gone back out on the piss. No one appeared to be working. The entire ship apart from only the very dedicated had decided to make the most of final big visit of the deployment. Junior rates, Senior rates and Officers. Everyone was out. I checked the post in my mail slot and found a letter which brought me crashing down to earth and hit me in the face like a brick. So far I had managed to avoid reality quite successfully but I now felt the lowest I have ever been in my life. Before I even opened it I knew how bad it was going to make me feel. A sure-fire reminder of how selfish and foolish I have been over the last few weeks. It was a letter from the UK, it was a letter from Abby.

I had the misfortune of Richie passing and casting his eyes over my shoulder.

"Fucking hell Tone is that from Abby?" He asked, barely able to contain his passion for scandal and gossip.

"Yeah." I sighed dreading what it would say.

"Open it then." He grinned.

I walked away from him and went to my gulch to get some privacy before my public execution.

I opened the letter, realising as I tore the envelope that I was shaking. The letter started normally and I felt for a minute that my anguish would be dragged out further. She hadn't received my letter, surely? After three pages of boyfriend, girlfriend chit chat the words, 'YOU BASTARD' leapt out at me scrawled in capitals diagonally across the page feelings of betrayal. At least she didn't hate me as much as I did. I was now at rock bottom. I put the letter into my locker and after dragging on my brown lace-up beer boots, my jeans and T-shirt from the day before I headed off to the Victoria.

"Hey Toneeeeeeey!" Bruce walked up and put his arm across my shoulders almost as soon as I entered the pub.

"I ain't fucking drinking Bruce," I told him, fighting to keep my tears in.

"What'll it be mate?" asked the stereotypical Aussie surf-dude bartender.

I looked at Bruce, then back at the Bartender.

"A beer with whisky chaser please."

"That's my boy!" Bruce shook my shoulders and wandered off.

I slammed back the unadulterated single malt and immediately asked for another. Tipping back the beer I found within moments all thoughts of the letter had passed. I had only been gathering strength at the bar for a few minutes when Bruce came back to tell me he was off again to Herbies to find Kylie and her mum.

"I'll catch you up mate, just gonna take my time here for a bit," I told him.

"No problem, you know where it is." He grinned.

Several drinks later I walked out of the bar. I was secretly hoping that Jo would turn up which is why I hung around there for longer. While waiting I sunk more beers complimented again with whisky chasers. I didn't want to just drown my sorrows, I was intent on committing sorrow genocide! A little later, and in the absence of Jo I decided to head for Herbies. Bruce was pretty good at finding ladies and he may have caught some more. I realised after about a quarter of an hour of walking that I didn't have a clue where I was going. My navigation skills for finding my way back to the ship when drunk were second to none. But tonight my Beer Compass was failing me and after another twenty minutes of walking around in circles I gave up and headed, instead, for the next available watering hole I could find.

Entering the large open plan bar I felt immediately at ease. Although there was, in common with most bars in Darwin, surprisingly few people in I still felt like those that were there weren't offended by the pissed Brit strolling in off the street. I took a seat at the bar and as the bartender approached decided on a change of poison as it was, apparently as good as a rest.

"Can I have a Guinness please boss?" I asked.

"Yep." replied the barman.

He reached behind to a fridge and pulled out a bottle of Guinness, cracked the top and handed it to me along with a glass.

"You're from Cornwall!" he said as I took hold of the bottle in one hand and the glass in the other.

He didn't so much as ask me, as tell me so. I was impressed, even Brummie cop only got the rough region by my dialect. This guy got the County right. He was roughly in his fifties with mostly grey hair, fairly shortish but by no means a short ass.

"Yeah!" I replied, confirming his suspicion.

"I'm from Gunnislake," he said.

"Bloody hell, small world." I smiled, "I'm from Padstow."

"Don't you recognise me?" asked my Cornish bartender.

I stared hard at him thinking he may be a long lost relative or something. He seemed pretty sure that I *should* recognise him.

I apologised, "Nope!"

He looked a little disappointed.

"Plymouth Argyle?" he continued.

"Nope, sorry mate don't follow football that much."

"Everton?" he said.

"Sorry buddy but I don't recognise ya." I still wasn't impressed, other than meeting a fellow Cornishman of course.

"I'm Mike Trebilcock!" he extended his hand.

"Tony Wilton." I shook it.

"Were you good then?" I asked.

Was then followed was a quick summary of the 1966 FA Cup Final.

"I scored two goals against Sheffield Wednesday during the second half of the match."

Mike explained how Everton had reached the final without conceding a single goal but in the last hurdle against Sheffield Wednesday, they found themselves two-nil down. During the second half, Mike stuffed one in the net from about twelve yards then five minutes later followed it with another after a free-kick by Sheffield Wednesday went astray. Now level at two-two it remained tight for a while until another Everton player stuck a third in giving Everton their first FA Cup win since 1933.

I was so impressed by the little bartender that I felt the very least I could do was to ask him for another Guinness, so I did.

A regular at the pub was sat propping up the end of the bar and sounded as though he'd heard Mike's story before, probably quite a few times. He was a huge bloke and looked like a cross between Shirley Crabtree aka Big Daddy and Windsor Davis. At his feet was a briefcase and after a bit of chat, Battery Sergeant Major

Tudor Williams told me that he was in town for a meeting.

"You don't look dressed for a meeting?" I pointed out, referring to his jeans, cowboy boots and lumberjack shirt.

"It's an Aussie meeting," he said, "I flew in earlier in me chopper."

"Oh right." I nodded, the pinch of salt going down well with my Guinness.

"You with that HMS Sheffield boat?" he asked.

Resisting the temptation to mimic my brother with, 'Boats go under the water, ships go on top!' so I agreed with Windsor Crabtree. I didn't wish to overcomplicate things besides by now I was smashed and speech was getting tricky.

"If you let me drive your boat, I'll let you fly me helicopter."

"Alright mate, no problem." I laughed.

After a couple hours of yarning and killing the pool table, happy in my new local and having given up on any chance of finding either Bruce or Herbies club, I stomped back to the Sheffield to get some food.

Returning on board about 18:00 hours I found that I didn't have the energy to eat. The fresh air of the walk had wiped me out and opted to crash out on the mess seats instead although collapse unconscious would've been more accurate. Luckily it was fairly empty and I met little resistance until however 'Evening Rounds' were due to be conducted. Tug was acting as Duty Weapons Engineer and as such had cleaned the mess deck ready for evening rounds. He had also placed me in the recovery position and gratefully put a bucket on the floor below my head which I was slowly filling with a black liquid which I kept bringing up from the depths of my stomach.

At bang on 19:10 hours, a long whistle blast or 'pipe' was heard at the top of the ladder to 3G mess and the Officer of the Day descended. The three or four lads who weren't braving Darwin on night two stood at attention for Lieutenant Phil Gascoigne Royal Navy. I just lay there, completely sparko. My ears started to absorb a conversation above me but I was unable to respond to it.

"Is he alright Tug?" asked Phil.

"It's Tony Sir." Tug replied.

"I can see that," it was obvious to see why Phil was a Lieutenant and Tug wasn't, "is he OK?' he repeated.

"Yes Sir, it's Tony," said Tug.

"Make sure he keeps breathing."

"Will do Sir."

With that, he was gone. Roughly an hour passed when I felt Tug give me a sharp slap across the face.

"Uh?"

It was the most intelligent thing I'd said all night.

"Better get to bed Tone, you're fucked."

I ignored Tug, stood bolt upright and picking up my bucket walked up the ladder and left the mess. Two minutes later I returned the bucket, washed out and clean from puke before striding off the ship and headed towards town to drink more beer.

I woke with a start the next day about five in the morning being shaken by the Bosun's Mate.

"Tony!" he shook my ears awake first.

"Tone!" he shook again.

"The fuck is it?" I complained.

"You're Duty LWEM today," he informed me.

"Yeah. think so, why?" I was praying for an easy question.

"There's some bloke on the jetty," the Bosuns Mate seemed a bit concerned, "he's been sleeping there all night."

"So?" I was a little puzzled as to why this should concern me.

"He dragged you back to the ship last night cos you could barely walk."

"Oh?" now I was puzzled.

"You were bought back about one in the morning, then the bloke lay on the jetty and went sleep, he said he's taking the ship for a spin and asked for you?"

His words helped me to recall being back in the bar with Mike and Windsor the night before. I'd gone there after leaving the mess in a semi-conscious drunken state.

"Right, fuck! I'll be up in a minute."

I grabbed my working rig out my locker and made my way up top to the gangway. The sun was already breaking through and as I approached the Quartermaster he pointed towards a figure on the jetty.

"Your mate?" he asked.

"Yeah, I think so." I nodded as much as my sore head would allow

I crossed the gangway and strolled down to see Windsor Crabtree who was looking intensely at the ship.

"How's your head mate?" he asked.

"It'll start to hurt in a while I expect," I told Windsor.

"You were doing well, knocking back the Guinness like a fish," he said, "then your legs went."

"We couldn't leave ya there so I picked ya up and carried ya back to the boat."

"Bloody 'ell mate, cheers!" I thanked him as I could barely remember anything from the evening.

"So when do I get to drive her?" Windsor asked.

"Drive what?"

"The boat," he pointed at the Sheffield, "You said I could drive her round the bay in exchange for a go in me helicopter."

I was suddenly aware of the Quartermaster and Bosun's Mate laughing their heads off behind me and I was beginning to appreciate how one of our artificers, Noddy, felt when he accidentally told some ex-pats in the Middle-East that he was a Captain only to find they had all arrived for a guided tour the following day.

"I was joking mate, you can't..."

"I'm taking the piss Tony, you take it easy pal," he laughed, "I needed to get a clear head before I flew home so I got me head down here for a bit."

"Thank fuck for that," I laughed nervously, "I thought you were serious."

"Tell ya what though Tone," he added.

"What?"

"She don't look too bad does she?" he said, eyeing the ship up and down.

"Brushes up well," I said agreeing with him.

"You wouldn't know she was hit by that Exocet in the Falklands," said Windsor, "It's amazing what you can do with a lick of paint. Anyway, cheers mate, see you on the ice."

With that final remark, Windsor turned and strolled off up the jetty. I didn't bother explaining that this was a different HMS Sheffield and I watched him wander off for a few yards before I walked back on board across the gangway. I'd spent just two minutes listening to the Quartermaster talking about Windsor sleeping off the beer on the jetty when we were interrupted by the sound of a whining turbine of some sort. As the noise increased we glanced in the direction of the racket and spotted a small yellow helicopter, a crop duster at most, in a far corner of a car park spinning it's rotors.

"Oh, it's his!" exclaimed the Quartermaster, "I was wondering who that belonged to?"

The small budgie had been there since we had and no one had taken any notice of it. In the following seconds, we watched Windsor lift off the ground and disappear.

"It's a different world down here innit?" said the Bosun's Mate.

"Sure is," I couldn't argue.

At least I was up early enough to get breakfast and after a strong coffee with full English, my only challenge for the day was to attend a duty-watch muster on the flight deck at 07:30 hours where I tried not to breathe too much alcohol on to the Officer of the Day. With all the fun being had in Darwin there was a very relaxed atmosphere surrounding the entire ship including those on duty. At the end of Duty Watch musters the Duty Petty Officer gets swamped by those wishing for an early heads-up on any forthcoming fire exercises that may be thrown at us during the day and today was no exception. In anticipation of such a question, the Duty Petty Officer turned to us and struck the flint on his Zippo lighter.

"For exercise, for exercise, fire, fire, fire! Fire on the flight deck!" he declared quietly.

With a sharp puff, he blew the flame out.

"Fire's out! End of exercise."

That was today's fire exercise over and done with.

Along with Bruce, several other lads on board gave cause for concern especially over their state of mind. Being tattooed in the dockyard at Manilla is one example. The sort of tattoo purchased can also convince your mates that your lift doesn't go all the way to the top floor.

Cheesy Bellringer, a Dabber from 3G, was also on duty today and as the mess filled with those fighting to get changed for a day out in Oz, Cheesy took the opportunity to show off his newly acquired 'arrow' tattoo he'd had in town the day before. Yes, a single vertical arrow. To help deter theft of government property from the dockyard all tools and equipment are marked with a rather crude arrow usually pointing straight up. In his wisdom, Cheesy had the same stick-like arrow tattooed onto his stick-like right leg. Nothing else, just an arrow to confirm he was government property.

Some other oddball behaviour which rose to the surface in Darwin was exhibited by Nick Devon, a Radio Operator from 3G. He had found a passion for collecting dead things. At least Bruce's chicken was alive when he bought it back to the ship. During his visit to Oz, Nick had so far had purchased a pair of horns from some cow-like thing, a small crocodiles head mounted on a wooden shield, a kangaroos head mounted in the same way, a wallaby skin and last but not least a purse made from the ball sack of a kangaroo. The duty day passed without hitch and the next day was soon upon us. Our final day in Darwin.

I spent that day considerably more sober than the first two. I saw it slamming back Sambruca's in the strip club followed by returning to the club that I'd found myself sleeping outside of in a camper van a couple of days before. The girl on the door even remembered me and bombarded me with questions about the UK. I did the 'oh if you're in town we can get together for a drink' bit and before I knew it she had told me her name and had written her phone number down for me. I wasn't sure if she realised how far Cornwall was from Darwin, either that or the local girls were as desperate to get out of Darwin as I was to get out the Navy.

The end of my last night saw me getting as much food as possible from a local takeaway, I had to use up the Aussie dollars after all. For those of us that collected foreign currency or had relatives that did, this abundance of ickies left over at the end of each visit was never a problem but the majority of us would either spend it or simply give away all that was left. This is common behaviour for Matelots running back to a ship on their last day in port. One little homeless bloke sat on the side of the road under a pile of newspapers during my visit to the Caribbean Island of Montserrat in 1991 got the shock of his life when he was caught on the direct flight path of the Matelots returning to the PAS boat from the town. The first two or three lads handed him their remaining ickies, about five pounds worth, followed by nearly every single Matelot that walked past him. It must've made his year. Even those who missed him were pointed back in his direction while they waited for the boat to turn up. In exchange for my loose change, he offered some friendly advice as it was clear we are in a rush for the boat. He told us in a slow Caribbean drool, "Hey *slooow doooooown*. If you walk too fast you'll run off da land and end up in da sea!"

Good advice for life in general.

We waved farewell to Australia, unhappy that we only had the one visit there but happy that the one we did have was Darwin. We all had our souvenirs to take home which meant by now, considering the stops we'd made elsewhere along the way, our lockers were bursting open but one of the lads had found the icing on the cake! Zipp Fly had got hold of a Rolf Harris greatest hits tape and it would soon prove to be very useful on the way home.

Chapter Thirteen

Hello Glastonbury

A ship homeward bound, for reasons that don't need explaining, is an environment of high emotion and charged positivity. It's a time to let your hair down a bit or even time for some to let their hair grow a bit. Although on the other side of the world we were still turning around and heading home. We had a very quick stop in Singapore planned but aside from that we were leaving the Far East behind us. It had become our Devonport dockyard of the Far East, much like Jebel Ali was for the Middle East. After this visit, we would be permitted the traditional beard-growing competition which gave young sailors the chance to see if they could manage to squeeze something credible out of their silky smooth faces and an excuse for some of the others to grow the most ridiculous beard possible.

There was a forthcoming SOD's Opera, Ships Operatic and Drama Society, to plan for as well. This was an opportunity, or rather an excuse, for all on board to have a dig at everyone else including the Captain and hierarchy. We could get away with being as un-politically correct as possible but the reality was that it was a good, whole ship, belly laugh with lots of beer to mark the end of the deployment. We needed an idea for 3G mess.

We slipped into Singapore one last time. This was our last chance to buy cheap electrical gear. I already had a car stereo I'd bought on an earlier stop in the trip when I was here so didn't need anything else however I took the opportunity to get hold of a beard trimmer for the forthcoming competition as I was intending to keep my facial fuzz once the fun was over.

It was fair to say that most of us just wanted to chill out in Singers and have a quiet beer. Well, why break the habit of a deployment. The stop was brief and uneventful. The parties carried on into the mess after we returned from ashore and the usual suspects like the fleet dentist, Nigel Somerset, were present.

Without paying much attention the deployment CD's, by either Jimmy Nail or The Eagles, were replaced temporarily by Rolf Harris and his greatest hits, 'ROLF RULES OK!'. The classic 'Tie Me Kangaroo Down Sport' was on the album along with a couple of others that wouldn't normally be associated with Rocker Rolf namely, his covers of 'Stairway to Heaven' and 'Satisfaction'.

It was these last two in particular that stood out and the introduction to his 'Stairway to Heaven' was all the inspiration we needed.

'There was an old Australian Rock Band, trying but dying. They get themselves up off their collective elbows, revert to their sixties instrumentation, and they try again.'

Bingo! We were going to put together an Australian Bush Band for 3G's entry into the SODs Opera. As I was the closest thing to a musician in the mess I took the responsibility of trying to organise something. Zipp Fly volunteered to take the lead role as Rolf and between us, we took the Rolf CD along with a CD player to the forward Seawolf Launcher office, somewhere we hoped we couldn't be snooped upon, and set about bastardising the lyrics to Satisfaction. We tried to make a tune dedicated to those dearest to us on board.

Chorus I can't get no satisfaction,
I can't get no split reaction,
'Cos I try, 'cos I try,
And I try, and I try,
And I try, and I try,
And I try, and I try,
I can't get no,
I can't get no.

When I'm lying in my rack,
And this bloke comes on the main broadcast,
And he's given me loads and loads and loads,
Of useless information,
S'pose to drive my imagination.
I can't get no,
No no no,
Hey hey hey.

Chorus

When I'm watching S.R.E.
Not tuned in by Jack Hatty,
And this bloke comes on and tells me,
What a big dog he can be,
But he can't be a dog 'cos he doesn't eat,
The same shit as me
I can't get no,
No no no,
Hey hey hey,
That's what I say.

Chorus

When I'm sailing round the world,
And I'm shagging this,
And I'm shagging that,
And I'm trying to take a days sea leave,
But the HODs say come back maybe next week,
CINC Fleets permission you must seek.
I can't get no,
I can't get no,
Satisfaction.

Actually, I can't get any!

The second line of the chorus, 'can't get no split reaction' was a reference to our female colleagues, while the first verse mentioned some old fart, the Jimmy, going on and on and on over the main broadcast. The second included our wonderful TV maintainer Jack Hatty and his inability to get us a decent picture when alongside in foreign ports. The same verse also popped a shot at our Supply Officers hopeless and quite bizarre big dog, little dog impressions and as he was in charge of the ship's stores including the food supplies it was only fair we had a dig at him for the food as well. The final verse dug at the general hierarchy and their reluctance to let us have more time off than they actually did. The whole concoction was sung to the tune of the Stones' Satisfaction with my accordion as the main instrument accompanied by Reggie on the sticks and Tug, Gary and Robbie with Didgeridoos. For a second song, we picked an Aussie style, Rolf Harris version of 'Stairway to Heaven'. We felt we couldn't change the lyrics, it was too much of a classic. The final song would be 'Two Little Boys' which we altered into a sexually explicit version about two little Wrens, another reference to our female colleagues, the double-breasted Matelots, and our broad imagination. For the intervals between songs, it was only fair that Rolf painted one of his famous masterpieces on a huge piece of white card at the rear of the stage. *D'ya know what it is yet?*

We were about a week away from the Sods Opera and as Zipp had no drawing ability what-so-ever I stuck together a couple large pieces of card and drew a very faint pencil outline of an object onto it. Only Zipp would be close enough to see it and he could then use a fat magic marker pen to go over the light pencil markings and, hey presto! The illusion would be complete. We made false beards and those of us who had bought Aussie bush hats dangled corks from the brims on strings. I dug out the one I'd got for my brother and did likewise.

Reluctant to leave people out, which was our excuse for getting as many people up on stage as possible thereby reducing the individual numpty factor for each of us, we made some wobble boards which could be wobbled in time with the tune. Each one had a Rolf-a-Roo drawn on masterfully by myself on the side. The practice run went better than expected and we were in danger of looking like we knew what we were doing. The acts were shrouded in secrecy to ensure maximum impact on the night but most people were so wrapped up in their party pieces that they weren't bothered about what other messes were doing.

The night was soon upon us and the evening couldn't have been better for it. A very gentle warm breeze was crossing across the flight deck as we cut through the water sailing west across the Indian ocean. Sailing smoothly on a flat calm sea with just moonlight for company allowed the lights from the stage to dazzle and give a fantastic atmosphere. The Petty Officers constructed a large stage on which the acts would appear complete with red and white curtains on either side that were drawn between performances. The thespians among us came out of the woodwork. Chairs were placed rows in front of the stage and beer crates appeared from nowhere. On the port side of the stage was the hi-tech equipment that would be used to measure the amount of applause each act received. In this case, the scale was known as the Clap-o-Meter and was an eight-foot penis the centre of which consisted of an arrow which climbed the height of the hard-on to indicate the success of the act. It was operated by the lovely Denise who wore a white Basque, mini-skirt and stockings with a blonde wig and looked a lot like our catering Petty Officer, Dennis. The tame acts were awarded with the pointer lifting to 'slight discharge' followed closely by 'squeezing.' The better acts crept up to a 'dribbling' followed by 'oozing' and finally the top acts were awarded with a 'pissing razor blades.' The final judge however would inevitably be the Captain so maybe it wasn't a good idea to dig at him too much.

The already well-oiled audience sat patiently until a loudspeaker announced the arrival of our host. Making a special trip out from the UK to visit us, we were honoured to be in the presence of Leading Seaman Micky Goble the 'HMS Brilliant reality TV star' or rather a Petty Officer dressed up to be Micky. He leapt through the gap in the curtains and failed miserably to inflate a condom that was stretched over his head. After it didn't work he sprayed the audience with his water pistol before beginning his introduction. After explaining the Clap-o-Meter the first act was introduced and on walked Crashy and Spicey, two of the chefs wearing thick jumpers and equally thick wigs, to the sound of 'Fanfare for the Common Man.'

Crashy kicked things off.

"Hello you seafaring, wave hopping, mega-ship tastic, get up at seven o'clock in the morning, type twenty-two people." he blurted through his pretend Radio DJ microphone.

They followed by having a chat about what each other had got up to the night before. Coriander Spice revealed how he was debating over a quiet night in or a quiet night out but as he didn't fancy wearing waves around his neck opted for a quiet night in his 'twenty-four man, can't see the TV for the smoke, livingroom mate!'

"Good Job," replied Crashy, "what a sight it would've been to see you wearing one of those darker than dark, clings to the skin so tight it looks like it was sprayed on, hydro-tastic, wear under the water wetsuits mate!"

The 'Smashy and Nicey' jibes continued until they introduced the next act, the Swillage People consisting of a navy fire-fighter, an NBCD man, a flight deck controller, a dockie and a first aider. They sang in the style of YMCA, 'It's fun to exercise NBCD!'

Then followed Crashy playing a bit of rock guitar as a piss-take of one of the rather large killick Stewards 'Buster' as he strutted around the stage eating pies. The Supply department certainly put a lot of work into their show and managed, in true comedy fashion, to poke most of the fun at themselves.

The Petty Officers jumped on next with the stumpy Matelot act involving a man stood on stage, his lower half hidden below a table and his arms disguised to look like his legs. Another man stood behind and put his arm around the outside of the shoulders of the man in front. The background was arranged in such a way that only the front man could be seen and the rear man's arms acted as those of the man in front. This presented an image of a 'Stumpy Matelot'.

The Petty Officers firstly proceeded to dig at the Navigation Officer, the Executive Officer and then the Wrens. The stumpy Matelot was charged before an imaginary Captains Table with misuse of government property, namely forcing a Wren to conduct an unnatural sexual act in the forward Tracker Office. He was instantly found guilty and given the maximum punishment, his draft on the Sheffield was extended until the completion of the following year's deployment. Stumpy Matelot then endured a costume change to play the part of a Wren, this included lipstick and a pair of inflated condoms pinned to the front of his shirt. The stumpy Wren was next in front the Captain's table facing the same charge of misusing government property, namely one Matelot and although she had, 'been cocked more times than the starboard twenty-millimetre gun', she was found not guilty, awarded ten pounds from the Captain's fund and given a Make 'n'

Mend in which to spend it. A stab at the *unintentional* use of kid gloves which the lads perceived were worn when the hierarchy dealt with some of the females on board. After the Table had concluded stumpy Matelot did a bit of circuit training flirting around the girls followed by a night out on the piss.

The Wrens were next up and had a tough job fighting through the heckling. Their sketch looked to be a serious observation of what a Matelot wants from a perfect Wren. A rather hand-carted young Wren continued to undergo cosmetic enhancements to satisfy her Matelot boyfriend, played by one of the Wren WAFU's. To the frustration of the Wren, once she had suffered the pain of her cosmetic changes the Matelot still wasn't happy with her. She asked what made the perfect Wren for him and on walked the Chief Gunnery Instructor, Bear, dressed in a grass skirt, sporting a black bra and a blonde wig. He stormed over and lip-locked the Wren WAFU to a round of applause.

The Chief's mess were next on and performed a Royal Navy careers office sketch. The first person to ask for a job in the Andrew was a young man who claimed to have been driving round and round in his battleship grey Skoda for hours. He was now lost and had run out of petrol. The Careers Officer, aka our WE Charge Chief, asked the chap three basic recruitment questions.

"Question one, moral is most important in the RN, how would you contribute to that?" asked the careers officer.

"That's very easy," replied the candidate, "I think a few high speed turns at mealtime should sort that out."

"Question two, you are required to rendezvous with a tanker in twenty-four hours, what would you do?"

"Go balls out, arrive early and steam around in circles to waste as much fuel as possible to make the replenishment worthwhile!" he answered.

"Question three, how many satellite navigation systems would a warship require to prevent it from getting lost?"

"Errrr, three minimum!" came the quick reply.

"What you have to bear in mind here is that Christopher Columbus discovered the new world with a needle floating on the top of a bucket of water," added the careers officer.

"Well, in that case, I don't think it really matters how many nav-aids you have, if the right man is at the chart you will still get lost!" declared the candidate.

The candidate was snapped up by the careers officer and sent to the Royal Naval School of Navigation. Three further candidates stood in front of the careers officer and were promptly ripped up for arse paper.

A few acts came and went before the Wardroom came on stage with their performance. It consisted of the younger junior officers popping shots at the older senior officers, but mainly the Jimmy who whilst wearing a camouflage jacket, United Nations beret and Bermuda shorts declaring how he would burn all the mail on the flight-deck before having a huge nervous breakdown and running around the stage shouting like a Dalek from Doctor Who.

Before I could get to see more acts I was dragged away to get the guys together for 3G's Bush band. False beards were fitted however as the beard competition was now well underway Gary and myself had something beginning to resemble beards of our own. Tug amusingly discovered when wearing his that he resembled Sinn Fein President Gerry Adams. We adjourned to the confines of the helicopter hanger, waited our turn and on cue set ourselves up behind the large closed curtains.

Through all of the heckling and cheering that other acts had received we noticed an eerie silence from the audience on the other side of the curtain. This spooky feeling made even more so by the sounds of Tug, Gary and Robbie on the port side of the stage blowing air through their Didgeridoos. This was subtle enough to make the audience sit still and listen rather than shouting us down before we started. Zipp was centre stage with his large piece of card placed upright behind him and the remainder of us stood on the starboard side, me with my accordion and the others with the wobble boards and sticks.

After a minute of Didgeridoos, Gary shouted to the audience from behind the curtain.

"HELLO GLASTONBURY!"

It was the signal for the curtains to be opened and there stood the 3G mess Australian Bush band in all its glory. Zipp gave a Rolf cough and turned to crack on with drawing his masterpiece. He started by filling in a small black upside-down triangle in the middle of the board. He then drew over a few of the lines either side but did just enough for the picture to remain a mystery.

"D'ya know what it is yet?" he asked the audience in his best 'Rolf'.

With that, I struck up the squeezebox and the lads cranked up the wobble boards.

"I can't get no, satisfaction, I can't get no split reaction!" sung Zipp Harris.

We decided to get the tricky one out of the way first, it also contained nice digs at some of the ship's company so hopefully it would get some laughs.

Zipp strutted around the stage in a fantastic Rolf walk that even Rolf Harris wouldn't attempt, shrugging his shoulders in time with the music and giving it lots of loud, *'OOO AAH! OOO AAH's!'*

After knocking out our version of 'Satisfaction' and receiving a very reassuring round of applause and cheers, Reggie cleared the lyric boards from the stage floor and replaced 'Satisfaction' with 'Stairway to Heaven'. Zipp turned to continue his artwork drawing two large breasts and long hair.

"A little bit here, a little bit there," Zipp faced the audience, "D'ya know what it is yet?"

"YEEEEEAHH!" came the universal yell followed by more applause.

That was the cue once again for my squeezebox, the wobble boards and Reggie with his sticks.

"There was an old Australian Rock Band..." started Zipp.

We broke into 'Stairway' and went through without a hitch. The classical rock anthem cowered under our tuneful voices. On completion of that the curtains were drawn across and the SODs Opera host, now wearing a smart suit, emerged onto the front of the stage and asked the audience if they wished for an encore.

"YEEAAAH!" came the unanimous reply.

We must've been doing something right. The curtains parted again signalling the final song of the 3G Aussie Bush band's first, and last, live performance.

This time with no musical accompaniment we all sang, "Two little Wrens, had two little toys, each had a rubber cock."

Three songs sang and it was over before we knew it. Ladies and Gentleman, Elvis had left the building. After a short pause the results came in, Crashy and Spicey deservedly won the night with their performance and the Wrens mess picked up the wooden spoon. 3G's Australian Bush band came in a respectable second place. We were happy.

After the fun of the SODs Opera, it was back to normal running. A few days passed and the beard competition concluded with those who had grown a real beard being given the option to keep it if they wished. The Navy insists that its men shave daily and although moustaches are not allowed, full beards are. The permission to 'cease shaving' must be written on a request chit and submitted to the hierarchy via department head. The sailor is then given two weeks to grow a beard before it is inspected by the Joss to see if it is satisfactory. Those whose beards are not up to scratch have to then shave them off.

HMS Sheffield sat patiently in the Red Sea awaiting the traffic lights in the Suez Canal to go green signalling a mass one-way charge north of ships transiting the narrow passage. It was time for all those who didn't get to see the Pyramids on the trip south to disembark the ship and jump on a coach. Tug, Jack Daniels and me were included on this excursion. Along with a handful of others, we left the Sheffield and after a long coach trip north, stopped at a papyrus paper factory and were given the opportunity to buy some freshly made traditional Egyptian notepaper. The coach then drove us to watch the fabulous pyramid light show which featured in the James Bond film 'The Spy Who Loved Me' when the villain's henchman Jaws ate some poor little local chap who'd been waiting for Mr Bond, told the story behind the Great Pyramids of Giza and was well worth the visit.

It was an impressive affair with huge coloured lights exposing the pyramids in all their glory accompanied by a huge booming narration. The show over we were allowed to wander about Cairo and get a taste of local life. This was relaxed and worry-free until one Matelot bought some postcards from a local trader for a pound, he handed over a one pound coin to the immediate fury of the local who was only able to change notes at his local currency exchange, not coins. We were not able to convince the trader that one pound notes no longer existed and he followed us into a nearby cafe ranting and raving how we had ripped him off. After a spot of negotiation, a Scottish pound note was exchanged for the pound coin. Wandering back to our hotel we stumbled across Sheffield's helicopter pilot looking a little on the wasted side. He was sat on an old creaky chair all on his own, his lips clamped firmly around the working parts of a hubbly-bubbly pipe.

Our hotel was a good one with all of the typical tourist mod-cons and offering a view over Cairo. I was sharing a room with Jack Daniels and after pissing about with the bidet bum washer, 'Crocodile Dundee' in the bathroom we set about destroying the mini-bar.

The next day saw us on the coach and off to the pyramids themselves. They were, as to be expected, a magnificent sight and I was surprised to discover that we were allowed inside one. This wasn't as much fun as climbing up the outside but soon found that there were large signs everywhere telling us not to do that. Whoops, must have missed them. The tourist Police were very nice about it all the same. Tug and me opted for a quick camel ride but found the operator to be a rip off merchant. As we admired the view we noticed that the camel was being taken further and further away from the pyramids, the operator then insisted on a second payment for us to get off. We refused and threatened instead to re-arrange his face and break his legs if he didn't let us down which worked quite well. The universal fist signal never fails and works even better when accompanied by 'FUCKING FUCKER FUCK YOU FUCK TWAT!' is shouted at the subject. The tour of the Pyramids concluded we jumped back onto the coach and went to the Museum of Cairo which was as spectacular as the Pyramids themselves. Once there we saw the Mask of Tutankhamun along with some important dead people wrapped up in bandages. They had clearly been to a Navy Sick Bay for a plaster.

That was Cairo out the way. In Summary, some Pyramids, some old stuff, something called a sphincter and a quick overnighter with no time to get properly pissed. Joking aside it was a refreshing change to see some culture instead of the bottom of a bottle. We met the Ship at the top of the Suez, Port Siad, and were then off into the Mediterranean Sea. Mainland Europe was within paddling distance.

The sense of excitement on board would have been obvious to any alien species dropping in for a visit. Letters from loved ones asked about what time they should be at Devonport Dockyard to greet the ship and where they should park. The Fleet Form 3's, a form allowing friends and family entry to the confines of Her Majesties dockyard, were being stamped and sent home. Many of the lads were writing their last letters home, signing them, 'See ya shortly!' or 'See ya in a couple of weeks'. We only had Gibraltar to stop in at and then it was North across the Bay of Biscay for Plymouth. The old and worn-out clothes which had looked after us so well on the trip were being thrown into the ship's incinerator, the souvenirs were being checked over and some were being bought out from their storage in the depths of the ship. The evening piss ups became heavier and heavier but no one cared. The atmosphere on board was electric.

In the middle of the Mediterranean, we were permitted a 'Hands to Bathe'. The ship stopped dead in the water and applied the hand brake, scramble nets were dropped over the waists enabling us to climb back on board from the sea. The Bear took up the role as shark sentry and stood on the aft Seawolf Launcher deck with a whistle and an SA80 Rifle. Those who wished to go for a dip made their way to the upper deck armed with speedos, bikinis and Bermudas. The brave ones among the ship's company took headfirst dives from the highest possible platforms, usually the aft Tracker deck. I was happy to jump in from the flight deck. The only thing we had to remember was that a long blast from the ship's siren indicated that time was up for our swim and a long blast on the whistle from the shark sentry meant, *'SHARK!'*

We also had the ever-watchful rigid-inflatable boat whizzing around nudging back any Matelots who floated too far from the ship.

Hands to Bathe could last anywhere between half-hour to an hour depending on the weather, shipping and generosity of the Captain. Ours lasted about twenty minutes.

Bear, being one of the most efficient Chief Petty Officers ever to hold the rank, was religiously strict when it came to his professional standards, even more so surrounding the use of firearms and would never allow skylarking of any sort with a weapon. Therefore it came as a surprise when he blew his whistle.

"Bear's fucking about, a quick way to get us out the water!" came a throwaway remark from one of the heads bobbing about in the sea.

But it was soon obvious that the remark was made by someone who wasn't watching what Bear was doing. Those of us who decided to watch Bear saw that he, in turn, was watching an area of water just off the port side of the waist. He looked as though he was concentrating on this area quite heavily. Most of the lads started to swim casually towards a ladder that had been dropped from the Quarter-deck. Bear blew his whistle again and those of us that looked up at him saw him make ready his SA80 rifle by pulling back on the cocking lever and chambering a round. Bear then aimed at a patch of water. The site of fifty Matelots all doing a Sharon Davies back to the ship was something to behold. We scrambled up the nets and fought for spaces on the ladder. 'I'm alright Jack' is the phrase most appropriate at this point. The sea was vacated in about two minutes. When we eventually caught up with Bear he expressed his concerns over the guest.

"I blew the first whistle when I saw it. It was a little one, a baby," he said, "but then Mum appeared so I the whistle again."

Hand brake off, up revs, away we go.

What can you say about Gibraltar? Well, the wonderful thing about 'Gib' is that it feels like the front gates to the UK, more so for Matelots than anyone else. A stop here when deploying hammers home the message that you've left Blighty whereas a stop on the way home feels like you're as good as home. My brother was based here on board the concrete warship, HMS Rooke, for some length of time. A draft which appealed to me as I felt Gibraltar was a piece of Britain with some nice bits of Spain thrown in for good measure. We were dropping in for a night to refuel and it presented an opportunity for the ship's company with leave to taste some British beer in British Pubs, eat Fish and Chips and generally have one final blow-out before they would have to exercise restraint in front of loved ones and family at home. Gibraltar, a half-way house for deployment orphans.

One formality conducted before entering any 'foreign' port is for the ships writers to post a list requesting all who require currency for that port to enter their names and an approximate amount of foreign ickies required. This was imaginatively referred to as the 'money changing list'. As the ship purchased foreign currency before arrivals, the only time the list was not published was when the ships writers felt they had enough foreign currency to cope with the demand. Such was the case in Gibraltar. The remaining few days steaming across the Med had not heard a whisper about money changing but the day before entering Gib the following pipe was broadcast.

"D'ya hear there! Money changing for Gibraltar will take place at the ship's office in five-minutes time, all those wishing to change money are to muster there now!"

There was nothing unusual about this pipe, it had been heard countless times during the deployment and within minutes there was a considerable queue from the ship's office stretching along the length of the flat. About thirty people were gathered with their cheque books at the ready, some folk profiling the cheques to speed the whole process along. Every so often a Matelot would walk past the queue and ask, "Money changing for Gib? How much you getting?"

This was followed by sniggers and those in the queue puzzling as to why. It would usually take about fifteen minutes before someone decided to ask the Ships Writer in the office, who wasn't showing any of the normal signs of opening the cash safe for business, what currency was used in Gibraltar and when they were told they used British Pounds like 'we use in the UK' that the ruse was rumbled. The line quickly dispersed with the gullible sailors all trying desperately to conceal cheque books in their pockets as they hurried back to their lockers. It was a cheap laugh at the deployment virgins on their first visit to 'The Rock'.

This was our last chance to go out in some decent sunshine, were we four days from home but the weather couldn't have been more different. The bars in Gibraltar are countless and we visited as many as possible throughout the night, the joys of having a pint of ale instead of a bottle or a litre of trendy lemon-infused lager were enormous. The local girls were well used to the Navy and to try and chat one up was a pretty daunting task. Once a few beers had gone down though I thought I would give it a try. Well, when in Gib!

I got chatting with Maria who was popping out for a few beers with her mate. She was a couple of years younger than me and looked every bit the sexy Spanish girl although she was a patriotic Giblet. I seemed to be doing quite well with her but the moment of truth came towards the end of the night when she offered to give me night-time tour of the rock on the back of her moped. An offer not to be refused. A slight reversal to what I was familiar with I took the pillion seat and also full advantage of the situation by going for a grope while her hands were occupied on the handlebars. After about two miles I managed to break her concentration and after striking a kerb with her wheel plus the additional weight of myself the rear tyre finally gave up life and deflated. We were in the back of beyond and after pushing the moped clear of the road Maria offered me some true Gibraltar hospitality against a wall at the side of the road.

The day before our arrival at our home port Plymouth and the Sheffield in common with all Naval ships had to clear customs and to do this we sailed down to Falmouth where HM Customs Officers came on board to go through the necessary. This was frustrating mainly because we are so close to home, especially being a Cornish boy I could see my home County albeit from a distance. It is also frustrating because one perk of having to spend so much time away from the UK on one of Her Majesty's big grey war canoe's should be that we're able to avoid the Government's pursuit of extra pennies at every single opportunity. To clear customs faster a list is requested from each sailor as to the items that he or she has purchased abroad and now intends to declare. I put on the souvenirs I had bought along with a small camera I'd picked up in Dubai and the car stereo from Singapore. I was charged a pittance for items, more of a token gesture and a 'thanks for declaring *some* stuff.' After this ritual from the Tax Man, the night was our own for our final night at sea, a night the Navy call 'Channel night'.

It is difficult to explain how time appears to pass on board a ship during a deployment such as the seven month Australasia '95 trip. Every single day takes an eternity, and those at either end of the deployment longer still. Seven months is by no means the longest deployment in the Royal Navy, not even close. History is however beginning to repeat itself and deployments are getting longer, especially as the ships are getting fewer. It is becoming commonplace for nine-month deployments especially but this is still thankfully a long way from the older Navy of thirty or forty years previous when a two-year deployment could be expected but at least then the men could rely on a tot of Nelson's blood at around 11:30 hours each day.

Knowing that we were now steaming along the East coast of Cornwall gave everyone on board the excuse that was needed to celebrate channel night, when we got closer to Plymouth we would take a position out in the channel waiting for the following day when we would sail into Devonport dockyard. This night was originally known as Channel Fever and was the term for the feeling of general excitement over the ship when approaching home port. The beer bosun had saved as much beer as possible over the last few days and with the stereo's on full volume in each mess deck the parties erupted. After the homecoming the following day, the bonding of the last seven months would disappear and we would refer to each other by rank instead of name once again. Nigel the Dentist and Phil the DWEO would be 'Sir' again and no longer 'mate'. Bear would be 'Chief' and Brum would be, well, Brum would still be a twat.

When leaving Plymouth seven months earlier it felt like this night would never come. The 'days to go' charts which a few lads had started usually never got past the first month before they would be ripped from the wall in desperation. Those who managed to keep one going filled in the final box with a felt tip, slowly and ceremoniously.

With Jimmy Nail and The Eagles playing away at full volume we all got very, *very* drunk!

October 13th 1995 and the last official day of Australasia '95 started early on-board HMS Sheffield.

"Clear lower deck, clear lower deck. All personnel are to muster on the flight deck in five-minutes time."

The 'clear lower deck' was a quick 'well done' chat from the Captain but tainted slightly by the 'enjoy your three weeks off lads but be ready to work your arses off when you come back in November' speech which he tagged skilfully on to the end. With that formality out of the way it just remained for us to get back down below and drag our Number 1's from the suit lockers.

"Hands to harbour stations, hands to harbour stations, assume NBCD state one condition yankee. Close all screen doors and hatches. All hands to muster on the upper deck for procedure alpha."

After a slow sail along the River Tamar, the feeling of accomplishment and joy cannot be explained, Matelots who would normally stand upright to attention come hell or high water, were waving their arms about like demented five-year-olds home from a school trip. Two tug boats pulled up and threw lines across to help us in for the final few metres. Those who had already spotted their loved ones were running to the part of the ship which was nearest to them and yelling. The families on the dockyard wall were doing likewise. I had kept the beard with the full intention of giving my family a laugh when I got home and as I stood on the port side of the boat deck I watched my mum, dad and big brother busily searching the length of the ship with their eyes, trying to find me in the sea of square rig uniform. The band of the Her Majesty's Royal Marines marched up and down the jetty playing, 'Heart of Oak' showing off proudly why, in my opinion, they are the best military band in the world. I knew for sure Abby wouldn't be there but I secretly hoped in some crazy 'I forgive you' act that she would be.

As the tug boats nudged us ever closer to the wall at Frigate alley I stood adjacent my family gripping the guard rail. I watched them, smiling to myself. I waited.

"Fifty feet!" I heard the captain radioing someone elsewhere on the ship as he looked over the edge to judge the gap between us and the jetty.

I was beginning to wonder how long it would take for my folks to recognise me...

"Thirty feet!"

...I was no longer sure that I was able to recognise myself, not after this trip.

"Twenty feet!"

Then from the jetty, my Mum looked straight at me and smiled.

Epilogue

'Pull up a bollard and I'll spin you a dit!'

Ask any 'Old Salt' to talk about his deployments and, providing you have their trust I guarantee that you will be privy to some tales of the most hilarious and insane behaviour imaginable. It usually helps if you request is accompanied by liberal quantities of real ale and quality spirits. It will be nearly impossible for him to tell you about anything other than the good times as the bad times seem to fade and disappear quickly from memory.

No doubt some Matelots will tell you how they have dined with Royalty, drank a bar dry with Hollywood A-listers, fought with locals, stolen a car, inadvertently foiled a bank robbery or re-built a town after a disastrous earthquake and maybe some have. I expect a few stories have been embellished slightly but will be based heavily on true events.

Sailors come from many different backgrounds but with just a beer fridge to keep them company for long periods until they reach the safety of a port it is easy to see why their sense of humour is somewhat 'unique'.

The Royal Navy continues to change daily, old sailors retire and new Nozzer's take their place. Old ships are sold to foreign powers and new ones (that, let's be honest, are never as good) replace them. The traditions however will always continue within the spirit of her men.

'Hearts of Oak, Men of Steel.'

Glossary

Jack-Speak is a commonly used collection of words and phrases many of which have found their way into everyday use in both the naval and civilian language. This glossary is by no means the definitive guide to Jack-Speak. There are, no doubt, historical and more in-depth meanings for many of the terms used in this book. This glossary is merely an aid to their layman's use within 'Groovers On Manoeuvres'.

AB	Able Seaman, a naval rank.
Adrift	Late, not on time.
Aft or After	The Rear, to the rear of.
AGR	Gas Mask.
Alongside	Tied up in port or in harbour.
Andrew (The)	The Royal Navy.
Anti-flash	Protective clothing worn on the face and hands to protect against radiated heat
AWOL	Absent Without Leave.
BASCCA	Breathing Apparatus Self-Contained Compressed Air.

Berth	Where we park the ship!
Bezzie Ops	Best Mate.
BM	Bosun's Mate.
Boot-neck/Royal	Royal Marine Commando.
BOST	Basic Operational Sea Training.
Bosun	Abbreviation of Boatswain, responsible for seamanship functions.
Bridge	The compartment with the windows at the front from where the ship is driven.
Brunch	Late breakfast/Early Lunch.
Budgie	Helicopter.
Buffer	see CBM.
Bulk-head	Compartment wall.
CAAIS	Computer Assisted Action Information System.
CACS	Computer Assisted Command System.
Captain's Table	A Disciplinary Hearing.
CBM	Chief Bosun's Mate.
Cheers Easy	Thank you very much!
Chit or Chitty	Note or Piece of paper usually with instructions or directions written on it.
CINC Fleet	Commander In Chief of the Fleet (An Admiral in charge)
Citadel	Airtight condition employed by a Royal Navy warship to help combat a nuclear, biological or chemical threat.
Civvies	Civilians/Civilian clothing.
CPO	Chief Petty Officer.
Dabber	Seaman.

Deck	Compartment floor.
Deck-head	Compartment ceiling.
Dhobey	Derived from Hindi refers now to the act of washing. Also name given to the Chinese 'Laundry' contractor on board
Dits	Tales or stories.
Divisions	Parade.
Draft	Posting to ship or shore establishment.
DWEO	Deputy Weapons Officer.
Ex-Pats	Ex-patriots, British Citizens living abroad.
Flat	Open space between compartments.
Fleet Form 3	Official Pass enabling a member of the public into the dockyard to visit a specific ship.
Flight deck	Part of ship for the landing and taking off of helicopters.
FMG	Fleet Maintenance Group.
Fore or Forward	The Front, to the front.
Fo'c's'le	Forecastle (pronounced folksel).
Galley	Ships kitchen.
Gangway	The walkway placed from the ship to jetty
Gash	Rubbish.
Gizzit	A souvenir obtained usually under difficult circumstances often without the owners permission. *"Give us it!"*
Greenie	Weapons Engineer/Electrician.

Gulch	WalkwayGap between a set of bunks.
Guzz	Devonport Dockyard
Half blues	see "Nos 5's"
Hands to Bathe	When the ship stops in the middle of the sea for the crew to have a swim
Harry black maskers	Black masking tape.
Heads	Ships toilets, which were historically situated at the ship's head.
Helo	Helicopter.
HMS	Her Majesty's Ship.
HMS Raleigh	Royal Navy basic training establishment located at Torpoint, Cornwall.
HOD	Heads of Department.
Hooky	Leading Rate, derived from the small anchor worn on the arm.
HQ1	Head Quarters 1.
Icky (Ickies)	Any foreign currency.
Jack	Member of the Royal Navy.
Jack with Bumps	Female Matelot.
Jack Dusty	Naval Stores
Jossman or Joss	Master-at-Arms.
Keel Hauled	Unconfirmed historical Naval punishment involving a person being dragged underneath the Keel of a vessel on a rope. Usually fatal.
Killick	Leading Rate, derived from the small anchor worn on the arm
LH or LS	Leading Hand, Naval Rank.
Lusty	HMS Illustrious.

Make 'n' Mend	An afternoon off work, traditionally a period set aside for Jack to repair his kit, 'to make and mend'.
Matelot	Serving member of the RN from middle-French pronounced 'mat-low'.
MEM	Marine Engineering Mechanic (see stoker)
Mess/Messdeck	Personnel recreation living quarters
Mob	Royal Navy.
MOB	Man overboard.
MOD	Ministry of Defence.
Nos 1's	Best uniform.
Nos 5's	Evening rig.
Nos 8's	Working rig.
Nozzer	New recruit
Oily	WEM (Ordnance).
OM	Operator Mechanic.
OOD	Officer of the Day.
OOW	Officer of the Watch.
Oppo	Mate, derived from opposite number. (see Bezzie Ops)
PAS Boat	Passenger boat.
Pinky	WEM (Radio).
Pipe	Main broadcast announcement on board ship.
Pit	Bed.
PO	Petty Officer.
Pongo	Army
Port	Left hand side (Red).
Procedure Alpha	Entering harbour routine consisting of all available members of the ships company

	stood to attention on the upper deck.
QM	Quartermaster.
Quarterdeck	Historically the raised deck behind the mast of a ship. Now refers Part of ship located towards the stern usually below the flight deck.
RADAR	Radio Aid to Direction and Ranging.
RAS	Replenishment At Sea.
Rate	Rank.
Rating	Non commissioned personnel.
RDP	Run Down Period - Term used to describe the period of running down a ship due to be decommissioned. Now more commonly used for Jack when they lose interest in their work due to imminent draft or retirement or resignation.
RIB	Rigid Inflatable Boat.
Rig	Attire or uniform.
Rig-Run	A 'run ashore' in uniform.
RN	Royal Navy.
RO	Radio Operator.
ROSPA	Royal Society for the Prevention of Accidents.
Run Ashore	A night out on the town.
SCC	Ships Control Centre.
Scran	Food.
Scratcher	Bed.
Sea Bear	Neptune's Henchman.
Shiny Sheff	HMS Sheffield.
Shippers	Shipmate.

Signal	Radio Message.
Singers	Singapore.
Skimmer	Submariner's term for us surface Matelots and our ships.
Skipper	Captain.
Skylark	Fool around.
SLUT	Sub-Lt. Under Training.
SONAR	Sound Direction And Ranging.
Spinning Dits	Telling stories.
Square Rig	Sailors uniform.
SRE	Ships Recreational Equipment.
SSD	Special-Sea-Dutymen.
Stand Easy	20 minute break or rest from work.
Starboard	Right hand side (Green).
Stoker	Marine Engineer (see MEM)
Turn To	Start work.
WAFU	Slang term for members of the 'Fleet Air Arm' standing for 'Weapon And Fuel User's', A reference to their equipment but more affectionally changed to 'Wet And Fucking Useless' by other branches in the RN.
Waist	Side of the ship.
Wardroom	Officers messdeck.
WEM	Weapon Engineering
Wet	A beer.
WIGS	West Indies Guard Ship.
WRN's or Wrens	Women's Royal Naval Service.
XO	Executive Officer
X-Ray	Condition of ships watertight integrity referring to which watertight hatches and doorways should be closed.

Yankee (NBCD	Next stage up from X-Ray - Increased level of watertight integrity used for time when there is an increased risk of collision.
Zulu	Maximum level of watertight integrity where all watertight hatches and doorways are closed usually during time of high risk/attack.
Zulu-Alpha	As per Zulu but in addition incorporates the 'citadel' for air tight integrity.

Printed in Great Britain
by Amazon